THE READER'S LIBRARY

THE GREAT ENGLISH ESSAYISTS

WITH INTRODUCTORY ESSAYS AND NOTES

BY
WILLIAM J. DAWSON
AND
CONINGSBY W. DAWSON

HARPER & BROTHERS PUBLISHERS
NEW YORK AND LONDON
MCMIX

Contents

THE GREAT ENGLISH ESSAYISTS

The Genesis of the Essay

THE essay, like almost all forms of literary art, has its roots in remote antiquity. It is in origin a brief discourse, a compact homily, a compendium of thought, experience, and observation. Its relation to the spoken word is obvious. Even in our own day the public address, reduced to writing, is accepted as an essay; and it is tolerably certain that the essay commenced its career as an oral utterance.

Thus, for example, although Socrates wrote no books, he is nevertheless related to the origin of the essay. From the memorabilia of two of his disciples, Xenophon and Plato, we learn all that we know with certainty concerning his personality and method of thought. Of Aristotle, Plato's disciple, the same is true, although in a more limited sense. Aristotle taught by means of the spoken word, and "even of his most famous and undisputed works, the structure is so irregular, and the style so unequal, that it has been with great probability supposed that they are to a large extent not finished writings, but notes and rough jottings edited by his disciples." In the fifth and fourth centuries B.C. a race of wandering wisdom-dealers arose, who, in the scarcity of written knowledge, taught men orally, in return for money, that which we should now learn in a library. These men were known as the Sophists, a name which means the skilled or the wise. They passed from city to city, imparting knowledge, disseminating philosophies, founding schools of thought, acquiring influence and reputation, much as a university-extension lecturer of to-day might do; but while they thus used the spoken word, their prelections, wherever they have been preserved, observe either the dialogue or the essay form.

The essay also derives itself, upon even clearer evidence, from the Chokhmah—or wisdom-literature of the Hebrews. To this wisdom-literature belong such books as Proverbs, Ecclesiastes, the Wisdom of Jesus the Son of Sirach, and the Wisdom of Solomon. The love for wise sayings had always been present in Hebrew literature (*e.g.*, II Sam. xiv), but during the Post-Exilic period, and especially after the Greek influence had begun to fashion thought, it found its most remarkable expression and became a literary form. Mr. R. G. Moulton, in his admirable *Modern Readers' Bible*, has rendered a great service to literature by enabling the reader to distinguish the great variety of method practised in these wisdom-books.   What appears at first a disconnected and disorderly whole resolves itself under his skilled analysis into a series of sonnets, epigrams, maxims, but especially of deliberate essays on set themes. The themes are poverty, riches, gluttony, inordinate pleasure, friendship, gossip, wives, children, the choice of company, consideration for the high and low, and so forth; and it is curious to remark how closely they forecast the exact method of the modern essay.   They are homiletic in spirit, as most good essays are, but they transcend the homily in their shrewdness of observation, their note of personal experience, and their frequent ironic wit.   It is probable that no inconsiderable portion of these books consists of the oral sayings of wise men memorised and written down by their disciples.   It appears certain that they set the model for Bacon.   Printed side by side, Bacon's essay on *Truth*, and the essay of Jesus the Son of Sirach on *Gossip*, reveal astonishing similarities, particularly in the terseness of the style and the depth of worldly wisdom which they display. For Bacon also was an ironic observer of men and manners, who sought to express the wisdom of a lifetime in apothegms.

The essay as *the written word* made its earliest appearance not as a single effort, but as a passage interpolated in a larger work, as a reflection, or side remark, of the author upon the events which he has been narrating. Instances of this may be found in all the Greek or Roman historians. Many of the speeches which Thucydides attributes to his orators if divorced from their setting and given a title, such as, "On Patriotism," "On a Soldier's Death," etc., would be excellent essays. Pericles' speech at the funeral of the Athenians who fell in the first campaign of the Peloponnesian War might well pass for a modern essay, entitled, "The Athenian Ideal." "We aim," Thucydides makes him say, "at a life beautiful without extravagance, and contemplative without unmanliness; wealth is in our eyes a thing not for ostentation, but for reasonable use; and it is not the acknowledgment of poverty we think disgraceful, but the want of endeavour to avoid it." In this and many similar passages we have a form of literature that suggests the essay while preserving the unmistakable note of oratory.

Gradually, however, we find this oratorical note declining, in the degree that the essay vindicates itself as a separate and recognised form of literary expression, until in Cicero we come to the greatest of ancient essayists. We have already seen (*vide Great English Letter-Writers*, vol. i, p. 14) that Cicero was a pioneer in the art of letter-writing, who set the standard of form and excellence for all future ages. As an essayist his work is even more remarkable. His *De Amicitia, De Senectute, De Officiis, De Finibus*, and

De Natura Deorum are productions so admirable in style
and so perfect in method that they created the pattern
which all succeeding generations of scholars have sought
to emulate and imitate. But the day was yet far distant
when the essay and the oration were to be finally separated.
During the mediæval period of European history the extreme costliness of books made oral instruction the only
available method of literary publication for the vast
majority of men. It must be remembered also that culture
was very largely confined to ecclesiastics, who naturally
found the spoken word the most convenient vehicle for
imparting ideas. One of the few blessings which Christendom derived from the Crusades was the creation of universities throughout Europe. A new passion for learning,
a mediæval renaissance, sprang up in the West as a direct
result of its contact with the wisdom of the East. The
natural mother and protector of this movement was the
Church; she alone of all feudal institutions had created
and preserved cloisters and quiet places in the midst of
baronial contentions, where men might seek other than
material gains, and have the " leisure to grow wise, the
shelter to grow ripe." Such men were Lanfranc, and
Anselm, his pupil and successor at the Abbey of Bec.
Such an one was Abelard, the most famous teacher
of his generation, the mere whisper of whose name
stirred the pulse of intellectual Europe, and made Paris
for a brief space as conspicuous a seat of wisdom as
Bologna, the most renowned of all mediæval universities.

It is extremely interesting to remark this vast influence
which the Church has exercised on the growth of literature,
and the more so because the more common temper has been
to fix the attention upon certain instances in which the
Church displayed hostility to new knowledge. The general

reprehension of these errors ought not to blind us to the
fact that throughout the mediæval period the Church was
not only the generous and almost sole patron of art, but
was equally the foster-mother of literature. Learning
lived in monasteries, and the universities which presently
sprang up beside the monasteries were themselves ecclesiastical institutions. The same hand which dispensed
the bread of eternal life held in jealous custody the pearl
of earthly wisdom; within the same walls the priest practised the mysteries of his religion and inculcated the rudi-
ments of literature; and to these centres of "light and
leading" the whole studious youth of Europe flocked.
That same noble curiosity and spirit of inquiry into the
traditions of mankind which had hurried Christendom
across the breadth of a continent, armed and militant,
sceptical or penitent, to the sepulchre of its Lord, now
crowded the highways and the forests with thousands of
eager students, who had forsaken all at the sound of the
whispered fame of some far-distant scholar. The romance
and hardship of this strange quest are both undeniable.
In a day when society was sharply territorialised, and any
man found beyond the boundaries of his own district without authentic credentials was regarded as a possible criminal,
the Church alone stood for a larger and more liberal cos-
mogony. Feudal law presented a thousand hindrances to
the poor scholar. He often had to beg his way from city
to city. His sole defence against interference and exaction
was a letter given him by the chancellor of a university,
proving his identity, and differentiating him from the
ordinary beggar, who was regarded as a criminal. One
of the enactments regulating the student's status in England as distinct from the beggar's reads "and that the
scholars of the universities that go so begging have letters of testimonial of their chancellor upon the same

"pain"[1]—*i.e.*, the penalty inflicted on the vagrant. Books
the student could rarely possess, for this was a day when,
as Carlyle says, "a man, for a single book, had to give an
estate of land." But his destitution of books was atoned
for by the eloquence and learning of a great race of
scholars, who made the spoken word the vehicle for every
form of literary expression.

It will be readily perceived that the lectures of these
mediæval teachers must have borne a strong resemblance
to the essay, and were indeed spoken essays. The teachers
themselves belonged for the most part to some religious
order; they were preachers, and their utterances naturally
bore the stamp of the sermonic mind. Here, again, is a
point in the history of the essay which is worthy of careful
note. If we find that the essay is still sermonic in form,
that it is in the nature of a secular homily or dissertation,
the reason is obvious; the essay in its European development has been closely associated with the pulpit. Had
books been never so accessible in mediæval times, they
would have been of no value to the bulk of society, among
whom very few could read or write. The man was the
authority, not the book, and the clerk with his sermon in
the neighbouring church was the utmost culture which most
men could either attain or afford. It must be remembered,
also, that the mediæval sermon was a creation of much more
generous proportions than the pulpit discourse of our own
day. It was a medium of singular elasticity, and capable
of the widest variation. The scholar delivered a learned
disquisition, seeking to reconcile the teachings of some great
pagan like Aristotle with the teachings of Christ. The
enthusiast uttered an impassioned appeal, rebuking men
for their sins, and calling on them to repent. The com-

---

[1] 12. *Rich. II*, cap. vii.

fortable parish priest or jolly travelling friar,[1] anxious to gain the good-will of his hearers, that he might be the more generously entertained, often told a short story, relating some fanciful legend, or described some scandalous temptation of the Saints, the whole wittily touched and virile with broad humour.   Sometimes the discourse was in reality a racy fable, rich in local allusion, and excusable only by

---

[1] The Friars first landed in England in 1221. The two most important orders were the Black Friars of Dominic and the Gray Friars of Francis. They were pledged to perpetual poverty, that so they might live more close to the common people. They often chose the site of their homes among the lepers. At London they established themselves in the noisome shambles of Newgate; at Oxford on the swampy land between the Thames and the city's walls. As time went on, their outward profession of poverty made them a conspicuous object of munificent benefaction, enabling them to acquire wealth; riches led to frequent hypocrisy. Thus we find Chaucer portraying the Friar of his day as a fore-runner of Falstaff, clad in a disguise of religion:

> "A Frere ther was, a wantoun and a merye
> .   .   .   .   .   .
> Ful sweetly herde he confessioun,
> And pleasaunt was his absolucioun.
> He was an esy man to yeve penance,
> Ther as he wiste to han a good pitance;
> For unto a povre order for to geve
> Is signe that a man is wel i-shreve.
> .   .   .   .   .
> He knew wel the tavernes in every toun,
> And every ostiller or gay tapstere."

Such an one was the teller of the ribald jest and scandalous legend at street-corners, in the market-place, and in church portals; he was the forerunner of the short-story essayist. But others there were, more important and more typical of their order; the John Bulls of history, who, out of a full knowledge of the misery of the villeins, had grown fanatic and preached with indignant compassion a social message. These honourably belong to the class of originators of the spoken impassioned essay. (For a fuller treatment of this subject, *vide* Part III. of J. J. Jusserand's masterly book on *English Wayfaring Life in the Middle Ages*.)

the pertinent moral which it conveyed. But each was in
its way a spoken essay: the scholar's a learned essay, the
enthusiast's an impassioned essay, the priest's a short-story
essay, the friar's a satirical essay. This distinct influence
of the sermonic mind upon the essay has never been outlived. Hazlitt and Leigh Hunt are as truly preachers as
Fuller and Baxter. Of the thirty-eight essayists who contribute to this volume, no less than fifteen were either
ordained clergymen or were educated with a view to the
clerical profession. When Coleridge, who began his career
as a Unitarian preacher, asked Lamb if he had ever heard
him preach, Lamb replied that he had never heard him do
anything else. Even so late as Carlyle and Thackeray, the
finest essays which they wrote were first given to the world
as the spoken word, while Emerson's essays were in almost
every instance lectures, and he himself, like Coleridge,
was a Unitarian minister.

The transition from the spoken mediæval essay to the
more deliberate written essay obviously dates from the
invention of the printing-press. On the day when Caxton
set up his wooden printing-press at Westminster (*vide
Great English Letter-Writers*, vol. i, p. 22), the real enfranchisement of literature began. Books now superseded
the pulpit and the scholar's rostrum. The ministry of the
spoken word declined; to the man armed with a pen there
was given an audience as wide as the limits of the language
in which he wrote. And the first great essayist to avail
himself of this enfranchisement was Montaigne, who not
only set the model for all succeeding essayists, but remains
after the lapse of three centuries their undisputed master.

Montaigne was no doubt influenced by the tradition of
the Hebrew Wisdom-books, and still more by the examples
of classical antiquity and the great Italians of the Renaissance; but he contributed an entirely new element—

viz., the personal note. In his hands the essay approaches to conversation, conversation that is frankly and genially egoistic. He writes to please himself, he follows with delighted curiosity the vagrancies of his own mind, he is obsessed by no homiletical responsibilities, he is by turns familiar and profound, the scholar and the jester; but in all he is Montaigne, and his essays are the exposition of a temperament capable of a great variety of moods. He himself has expressed admirably his own conception of the essay in his quaint address to the reader. "Reader," he writes, "loe here a well-meaning Booke. It doth at the first entrance forewarne thee, that in contriving the same, I have proposed unto my selfe no other than a familiar and private end. . . . Had my intention beene to forestal and purchase the world's opinion and favour, I would surely have adorned my selfe more quaintly, or kept a more grave and solemne march. I desire therein to be delineated in mine owne genuine, simple and ordinarie fashion, without contention, art or study; for it is my selfe I pourtray. My imperfections shall therein be read to the life, and my naturall forme discerned, so farre-forth as publike reverence hath permitted me. For if my fortune had beene to have lived among those nations, which yet are said to live under the sweet liberty of nature's first and uncorrupted lawes, I assure thee, I would most willingly have pourtrayed my selfe fully and naked. Thus gentle reader my selfe am the groundworke of my booke."

No exposition of Montaigne's method could be so clear as this which is afforded by his own words. He proposes to himself "a familiar and a private end"; his subject is "himselfe," and his sole regret is that public opinion forbids him to reveal himself as nakedly as he could wish. Lamb might have said the same thing; Stevenson even more emphatically. As a method of self-revelation, not even poetry surpasses the essay. The tradition established by Montaigne has been among the most fruitful of all traditions. He presented to his own contemporaries a novel—thanks to his example, to us a familiar—picture of the true essayist; the genial egoist, the man who sits apart from life, divorced from its mean perturbations, yet shrewdly conscious of their causes; a fugitive without prejudice, a prophet without passion; above all, a very human creature, wise beyond others, and yet full of amiable weaknesses, who with the unabashed candour of the child, totally unacquainted with the prudishness which begets shame, is willing to present us with the substance of his own most private thoughts, his subtlest emotions, his most endearing follies, in the assured faith that we cannot be less interested in himself than he is.

The influence of Montaigne on English literature has been so great that it would involve no very serious straining of exactitude if we numbered him among the English essayists. His essays were read by English people in their original tongue for at least a hundred years, and in their popular translations have endured to our own day. Mr. Saintsbury expresses the opinion that no book has exercised so much influence on the English mind, with the exception of the authorised version of the Bible and certain religious books. It should be added also that the inimitable translation of John Florio, published in 1613, is less a translation than a rendering. Florio, while preserving the spirit of Montaigne, nevertheless has given the book an English dress so admirably quaint and idiomatic that to all intents and purposes it is an English classic. The knowledge of Montaigne among English readers has undoubtedly been obtained for the most part from Florio, whose rendering of the great Frenchman attains this highest merit of translation that it produces "on the reader the effect which the original produces on the reader of that original."

In spite, however, of the magnificent achievement of Montaigne, and the subsequent success of Bacon, the essay, for an inordinately long period, was considered an inferior form of literature. Doctor Johnson speaks of it in terms which are almost contemptuous, describing it as "a loose sally of the mind; an irregular, undigested piece; not a regular and orderly composition." The reason for this depreciation probably lay in the brief and fugitive nature of the essay. If lyric verse may be described as a swallow-flight of song, the essay may equally be described as a swallow-flight of prose. Compared with the ponderous labour of the lexicographer, it appears an indolent pursuit; placed beside grave and solemn works of history and philosophy, it appears insignificant. It is a carving of cherry-stones contrasted with a Phidian statue. But this is to apply to works of art the test of bulk, than which no test can be more absurd. It needed a more delicate taste than Johnson's to perceive that the highest art may be found in an intaglio as well as in a statue; that, in fact, weighed in the scales of a true critical discernment, Goldsmith's exquisite touch and fugitive charm have a much rarer value than Johnson's own laborious magniloquence.

Nevertheless, the Johnsonian tradition held sway over his own generation, and until relatively recent times the essay has been regarded with indifference, as a sort of literary by-product. One reason for this misjudgment undoubtedly lies in the fact that few great writers have been *essayists only*. Montaigne occupies this sole eminence, but he has few followers. Bacon was the author of the *Organum*, Cowley was a poet, Swift a statesman and a satirist. Hazlitt wrote biographies, even Lamb produced plays and poems; while the fame of Carlyle and Macaulay is based upon their histories, and the monument of Thackeray's genius is found not in his essays, but his novels. In the case of Carlyle and Macaulay, the essays clearly owe themselves to the opportunities afforded by periodic publication; in the case of Thackeray, to the platform of the lecturer.   Hazlitt and Lamb undoubtedly devoted their best genius to the essay, and regarded it as cardinal in their work; but neither of the great writers named above regarded the essay as other than a by-product of their intellectual activity.   If they did not regard it as deserving of Johnson's harsh terms, they certainly did not rank it higher than a fugitive form of literature.   To Carlyle and Macaulay, as truly as for Bacon and Swift, the essay was a relaxation from heavier pursuits, "a sally of the mind," as Johnson called it, though certainly neither loose nor undigested: something that served the exigency of the moment, expressed a passing phase of opinion, attained an immediate end; something which might add a value to the final edifice of their endeavour, but not the kind of work which has a high intrinsic value of its own, or is meant to be judged alone.

Gradually, however, the world has come to see that this estimate of the essay is wholly incorrect.   The stone rejected by the builders has become the chief stone of the corner.   Bacon's essays survive, while his *Organum* is unread; Cowley's essays are admired when his poetry is forgotten; and even of Carlyle and Macaulay it is true that their deliberate and largely planned histories are less appreciated by the great majority of readers than their essays.   For one man who has read Carlyle's *Frederick the Great*, a thousand are familiar with his *Heroes and Hero Worship;* and while no intelligent reader can afford to neglect Macaulay's *History*, yet there are few readers who would not confess that they had derived far more pleasure from the reiterated reading of his essays on Milton, Johnson, and Clive. Even of Johnson himself it is true, in spite of his disclaimer, that of all his voluminous labours, nothing is so likely to survive as his *Lives of the Poets*, which are critical essays. These "sallies" of a full mind, written with an easy sense of power and complete command of wide resources, bring us nearer to Johnson than anything else which he has written. It is perhaps not surprising that Johnson set the most value on the work that cost him most, for this is a common habit with authors; it is, however, a matter for amazement that he did not perceive that, of all forms of literature common to the eighteenth century, the essay had already proved itself the most popular and characteristic. So far was it from being an irregular and disorderly composition, that it had already established an ideal and created a model. Addison had made it the vehicle of both solemn reflection and delightful humour; Steele and Goldsmith had used it in a great variety of ways, thus illustrating its extreme flexibility; and earlier than these was a man who has never yet received his full meed of recognition, Daniel Defoe, who attempted every form of literature common to his day, and achieved remarkable results in each. Defoe, as a realistic novelist, was the instructor of Fielding, as a satirist the preceptor of Swift, and as an essayist had suggested the methods of the *Tatler* and the *Spectator* several years before either had come into existence. It is surely one of the ironies of literature, and one of the worst instances of the injustice of fame, that a man who originated so much has been all but totally ignored, and that even Lamb, while acknowledging that his novels "from their deep interest are worthy to find a shelf in the libraries of the wealthiest and the most learned," limits his praise by the statement that they are "capable kitchen reading," and that *Robinson Crusoe* in its phraseology is peculiarly adapted to the understanding of "seafaring men, poor boys, and servant maids."

The peculiar value of the essay in the latter half of the eighteenth century was that it afforded the most complete mirror we possess of contemporary life and manners. The same claim may be made for the novel, in so far as it followed the tradition established by Defoe and Richardson, Fielding and Smollett; but this tradition was soon neglected. With the rise of what may be termed the Gothic school of fiction, invented by Horace Walpole and carried out by such writers as Clara Reeve, Mrs. Radcliffe, and Maturin, the novel ceased to be a mirror of anything but a romantic and hysteric imagination. It had no relation whatever to real life. It was then that the essay assumed the function of the novel of life and manners. It painted with fidelity the incidents of real life. The characters and portraits in Goldsmith's essays are as vital as any in his *Vicar of Wakefield*, and are sketched in the same method. So close is the resemblance that Mr. Gosse has declared of the *Vicar of Wakefield* "that it is more like an extended episode in the *Spectator* manner than a story." And to Goldsmith must be attributed also that artless art of self-revelation so notable in Montaigne, but much more unaffectedly manifest in the glorified drudge of Brick Court, who consciously or unconsciously coloured every page he wrote with the reflection of his own amiable simplicity, deep tenderness, endearing follies, and pitiable misfortunes.

These observations, however, carry us beyond the immediate purpose of this introduction, which is simply to trace the genesis of the essay. The various forms which the essay has taken can be best studied in their examples, and it is in relation to these that any criticism of the essayists themselves finds its proper place. It is sufficient for the present purpose if we observe that no existing form of literature exhibits so much flexibility or allows so wide a field for the display of idiosyncrasy. The essay may obey its earliest impulse and be sermonic, as is distinctly the case in Carlyle's *Hero Worship;* it may follow the tradition of the mediæval fabulist and be a short story, as in Addison's *Vision of Mirza;* it may be a letter, as in Leigh Hunt's *World of Books;* but, whatever form it takes, its supreme characteristic is that it allows a freer expression of personality than any other mode of literary expression excepting the letter. The true essay may deal with historical matter, but it is not history; it may use the materials of biography, but it is not biography; it may criticise life, but it is more than criticism. If we except the purely critical essay, which constitutes a class by itself, we shall find that the outstanding characteristic of the essay is the room it affords for the play of personality. It is this quality, so entirely inadmissible in graver forms of literature, which constitutes the virtue of the essay. It is the perfect display of this quality which gives the essay its charm, rarity, delicacy, and makes it one of the most difficult forms of art. The essayist is thus among the freest of all literary practitioners. There is imposed upon him no limit of either method or theme. There are no imperious and autocratic unities to trouble him. There are no conventions to curtail the liberty of his spirit. He may select any theme, treat it in any way, intrude his own opinions or reflections, insist upon his own prejudices, intersperse his most serious passages with grotesque humour, pass at will from familiar gossip to impassioned eloquence, act in all things as he pleases, with a complete disregard of any will but his own, and no one will complain so long as his page is interesting. He is the Ariel of literature, and sometimes even the Puck. That very irresponsibility, which in graver writers would be counted a misdemeanour, in him becomes a charm. With the single exception of the letter, the essay is the friendliest form of literary art. The essayist either wins our intimate regard, or he fails altogether. And thus it happens that when the mind wearies of the large discourse of the Olympians, the intimate voice of the essayist secures our attention by its friendliness; it has a fireside familiarity; and should that unhappy day come, as it came to Ruskin and has come to many others, when books themselves no longer charm us, we may be sure that among the books which stay longest and are the last to fail us will be found the essay.

I

The Classic Essay

THE CLASSIC ESSAY

FRANCIS BACON, the father of the English classic essay, explains the purpose of his essays when he writes that they are "certain brief notes set down rather significantly than curiously; not vulgar, but of a kind whereof men shall find much experience and little in books." His aim, therefore, is akin to that of the preacher, only he selects *lay topics;* many of his own results, and those of the inheritors of his tradition, differ very little from sermons save in this, that they lack scriptural texts. The intention of Bacon's essays is to instruct; to this end they are made solemn with a large display of scholarship, and have for theme some abstract subject. Consequently, their remoteness from matters of general experience safeguards them from being *vulgar;* but at the same time, because of their pedantic gentility, narrows their scope of achievement. How much more generous was Montaigne's method, who took *himself for the groundwork of his book*—himself, if need be, in his nakedness! Yet Montaigne was undoubtedly Bacon's instigator: both illustrate their meaning with copious extracts from the classics; both go repeatedly to Machiavelli and Philip de Comines for their lessons in history and knowledge of men; both take high-sounding moral themes for their subjects. But Bacon and his followers miss the unabashed friendliness of their inspirer, being hampered by reserve or carried away by earnestness in delivering their message. Compare, for example, Bacon's essay entitled *Of Friend-*

ship with that of Montaigne. Bacon cites Lucius Sylla and Pompey, Julius Cæsar and Decimus Brutus, Augustus and Agrippa, Septimus Severus and Plantianus as illustrations of great friendships, *but he never cites himself.* Montaigne does little else; he takes for subject his own love for Steven de la Boitie, who, at the time of writing, has been long dead. "Truly," he says, "if I compare all the rest of my forepassed life unto the foure years, I so happily enjoied the sweet company, and deare-deare society of that worthy man, it is nought but a vapour, nought but a darke and yrksome light. Since the time I lost him, I doe but languish, I doe but sorrow. . . . All things were with us at halfe; me thinkes I have stolne his part from him." Bacon is never less than a teacher, to whom the attitude of the reader is that of a school-boy in the presence of a sage. Montaigne is always frankly fallible, and seemingly takes delight in owning to his errors; he approaches his reader on terms of equality as a confiding friend. Not for one hundred and fifty years, until Laurence Sterne commenced to write, did the English essay arrive at this thorough-paced first-person self-revelation, and Sterne's revelations are for the most part fables. In the meanwhile the classic tradition as established by Bacon, with its semi-sermonic purpose, became the model; and, although no longer a popular form of literature, occasionally finds a casual exponent even to-day.

Robert Burton was one of the first to do something toward breaking down the Baconian tradition—he paganised the essay. Up to his day it had been the medium of piously philosophic or, at least, of moral expression. He enfranchised it by setting down in essay form almost whatever it pleased him to think about. He was interested in ideas, and did not trouble to test their worthiness by discovering their relation to established conventions and orthodoxies. He wrote for his own and not for his public's pleasure. *The Anatomy of Melancholy* was a life's work, composed "with a view to relieving his own melancholy, but increased it to such a degree that nothing could make him laugh but going to the bridge-foot [1] and hearing the ribaldry of the bargemen, which rarely failed to throw him into a violent fit of laughter." When he died, he was suspected of having encompassed his own death, "because he departed this life, at or very near the time which he had some years foretold, from the calculation of his own nativity, and which, being exact, several of the students did not forbear to whisper among themselves that, rather than there should be a mistake in calculation, he sent up his soul to heaven through a slip about his neck." Such was the man. If he did not communicate his thoughts with the unashamed nakedness of Montaigne, he at least surpassed Bacon in this, that he wrote less to instruct others than himself. Though his style is often cumbered and his secrets are sometimes rudely violent in their intimacy, his book may truthfully be said to be one of the kindest and most companionable in the English language. Doctor Johnson said of it that it was the only book that took him out of his bed two hours before he wished to rise. It is all about himself, being written as a cure for his own disease; yet in this it falls short of Montaigne's friendliness, that it tells us only what he thought, not what he did, he being solely interested in ideas. Bacon preaches *at* the world; Burton diagnoses his own emotions and then advises that he may remedy himself.

The *Religio Medici* of Sir Thomas Browne was written at Shipdon Hall, Halifax. The date of its creation is approximately determined as 1635 by the internal evidence

---

[1] Probably Folly Bridge, which crosses the Thames at Oxford.

contained in the following passage: "As yet," he says, "I have not seen one revolution of Saturn, nor has my pulse beat thirty years"—"a double mode of reckoning," says Professor Herford[1] in his excellent introduction to the Everyman's edition of this book, "in which we seem to catch the far-off murmur of generations of mediæval doctors, prescribing for the unhappy patient with their eyes on the midnight horizon, and cupping him at the bidding of the stars." In these few words lies the whole importance of Sir Thomas Browne's contribution to the evolution of the essay; he widens its borders when he uses it, by fixing his gaze upon the heavens. He was a man of sidereal modes of thought and helped to enfranchise the medium through which he worked, not by adding anything fresh to its mechanism, but by making it spacious with the largeness of his own imagination. At the same time, this *upward gaze* prevented him from attaining to any considerable knowledge of the world of men, by virtue of which knowledge Montaigne is so excellent. Though his long life covers the whole of the troublous period of the Puritan Revolution, he has left scarcely a reference to things political. Were his books, by some destructive accident, the only literary survivors of Commonwealth times, we could reconstruct from his pages no contemporary picture of the first half of the seventeenth century, when monarchy was overthrown and England resounded to the "drums and tramplings of conquest." Though a convinced Royalist, he preferred his quiet to the contentions of parties, and dwelt remote in spirit with *his eyes upon the stars*. At the opening of the war he published his *Religio;* when the Royal cause was already approaching its final ruin, he published his *Pseudodoxia Epidemica,* wherein he makes

[1] Prof. C. H. Herford's *Introduction* is one of the best short essays that has been written on Sir Thomas Browne and his writings.

grave inquiries into the existence of the phœnix, and questions whether swans do actually sing at the hour of their dissolution; when the Protector was dead and the Restoration was at hand, he gave to the world his *Urn Burial*. If his heavenly horizon was large, his earthly landscape was proportionately narrow; his essays are evidently the work of a gentlemanly dreamer, who was born and lived out his life in an old East Anglian town— one whose eyes attended the Eternal with so fixed a stare that they were allowed no opportunity of gazing on the nearer world.

It is astonishing to note that not until a hundred years after its introduction into the language did the essay become a recognised vehicle for humorous and emotional expression, which was one of the uses to which it was best adapted, as Montaigne demonstrated in his treatment of it. Indeed, much of the history of the evolution of the English essay may be summed up in the phrase " back to Montaigne." Thomas Fuller was one of the first to realise its humorous possibilities. He, like Sir Thomas Browne, who was three years his senior, was attached to the Royal cause, but, unlike him, was an inquisitive observer of the near-by world. He was an ordained clergyman, and seems to have accompanied the army for some time as chaplain to Lord Hopton. Many of his writings are definitely theological, and all of them bear the impress of the sermonic mind. But he was saved from becoming stilted and sedate by his evident joy of life. We are told that even when engaged in active service he busied himself in gathering materials for many of the books which he subsequently published; that his company was at the same time much courted, on account of the extraordinary intelligence which he had acquired and the strain of lively humour of which he was possessed, which seems to have been quite irrepressible;

and that he would sit patiently for hours listening to the prattle of old wives, in order that he might obtain snatches of local history, traditionary anecdote, and proverbial wisdom. The style of all Fuller's works is quaintly jocular. Bishop Nicholson, in speaking of his *Church History*, accuses him of being fonder of a good joke than of correctness, and says that he is not over-scrupulous in his inquiry into the foundation of any laughable story which Providence sends his way. "Even the most serious and authentic parts of it are so interlaced with pun and quibble that it looks as if the man had designed to ridicule the annals of our Church into fable and romance." Examples of this risible quality, combined with a profound insight, are seen in his characterisation of a negro as "the image of God cut in ebony," and again when he says of the Pyramids that "they themselves, doting with age, have forgotten their founders." He is a preacher like Bacon, but he carries the development of the essay one step further, inasmuch as he laughs while he preaches.

John Milton adds a new element—the political. Most of his prose writings deal with affairs of State, and in Puritan days affairs of State were largely affairs of religion. The *Areopagitica*, from which our selection is taken, had for subtitle *A Speech for the Liberty of Unlicensed Printing*. Though a written composition, it assumed the literary form of the *spoken word*. He outsteps the Baconian tradition of instructing in this much, that he accuses and upbraids.

Abraham Cowley, of all the seventeenth-century essayists, comes nearest in spirit to Montaigne. He is not so large a man, nor as recklessly garrulous, but his method is the same. He is either read out of affection for his personality, or is disregarded absolutely; there is no middle way. Lamb, in his essay on *Detached Thoughts on Books and Reading*, writes, "The sweetest names, and which carry a perfume to mention, are Kit Marlowe, Drayton, Drummond of Hawthornden, and Cowley." The note of real affection is there. And again, in a letter to Coleridge, he writes: "In all our comparisons of taste, I do not know whether I have ever heard your opinion of a poet very dear to me—now out-of-fashion—Cowley. Favour me with your judgment of him, and tell me if his prose essays, in particular, as well as no inconsiderable part of his verse, be not delicious. I prefer the graceful rambling of his essays even to the courtly elegance and grace of Addison; abstracting from this the latter's exquisite humour." There is something very modern about what is called, "the sweetness and old-world air of Cowley." In comparison with him, most of the eighteenth-century essayists seem relatively archaic. In his method he is the forerunner of the English familiar essay, though his diction is sedately quaint; he prepared the way for the fuller intimacy of Stevenson.

According to Boswell, Samuel Johnson's purpose in literature was "to come forth in the character for which he was eminently qualified, a majestic teacher of moral and religious wisdom." Johnson himself acknowledges this when he writes, "As it has been my principal design to inculcate wisdom or piety, I have allotted a few papers to the idle sports of imagination." For *idle sports of the imagination* his style was not best fitted; in attempting them, so far as it is possible for Johnson to fail, he fails. As is well known, on several occasions, when his means were straitened, he was driven to write sermons for a livelihood; here he was in his element, for he was a born preacher. His share in the evolution of the classic essay is most important as a contribution to periodic literature. When once this style of writing was called upon to stand the test of immediate popularity it proved its limitations.

William Hazlitt and Leigh Hunt are significant as the

last upholders of an old tradition. They were sensitive
of the modern movement toward wider boundaries, but
they went forward with a backward look and a half-regret
for things past. Both did much in helping to establish
the critical and biographic essay, Hazlitt in particular, but
they returned frequently to the old standards which the
world was abandoning. In Hazlitt we meet with none of
those emotional qualities which we now expect in the
essayist; there is strong egotism, but very little that is
personal. He does not reveal his circumstances, and only
partially reveals his mind. Where books and his apprecia-
tion of them are concerned, he is most communicative.
His reputation as a classic essayist must be chiefly based
on enthusiasm of thought and lucidity of style—not on any
newness of handling. The first essays of Leigh Hunt prove
clearly that he worked under the shadow of a past age.
Though in later life he came to be an able journalist, he
never quite threw off the earlier influence. He attempted
many styles of essay-writing, but in none of them did he
equal his model. When he preaches, the lesson which he
inculcates is not often very profound. His chief quality
is a consistent friendliness and pleasure in talking for
talking's sake. He is the last of the long line of men who
have attempted the classic essay with any measure of
success. He was also a practitioner of the newer forms
of essay which have come to take its place, and in many
cases blended successfully the old with the new. In so
doing, he was pioneering and not imitating; and it is then
that we see him at his best. His essay on *Deaths of Little
Children*, though cast in the classic mould, comes very near
to being impassioned prose. He was a timid innovator,
whom tradition restrained. Already the essay had
branched out into many new lines of development, as will
be seen in the succeeding chapters, many of which were

little more than *a leading back to Montaigne*. The Baconian tradition was stubborn and hard to die. Its death is largely attributable to that demand for livelier or more scientific styles of writing which grew out of the wider diffusion of periodic literature.

OF LOVE

Francis Bacon

The stage is more beholding to love, than the life of man. For as to the stage, love is even matter of comedies, and now and then of tragedies; but in life it doth much mischief, sometimes like a siren, sometimes like a fury. You may observe, that amongst all the great and worthy persons, (whereof the memory remaineth, either ancient or recent,) there is not one that hath been transported to the mad degree of love; which shows, that great spirits and great business do keep out this weak passion. You must except, nevertheless, Marcus Antonius the half partner of the Empire of Rome, and Appius Claudius the Decemvir and lawgiver; whereof the former was indeed a voluptuous man and inordinate; but the latter was an austere and wise man: and therefore it seems, (though rarely,) that love can find entrance, not only into an open heart, but also into a heart well fortified, if watch be not well kept. It is a poor saying of Epicurus: *"Satis magnum alter alteri theatrum sumus";* as if man, made for the contemplation of heaven, and all noble objects, should do nothing but kneel before a little idol, and make himself a subject, though not of the mouth, (as beasts are,) yet of the eye, which was given him for higher purposes. It is a strange thing to note the excess of this passion; and how it braves the nature and value of things by this, that the speaking in a perpetual hyperbole is comely in nothing but in love. Neither is it merely in the phrase;

for whereas it hath been well said, that the arch-flatterer, with whom all the petty flatterers have intelligence, is a man's self; certainly the lover is more; for there was never proud man thought so absurdly well of himself as the lover doth of the person loved; and therefore it was well said, that it is impossible to love, and to be wise. Neither doth this weakness appear to others only, and not to the party loved, but to the loved most of all; except the love be reciprocal. For it is a true rule, that love is ever rewarded either with the reciprocal, or with an inward and secret contempt: by how much the more men ought to beware of this passion, which loseth not only other things but itself. As for the other losses, the poet's relation doth well figure them; that he that preferred Helena, quitted the gifts of Juno and Pallas: for whosoever esteemeth too much of amourous affection, quitteth both riches and wisdom. This passion hath his floods in the very times of weakness, which are, great prosperity and great adversity; though this latter hath been less observed: both which times kindle love, and make it more frequent, and therefore, show it to be the child of folly. They do best, who, if they cannot but admit love, yet make it keep quarter; and sever it wholly from their serious affairs and actions of life: for if it check once with business, it troubleth men's fortunes, and maketh men that they can no ways be true to their own ends. I know not how, but martial men are given to love: I think it is, but as they are given to wine; for perils commonly ask to be paid in pleasures. There is in man's nature a secret inclination and motion toward love of others, which, if it be not spent upon some one or a few, doth naturally spread itself toward many, and maketh men to become humane and charitable; as it is seen sometimes in friars. Nuptial love maketh mankind; friendly love perfecteth it; but wanton love corrupteth and embaseth it.

REMEDIES OF DISCONTENTS[1]

Robert Burton

Whatsoever is under the moon is subject to corruption, alterations; and so long as thou livest upon earth, look not for other. Thou shalt not here find peaceable and cheerful days, quiet times, but rather clouds, storms, calumnies, such is our fate. And as those errant planets, in their distinct orbs, have their several motions, sometimes direct, stationary, retrograde, in apogeo, perigeo, oriental, occidental, combust, feral, free, and as astrologers will have their fortitudes and debilities, by reason of those good and bad irradiations, conferred to each other's site in the heavens, in their terms, houses, ease, detriments, etc.; so we rise and fall in this world, ebb and flow, in and out, reared and dejected, lead a troublesome life, subject to many accidents and casualties of fortunes, variety of passions, infirmities, as well from ourselves as others.

Yea, but thou thinkest thou art more miserable than the rest, other men are happy in respect of thee, their miseries are but flea-bitings to thine, thou alone art unhappy, none so bad as thyself. Yet, if as Socrates said: All the men in the world should come and bring their grievances together, of body, mind, fortune, sores, ulcers, madness, epilepsies, agues, and all those common calamities of beggary, want, servitude, imprisonment, and lay them on a heap to be equally divided, wouldst thou share alike, and take thy portion, or be as thou art? Without question thou wouldst be as thou art. If some Jupiter should say, to give us all content:

> *Jam faciam quod vultis; eris tu, qui modò miles,*
> *Mercator; tu, consultus modo, rusticus; hinc vos,*
> *Vos hinc, mutatis discedite partibus; eia!*
> *Quid statis? nolunt.*

[1] From *The Anatomy of Melancholy.*

> Well, be 't so then: you, master soldier,
> Shall be a merchant; you, sir lawyer,
> A country gentleman; go you to this,
> That side you; why stand ye? It's well as 'tis.

Every man knows his own but not others' defects and miseries
and 'tis the nature of all men still to reflect upon themselves,
their own misfortunes, not to examine or consider other men's,
not to confer themselves with others: to recount their miseries,
but not their good gifts, fortunes, benefits, which they have
to ruminate on their adversity, but not once to think on their
prosperity, not what they have, but what they want: to look
still on them that go before, but not on those infinite numbers
that come after; whereas many a man would think himself in
heaven, a petty prince, if he had but the least part of that
fortune which thou so much repinest at, abhorrest, and ac-
countest a most vile and wretched state. How many thousands want that which thou hast? How many myriads of
poor slaves, captives, of such as work day and night in coal-
pits, tin-mines, with sore toil to maintain a poor living, of
such as labour in body and mind, live in extreme anguish and
pain, all of which thou art free from? *O fortunatos nimium
bona si sua norînt;* thou art most happy, if thou couldst be
content and acknowledge thy happiness; *Rem carendo, non
fruendo cognoscimus*, when thou shalt hereafter come to want
that which thou now loathest, abhorrest, and art weary of,
and tired with, when 'tis past, thou wilt say thou wast most
happy: and, after a little miss, wish with all thine heart,
thou hadst the same content again, mightst lead but such a
life, a world for such a life; the remembrance of it is pleasant.
Be silent, then, rest satisfied, *desine, intuensque in aliorum
infortunia, solare mentem*, comfort thyself with other men's
misfortunes, and as the moldiwarpe in Æsop told the fox,
complaining for want of a tail, and the rest of his companions

tacete, quando me Oculis captum videtis; you complain of toys, but I am blind, be quiet. I say to thee be thou satisfied. It is recorded of the hares, that with a general consent they went to drown themselves, out of a feeling of their misery; but when they saw a company of frogs more fearful than they were, they began to take courage and comfort again. Confer thine estate with others. *Similes aliorum respice casus, mitius ista feres.* Be content and rest satisfied, for thou art well in respect of others; be thankful for that thou hast, that God hath done for thee, he hath not made thee a monster, a beast, a base creature, as he might, but a man, a Christian, such a man: consider aright of it, thou art full well as thou art. *Quicquid vult, habere nemo potest,* no man can have what he will: *Illud potest nolle, quod non habet,* he may choose whether he will desire that which he hath not: Thy lot is fallen, make the best of it. If we should all sleep at all times (as Endymion is said to have done), who then were happier than his fellow? Our life is but short, a very dream, and while we look about, *Immortalitas adest,* eternity is at hand. Our life is a pilgrimage on earth, which wise men pass with great alacrity. If thou be in woe, sorrow, want, distress, in pain, or sickness, think of that of our Apostle, God chastiseth them whom he loveth: They that sow in tears, shall reap in joy, *Psal.* cxxvi: 6. As the furnace proveth the potter's vessel, so doth temptation true men's thoughts, *Eccl.* xxv: 5. 'Tis for thy good, *Periisses, nisi periisses:* Hadst thou not been so visited, thou hadst been utterly undone; as gold in the fire, so men are tried in adversity. *Tribulatio ditat:* and which Camerarius hath well shadowed in an emblem of a thresher and corn:

> *Si tritura absit, paleis sunt abdita grana,*
> *Nos crux mundanis separat à paleis:*

> As threshing separates from straw the corn,
> By crosses from the world's chaff are we born.

'Tis the very same which Chrysostome comments, *Hom.* 2, *in* 3 *Mat.* Corn is not separated but by threshing, nor men from worldly impediments but by tribulation. 'Tis that which Cyprian ingerminates, *Serm.* 4, *de Immort.* 'Tis that which Hierom, which all the Fathers inculcate, so we are catechised for eternity. 'Tis that which the proverb insinuates, *Nocumentum documentum.* 'Tis that which all the world rings into our ears. *Deus unicum habet filium sine peccato, nullum sine flagello:* God, saith Austin, hath one son without sin, none without correction. An expert seaman is tried in a tempest, a runner in a race, a captain in a battle, a valiant man in adversity, a Christian in temptation and misery. *Basil. Hom.* 8. We are sent as so many soldiers into this world, to strive with it, the flesh, the devil; our life is a warfare, and who knows it not? *Non est ad astra mollis è terris via:* and therefore peradventure this world here is made troublesome unto us, that, as Gregory notes, we should not be delighted by the way, and forget whither we are going.

> *Ite nunc fortes, ubi celsa magni*
> *Ducit exempli via: cur inertes*
> *Terga nudatis? superata tellus*
> *Sidera donat.*

Go on then merrily to heaven. If the way be troublesome, and you in misery, in many grievances; on the other side you have many pleasant sports, objects, sweet smells, delightsome tastes, music, meats, herbs, flowers, etc., to recreate your senses. Or put a case, thou art now forsaken of the world, dejected, contemned, yet comfort thyself, as it was said to Agar in the wilderness, God sees thee, He takes notice of thee: there is a God above that can vindicate thy cause, that can relieve thee. And surely Seneca thinks he takes delight in seeing thee. The gods are well pleased when they see great men contending with adversity, as we are to see

men fight, or a man with a beast.   But these are toys in respect, Behold, saith he, a spectacle worthy of God: a good
man contented with his estate.   A tyrant is the best sacrifice
to Jupiter, as the ancients held, and his best object a contented mind.   For thy part then rest satisfied, cast all thy
care on him, thy burden on him, rely on him, trust in him,
and he shall nourish thee, care for thee, give thee thine heart's
desire; say with David, God is our hope and strength, in
troubles ready to be found.   *Psal.* xlvi: 1.   For they that
trust in the Lord shall be as Mount Sion, which cannot be
removed.   *Psal.* cxxiv: 1, 2.   As the mountains are about
Jerusalem, so is the Lord about his people, from henceforth
and forever.

The Shame of Death[1]

Sir Thomas Browne

I am naturally bashful; nor hath conversation, age, or
travel, been able to effront or enharden me; yet I have one
part of modesty which I have seldom discovered in another,
that is (to speak truely), I am not so much afraid of death,
as ashamed thereof.   'Tis the very disgrace and ignominy
of our natures, that in a moment can so disfigure us, that
our nearest friends, Wife, and Children, stand afraid and
start at us: the Birds and Beasts of the field, that before
in a natural fear obeyed us, forgetting all allegiance, begin
to prey upon us.   This very conceit hath in a tempest disposed and left me willing to be swallowed up in the abyss
of waters, wherein I had perished unseen, unpitied, without wondering eyes, tears of pity, Lectures of mortality,
and none had said,

Quantum mutatus ab illo!

[1] From the *Religio Medici*.

4

Not that I am ashamed of the Anatomy of my parts, or can accuse Nature for playing the bungler in any part of me, or my own vitious life for contracting any shameful disease upon me, whereby I might not call my self as wholesome a morsel for the worms as any.

Some, upon the courage of a fruitful issue, wherein, as in the truest Chronicle, they seem to outlive themselves, can with greater patience away with death. This conceit and counterfeit subsisting in our progenies seems to me a meer fallacy, unworthy the desires of a man that can but conceive a thought of the next World; who, in a nobler ambition, should desire to live in his substance in Heaven, rather than his name and shadow in the earth. And therefore at my death I mean to take a total adieu of the World, not caring for a Monument, History, or Epitaph, not so much as the bare memory of my name to be found any where but in the universal Register of GOD. I am not yet so Cynical as to approve the Testament of Diogenes; nor do I altogether allow that *Rodomontado* of Lucan,

>   ——*Cælo tegitur, qui non habet urnam.*

> He that unburied lies wants not his Herse,
> For unto him a Tomb's the Universe.

but commend in my calmer judgment those ingenuous intentions that desire to sleep by the urns of their Fathers, and strive to go the neatest way unto corruption. I do not envy the temper of Crows and Daws, nor the numerous and weary days of our Fathers before the Flood. If there be any truth in Astrology, I may outlive a Jubilee: as yet I have not seen one revolution of Saturn, nor hath my pulse beat thirty years; and yet, excepting one, have seen the Ashes and left under ground all the Kings of Europe; have been contemporary to three Emperours, four Grand

Signiours, and as many Popes. Methinks I have outlived my self, and begin to be weary of the Sun; I have shaken hands with delight, in my warm blood and Canicular days, I perceive I do anticipate the vices of age; the World to me is but a dream or mock-show, and we all therein but Pantalones and Anticks, to my severer contemplations.

It is not, I confess, an unlawful Prayer to desire to surpass the days of our Saviour, or wish to outlive that age wherein He thought fittest to dye; yet if (as Divinity affirms) there shall be no gray hairs in Heaven, but all shall rise in the perfect state of men, we do but outlive those perfections in this World, to be recalled unto them by a greater Miracle in the next, and run on here but to be retrograde hereafter. Were there any hopes to outlive vice, or a point to be superannuated from sin, it were worthy our knees to implore the days of Methuselah. But age doth not rectify, but incurvate our natures, turning bad dispositions into worser habits, and (like diseases), brings on incurable vices; for every day as we grow weaker in age, we grow stronger in sin, and the number of our days doth but make our sins innumerable. The same vice committed at sixteen, is not the same, though it agree in all other circumstances, at forty, but swells and doubles from the circumstance of our ages; wherein, besides the constant and inexcusable habit of transgressing, the maturity of our judgment cuts off pretence unto excuse or pardon. Every sin, the oftner it is committed, the more it acquireth in the quality of evil; as it succeeds in time, so it proceeds in degrees of badness; for as they proceed they ever multiply, and, like figures in Arithmetick, the last stands for more than all that went before it. And though I think no man can live well once, but he that could live twice, yet for my own part I would not live over my hours past, or begin again the thread of my days: not upon Cicero's ground, because I have lived them well, but for fear I should live them worse. I find my growing Judgment daily instruct me how to be better, but my untamed affections and confirmed vitiosity makes me daily do worse. I find in my confirmed age the same sins I discovered in my youth; I committed many then, because I was a Child; and because I commit them still, I am yet an infant. Therefore I perceive a man may be twice a Child, before the days of dotage; and stand in need of Æsons Bath before threescore.

And truly there goes a great deal of providence to produce a man's life unto threescore: there is more required than an able temper for those years; though the radical humour contain in it sufficient oyl for seventy, yet I perceive in some it gives no light past thirty: men assign not all the causes of long life, that write whole Books thereof. They that found themselves on the radical balsome, or vital sulphur of the parts, determine not why Abel lived not so long as Adam. There is therefore a secret glome or bottome of our days: 'twas His wisdom to determine them, but His perpetual and waking providence that fulfils and accomplisheth them; wherein the spirits, ourselves, and all the creatures of GOD in a secret and disputed way do execute His will. Let *them* not therefore complain of immaturity that die about thirty; they fall but like the whole World, whose solid and well-composed substance must not expect the duration and period of its constitution: when all things are completed in it, its age is accomplished; and the last and general fever may as naturally destroy it before six thousand, as me before forty. There is therefore some other hand that twines the thread of life than that of Nature: we are not onely ignorant in Antipathies and occult qualities; our ends are as obscure as our beginnings; the line of our days is drawn by night, and the various effects therein by a pensil that is invisible; wherein though we confess our ignorance, I am sure we do not err if we say it is the hand of GOD.

OF JESTING[1]

Thomas Fuller

Harmless mirth is the best cordial against the consumption of the spirits: wherefore jesting is not unlawful if it trespasseth not in quantity, quality, or season.

It is good to make a jest, but not to make a trade of jesting. The Earl of Leicester, knowing that Queen Elizabeth was much delighted to see a gentleman dance well, brought the master of the dancing-school to dance before her. "Pish," said the queen, "it is his profession, I will not see him." She liked it not where it was a master quality, but where it attended on other perfections. The same may we say of jesting.

Jest not with the two-edged sword of God's Word. Will nothing please thee to wash thy hands in, but the font, or to drink healths in, but the church chalice? And know the whole art is learnt at the first admission, and profane jests will come without calling. If in the troublesome days of King Edward the Fourth, a citizen in Cheapside was executed as a traitor for saying he would make his son heir to the Crown, though he only meant his own house, having a crown for the sign; more dangerous it is to wit-wanton it with the majesty of God. Wherefore, if without thine intention, and against thy will, by chance medley thou hittest Scripture in ordinary discourse, yet fly to the city of refuge, and pray to God to forgive thee.

Wanton jests make fools laugh, and wise men frown. Seeing we are civilised Englishmen, let us not be naked

---

[1] From *Holy and Profane States*.

savages in our talk. Such rotten speeches are worst in withered age, when men run after that sin in their words which flieth from them in the deed.

Let not thy jests, like mummy, be made of dead men's flesh. Abuse not any that are departed; for to wrong their memories is to rob their ghosts of their winding-sheets.

Scoff not at the natural defects of any which are not in their power to amend. Oh, it is cruelty to beat a cripple with his own crutches! Neither flout any for his profession, if honest, though poor and painful. Mock not a cobbler for his black thumbs.

He that relates another man's wicked jests with delight, adopts them to be his own. Purge them therefore from their poison. If the profaneness may be severed from the wit, it is like a lamprey; take out the string in the back, it may make good meat. But if the staple conceit consists in profaneness, then it is a viper, all poison, and meddle not with it.

He that will lose his friend for a jest, deserves to die a beggar by the bargain. Yet some think their conceits, like mustard, not good except they bite. We read that all those who were born in England the year after the beginning of the great mortality, 1349, wanted their four cheek-teeth. Such let thy jests be, that may not grind the credit of thy friend, and make not jests so long till thou becomest one.

No time to break jests when the heart-strings are about to be broken. No more showing of wit when the head is to be cut off, like that dying man, who, when the priest coming to him to give him extreme unction, asked of him where his feet were, answered, "At the end of my legs." But at such a time jests are an unmannerly *crepitus ingenii*. And let those take heed who end here with Democritus, that they begin not with Heraclitus hereafter.

The Search after Truth[1]

John Milton

Truth indeed came once into the world with her divine master, and was a perfect shape most glorious to look on; but when he ascended, and his apostles after him were laid asleep, then straight arose a wicked race of deceivers, who, as that story goes of the Egyptian Typhon with his conspirators, how they dealt with the good Osiris, took the virgin Truth, hewed her lovely form into a thousand pieces, and scattered them to the four winds. From that time ever since, the sad friends of Truth, such as durst appear, imitating the careful search that Isis made for the mangled body of Osiris, went up and down gathering up limb by limb still as they could find them. We have not yet found them all, lords and commons, nor ever shall do, till her Master's second coming; He shall bring together every joint and member, and shall mould them into an immortal feature of loveliness and perfection. Suffer not these licensing prohibitions to stand at every place of opportunity forbidding and disturbing them that continue seeking, that continue to do our obsequies to the torn body of our martyred saint.

We boast our light; but if we look not wisely on the sun itself, it smites us into darkness. Who can discern those planets that are oft combust, and those stars of brightest magnitude that rise and set with the sun, until the opposite motion of their orbs bring them to such a place in the firmament, where they may be seen evening or morning? The light which we have gained was given us, not to be ever staring on, but by it to discover onward things more remote from our knowledge. It is not the unfrocking of a priest,

[1] From the *Areopagitica*.

the unmitring of a bishop, and the removing him from off the presbyterian shoulders, that will make us a happy nation: no; if other things as great in the church, and in the rule of life both economical and political, be not looked into and reformed, we have looked so long upon the blaze that Zuinglius and Calvin have beaconed up to us, that we are stark blind.

There be who perpetually complain of schisms and sects, and make it such a calamity that any man dissents from their maxims. It is their own pride and ignorance which causes the disturbing, who neither will hear with meekness, nor can convince, yet all must be suppressed which is not found in their Syntagma. They are the troublers, they are the dividers of unity, who neglect and permit not others to unite those dissevered pieces, which are yet wanting to the body of truth. To be still searching what we know not by what we know, still closing up truth to truth as we find it (for all her body is homogeneal, and proportional), this is the golden rule in theology as well as in arithmetic, and makes up the best harmony in a church; not the forced and outward union of cold, and neutral, and inwardly divided minds.

Of Greatness

Abraham Cowley

"Since we cannot attain to greatness," (says the Sieur de Montaigne,) "let us have our revenge by railing at it": this he spoke but in jest. I believe he desired it no more than I do, and had less reason; for he enjoyed so plentiful and honourable a fortune in a most excellent country, as allowed him all the real conveniences of it, separated and purged from the incommodities. If I were but in his condition, I should think it hard measure, without being convinced of any crime, to be sequestrated from it, and made one of the principal officers of state. But the reader may think that what I now say is of small authority, because I never was, nor ever shall be, put to the trial: I can therefore only make my protestation:

> If ever I more riches did desire
> Than cleanliness and quiet do require:
> If e'er ambition did my fancy cheat,
> With any wish, so mean as to be great,
> Continue, Heaven, still from me to remove
> The humble blessings of that life I love.

I know very many men will despise, and some pity me, for this humour, as a poor-spirited fellow; but I am content, and, like Horace, thank God for being so.

> *" Di bene fecerunt, inopis me quódque pusilli,*
> *Finxerunt animi."* [1]

I confess I love littleness almost in all things. A little convenient estate, a little chearful house, a little company, and a very little feast; and, if I were to fall in love again (which is a great passion, and therefore, I hope, I have done with it) it would be, I think, with prettiness, rather than with majestical beauty. I would neither wish that my mistress, nor my fortune, should be a *bona roba*, nor, as Homer uses to describe his beauties, like a daughter of great Jupiter, for the stateliness and largeness of her person; but, as Lucretius says,

> " *Parvula, pumilio,* Χαρίτων μία, *tota merum sal.*"

Where there is one man of this, I believe there are a thousand of Senecio's mind, whose ridiculous affectation of grandeur, Seneca the elder describes to this effect: Senecio was a man of a turbid and confused wit, who could not endure to

---

[1] Horace, *Sat. I.*, iv : 17.

speak any but mighty words and sentences, till this humour
grew at last into so notorious a habit, or rather disease, as became the sport of the whole town: he would have no servants,
but huge, massy fellows; no plate or household stuff, but
thrice as big as the fashion: you may believe me, for I speak
it without raillery, his extravagancy came at last into such a
madness, that he would not put on a pair of shoes, each of
which was not big enough for both his feet: he would eat
nothing but what was great, nor touch any fruit but horse-
plums and pound-pears: he kept a concubine that was a very
giantess, and made her walk too always in chiopins, till, at
last, he got the surname of Senecio Grandio, which, Messala
said, was not his *cognomen*, but his *cognomentum:* when he
declaimed for the three hundred Lacedæmonians, who alone
opposed Xerxes's army of above three hundred thousand, he
stretched out his arms, and stood on tiptoes, that he might
appear the taller, and cried out, in a very loud voice: "I rejoice, I rejoice!" We wondered, I remember, what new great
fortune had befallen his eminence. "Xerxes," says he, "is
all mine own. He, who took away the sight of the sea, with
the canvas veils of so many ships"—and then he goes on so,
as I know not what to make of the rest, whether it be the
fault of the edition, or the orator's own burly way of nonsense.

This is the character that Seneca gives of this hyperbolical
fop, whom we stand amazed at, and yet there are very few
men who are not in some things, and to some degrees, *Grandios*.
Is anything more common, than to see our ladies of quality
wear such high shoes as they cannot walk in, without one to
lead them; and a gown as long again as their body, so that
they cannot stir to the next room, without a page or two to
hold it up? I may safely say, that all the ostentation of our
grandees is, just like a train, of no use in the world, but hor-
ribly cumbersome and incommodious. What is all this but a
spice of *Grandio?* how tedious would this be if we were al-

ways bound to it! I do believe there is no king, who would not rather be deposed, than endure, every day of his reign, all the ceremonies of his coronation.

The mightiest princes are glad to fly often from these majestic pleasures (which is, methinks, no small disparagement to them) as it were for refuge, to the most contemptible divertisements, and meanest recreations, of the vulgar, nay, even of children. One of the most powerful and fortunate princes of the world,[1] of late, could find out no delight so satisfactory, as the keeping of little singing birds, and hearing of them, and whistling to them. What did the emperors of the whole world? If ever any men had the free and full enjoyment of all human greatness (nay, that would not suffice, for they would be gods too), they certainly possessed it: and yet one of them, who styled himself lord and god of the earth, could not tell how to pass his whole day pleasantly, without spending constantly two or three hours in catching of flies, and killing them with a bodkin, as if his godship had been Beelzebub. One of his predecessors, Nero (who never put any bounds, nor met with any stop to his appetite), could divert himself with no pastime more agreeable, than to run about the streets all night in a disguise, and abuse the women, and affront the men whom he met, and sometimes to beat them, and sometimes to be beaten by them: this was one of his imperial nocturnal pleasures. His chiefest in the day was, to sing, and play upon a fiddle, in the habit of a minstrel, upon the public stage: he was prouder of the garlands that were given to his divine voice (as they called it then) in those kind of prizes, than all his forefathers were, of their triumphs over nations: he did not at his death complain that so mighty an emperor, and the last of all the Cæsarian

[1] Louis XIII.

race of deities, should be brought to so shameful and miserable an end; but only cried out, "Alas! what pity it is that so excellent a musician should perish in this manner!" His uncle Claudius spent half his time at playing at dice; that was the main fruit of his sovereignty. I omit the madnesses of Caligula's delights, and the execrable sordidness of those of Tiberius. Would one think that Augustus himself, the highest and most fortunate of mankind, a person endowed too with many excellent parts of nature, should be so hard put to it sometimes for want of recreations, as to be found playing at nuts and bounding-stones with little Syrian and Moorish boys, whose company he took delight in, for their prating and their wantonness?

> Was it for this, that Rome's best blood he spilt,
> With so much falsehood, so much guilt?
> Was it for this, that his ambition strove
> To equal Cæsar, first; and after, Jove?
> Greatness is barren, sure, of solid joys;
> Her merchandise (I fear) is all in toys:
> She could not else, sure, so uncivil be,
> To treat his universal majesty,
> His new-created deity,
> With nuts and bounding-stones and boys.

But we must excuse her for this meagre entertainment; she has not really wherewithal to make such feasts as we imagine. Her guests must be contented sometimes with but slender cates, and with the same cold meats served over and over again, even till they become nauseous. When you have pared away all the vanity, what solid and natural contentment does there remain, which may not be had with five hundred pounds a year? Not so many servants or horses; but a few good ones, which will do all the business as well: not so many choice dishes at every meal; but at several meals all of them, which makes them both the more healthy, and the more pleasant: not so rich garments, nor so frequent changes; but as warm and as comely, and so frequent change too, as is every jot as good for the master, though not for the tailor or *valet de chambre:* not such a stately palace, nor gilt rooms, or the costliest sorts of tapestry; but a convenient brick house, with decent wainscot, and pretty forest-work hangings. Lastly, (for I omit all other particulars, and will end with that which I love most in both conditions), not whole woods cut in walks, nor vast parks, nor fountain or cascade gardens; but herb, and flower, and fruit gardens, which are more useful, and the water every whit as clear and wholesome as if it darted from the breasts of a marble nymph, or the urn of a river god. . . .

"As riches increase," says Solomon, "so do the mouths that devour them." [1] The master mouth has no more than before. The owner, methinks, is like Ocnus in the fable, who is perpetually winding a rope of hay, and an ass at the end perpetually eating it.

Out of these inconveniences arises naturally one more, which is, that no greatness can be satisfied or contented with itself: still, if it could mount up a little higher, it would be happy; if it could gain but that oint, it would obtain all its desires; but yet at last, when it is got up to the very top of the Peak of Teneriffe, it is in very great danger of breaking its neck downward, but in no possibility of ascending upward into the seat of tranquillity above the moon. The first ambitious men in the world, the old giants, are said to have made an heroical attempt of scaling heaven in despight of the gods; and they cast Ossa upon Olympus, and Pelion upon Ossa: two or three moun-

[1] Eccles. v: xi.

tains more, they thought, would have done their business; but the thunder spoilt all the work, when they were come up to the third story.

> And what a noble plot was crost!
> And what a brave design was lost!

A famous person of their offspring, the late giant of our nation, when, from the condition of a very inconsiderable captain, he made himself lieutenant-general of an army of little Titans, which was his first mountain, and afterward general, which was his second, and after that, absolute tyrant of three kingdoms, which was the third, and almost touched the heaven which he affected, is believed to have died with grief and discontent, because he could not attain to the honest name of a king, and the old formality of a crown, though he had before exceeded the power by a wicked usurpation. If he could have compassed that, he would perhaps have wanted something else that is necessary to felicity, and pined away for the want of the title of an emperor or a god. The reason of this is, that greatness has no reality in nature, but is a creature of the fancy, a notion that consists only in relation and comparison: it is indeed an idol; but St. Paul teaches us, *"that an idol is worth nothing in the world."* There is, in truth, no rising or meridian of the sun, but only in respect to several places: there is no right or left, no upper hand, in nature; everything is little, and everything is great, according as it is diversely compared. There may be perhaps some village in Scotland or Ireland, where I might be a great man; and in that case I should be like Cæsar (you would wonder how Cæsar and I should be like one another in anything); and choose rather to be the first man of the village, than second at Rome. Our country is called Great Britainy, in regard only of a lesser of the same name; it would be but a ridiculous epithet for it, when we consider it together with the Kingdom of China. That, too, is but a pitiful rood of ground, in comparison of the whole earth besides: and this whole globe of earth, which we account so immense a body, is but one point or atom in relation to those numberless worlds that are scattered up and down in the infinite space of the sky which we behold.

THE ADVANTAGES OF LIVING IN A GARRET[1]

Samuel Johnson

SIR,—Nothing has more retarded the advancement of learning than the disposition of vulgar minds to ridicule, and vilify what they cannot comprehend. All industry must be excited by hope; and as the student often proposes no other reward to himself than praise, he is easily discouraged by contempt and insult. He, who brings with him into a clamorous multitude the timidity of recluse speculation, and has never hardened his front in public life, or accustomed his passions to the vicissitudes and accidents, the triumphs and defeats of mixed conversation, will blush at the stare of petulant incredulity, and suffer himself to be driven by a burst of laughter, from the fortresses of demonstration. The mechanist will be afraid to assert before hardy contradiction the possibility of tearing down bulwarks with a silkworm's thread; and the astronomer of relating the rapidity of light, the distance of the fixed stars, and the height of the lunar mountains.

If I could by any efforts have shaken off this cowardice, I had not sheltered myself under a borrowed name, nor applied to you for the means of communicating to the

[1] Appeared in No. 117 of *The Rambler* in the form of a letter, signed " Hypertatus."

public the theory of a garret: a subject which, except some slight and transient strictures, has been hitherto neglected by those who were best qualified to adorn it, either for want of leisure to prosecute the various researches in which a nice discussion must engage them, or because it requires such diversity of knowledge, and such extent of curiosity, as is scarcely to be found in any single intellect; or, perhaps, others foresaw the tumults which would be raised against them, and confined their knowledge to their own breasts, and abandoned prejudice and folly to the direction of chance.

That the professors of literature generally reside in the highest stories has been immemorially observed. The wisdom of the ancients was well acquainted with the intellectual advantages of an elevated situation: else why were the Muses stationed on Olympus, or Parnassus, by those who could with equal right have raised them bowers in the vale of Tempe, or erected their altars among the flexures of Meander? Why was Jove himself nursed upon a mountain? or why did the goddesses, when the prize of beauty was contested, try the cause upon the top of Ida? Such were the fictions by which the great masters of the earlier ages endeavoured to inculcate to posterity the importance of a garret, which, though they had been long obscured by the negligence and ignorance of succeeding times, were well enforced by the celebrated symbol of Pythagoras:

"ἀνεμῶν πνεόντων τὴν ἠχὼ προσχύνει."

"When the wind blows, worship its echo."

This could not but be understood by his disciples as an inviolable injunction to live in a garret, which I have found frequently visited by the echo and the wind. Nor was the tradition wholly obliterated in the age of Augustus, for Tibullus evidently congratulates himself upon his garret, not without some allusion to the Pythagorean precept:

"Quam juvat immites ventos audire cubantem—
Aut, gelidas hibernus aquas cum fuderit auster
Securum somnos, imbre juvante, sequi !"

"How sweet in sleep to pass the careless hours,
Lull'd by the beating winds and dashing showers!"

And it is impossible not to discover the fondness of
Lucretius, an earlier writer, for a garret, in his description
of the lofty towers of serene learning, and of the pleasure
with which a wise man looks down upon the confused and
erratic state of the world moving below him:

"Sed nil dulcius est, bene quam munita tenere
Edita doctrina sapientum templa serena;
Despicere unde queas alios, passimque videre
Errare, atque viam palanteis quærere vitæ."

'Tis sweet thy labouring steps to guide
To virtue's heights, with wisdom well supplied,
And all the magazine of learning fortified:
From thence to look below on humankind,
Bewilder'd in the maze of life, and blind.—*Dryden.*

The institution has, indeed, continued to our own time;
the garret is still the usual receptacle of the philosopher and
poet; but this, like many ancient customs, is perpetuated
only by an accidental imitation, without knowledge of the
original reason for which it was established:

"Causa latet: res est notissima."
The cause is secret, but th' effect is known.—*Addison.*

Conjectures have, indeed, been advanced concerning
these habitations of literature, but without much satisfaction to the judicious inquirer. Some have imagined that
the garret is generally chosen by the wits, as most easily
rented; and concluded that no man rejoices in his aerial

5

abode, but on the days of payment. Others suspect that
a garret is chiefly convenient, as it is remoter than any
other part of the house from the outer door, which is often
observed to be infested by visitants, who talk incessantly
of beer, or linen, or a coat, and repeat the same sounds
every morning, and sometimes again in the afternoon,
without any variation, except that they grow daily more
importunate and clamorous, and raise their voices in time
from mournful murmurs to raging vociferations. This
eternal monotony is always detestable to a man whose
chief pleasure is to enlarge his knowledge, and vary his
ideas. Others talk of freedom from noise, and abstraction
from common business or amusements; and some, yet
more visionary, tell us that the faculties are enlarged by
open prospects, and that the fancy is more at liberty when
the eye ranges without confinement.

These conveniences may, perhaps, all be found in a well-
chosen garret; but surely they cannot be supposed sufficiently important to have operated invariably upon different
climates, distant ages, and separate nations. Of a universal
practice, there must still be presumed a universal cause,
which, however recondite and abstruse, may be perhaps reserved to make me illustrious by its discovery, and you by
its promulgation.

It is universally known that the faculties of the mind
are invigorated or weakened by the state of the body; and
that the body is in a great measure regulated by the various
compressions of the ambient element. The effects of the
air in the production or cure of corporeal maladies have
been acknowledged from the time of Hippocrates; but no
man has yet sufficiently considered how far it may influence the operations of the genius, though every day
affords instances of local understanding, of wits and rea-
soners, whose faculties are adapted to some single spot,

and who, when they are removed to any other place, sink at once into silence and stupidity. I have discovered, by a long series of observations, that invention and elocution suffer great impediments from dense and impure vapours, and that the tenuity of a defecated air at a proper distance from the surface of the earth accelerates the fancy, and sets at liberty those intellectual powers, which were before shackled by too strong attraction, and unable to expand themselves under the pressure of a gross atmosphere. I have found dulness to quicken into sentiment in a thin ether, as water, though not very hot, boils in a receiver partly exhausted; and heads, in appearance empty, have teemed with notions upon rising ground, as the flaccid sides of a football would have swelled out into stiffness and extension.

For this reason, I never think myself qualified to judge decisively of any man's faculties whom I have only known in one degree of elevation; but take some opportunity of attending him from the cellar to the garret, and try upon him all the various degrees of rarefaction and condensation, tension and laxity. If he is neither vivacious aloft, nor serious below, I then consider him as hopeless. But as it seldom happens that I do not find the temper to which the texture of his brain is fitted, I accommodate him in time with a tube of mercury, first marking the point most favourable to his intellects, according to rules which I have long studied, and which I may, perhaps, reveal to mankind in a complete treatise of barometrical pneumatology.

Another cause of the gayety and sprightliness of the dwellers in garrets is, probably, the increase of that vertiginous motion, with which we are carried round by the diurnal revolution of the earth. The power of agitation upon the spirits is well known; every man has felt his heart lightened in a rapid vehicle, or on a galloping horse.

Nothing is plainer, than that he, who towers to the fifth story, is whirled through more space by every circumrotation than another that grovels upon the ground-floor. The nations between the tropics are known to be fiery, inconstant, inventive, and fanciful because, living at the utmost length of the earth's diameter, they are carried about with more swiftness than those whom nature has placed nearer to the poles; and, therefore, as it becomes a wise man to struggle with the inconveniences of his country, whenever celerity and acuteness are requisite, we must actuate our languor by taking a few turns round the centre in a garret.

If you imagine that I ascribe to air effects which it cannot produce, I desire you to consult your own memory, and consider whether you have never known a man acquire a reputation in his garret, which, when fortune, or a patron, had placed him upon the first floor, he was unable to maintain; and who never recovered his former vigour of understanding till he was restored to his original situation. That a garret will make every man a wit, I am very far from supposing; I know there are some who would continue blockheads even on the summit of the Andes or on the peak of Teneriffe. But let not any man be considered as unimprovable till this potent remedy has been tried; for, perhaps, he was formed to be great only in a garret, as the joiner of Aretæus was rational in no other place but in his own shop.

I think a frequent removal, to various distances from the centre, so necessary to a just estimate of intellectual abilities, and consequently of so great use in education, that if I hoped that the public could be persuaded to so expensive an experiment, I would propose, that there should be a cavern dug, and a tower erected, like those which Bacon describes in Solomon's house, for the expansion and concentration of understanding, according to the exigences of different employments, or constitutions. Perhaps, some that fume away in meditations upon time and space, in the tower might compose tables of interest at a certain depth; and he that upon level ground stagnates in silence, or creeps in narrative, might, at the height of half a mile, ferment into merriment, sparkle with repartee and froth with declamation.

Addison observes that we may find the heat of Vergil's climate in some lines of his Georgics; so, when I read a composition, I immediately determine the height of the author's habitation. As an elaborate performance is commonly said to smell of the lamp, my commendation of a noble thought, a sprightly sally, or a bold figure, is to pronounce it fresh from the garret; an expression which would break from me upon the perusal of most of your papers, did I not believe that you sometimes quit the garret, and ascend into the cock-loft.

ON THE FEAR OF DEATH[1]

William Hazlitt

" And our little life is rounded with a sleep."

Perhaps the best cure for the fear of death is to reflect that life has a beginning as well as an end. There was a time when we were not: this gives us no concern—why should it trouble us that a time will come when we shall cease to be? I have no wish to have been alive a hundred years ago, or in the reign of Queen Anne; why should I

[1] This essay appeared in the second volume of *Table-Talk* (1822). Hazlitt died at No. 6 Frith Street, Soho, on September 18, 1830. He was fifty-five years of age. "Well, I've had a happy life," were his last words.

regret and lay it so much to heart that I shall not be alive a hundred years hence, in the reign of I cannot tell whom?

When Bickerstaff wrote his essays, I knew nothing of the subjects of them; nay, much later, and but the other day, as it were, in the beginning of the reign of George III., when Goldsmith, Johnson, Burke, used to meet at the Globe, when Garrick was in his glory, and Reynolds was over head and ears with his portraits, and Sterne brought out the volumes of Tristram Shandy year by year, it was without consulting me: I had not the slightest intimation of what was going on: the debates in the House of Commons on the American war, or the firing at Bunker's Hill, disturbed not me; yet I thought this no evil—I neither ate, drank, nor was merry, yet I did not complain: I had not then looked out into this breathing world, yet I was well; and the world did quite as well without me as I did without it! Why then should I make all this outcry about parting with it, and being no worse off than I was before? There is nothing in the recollection that at a certain time we were not come into the world, that "the gorge rises at"—why should we revolt at the idea that we must one day go out of it? To die is only to be as we were before we were born; yet no one feels any remorse, or regret, or repugnance, in contemplating this last idea. It is rather a relief and disburthening of the mind: it seems to have been holiday-time with us then: we were not called to appear upon the stage of life, to wear robes or tatters, to laugh or cry, be hooted or applauded; we had lain *perdus* all this while, snug, out of harm's way; and had slept out our thousands of centuries without wanting to be waked up; at peace and free from care, in a long nonage, in a sleep deeper and calmer than that of infancy, wrapped in the softest and finest dust. And the worst that we dread is, after a short, fretful, feverish being, after vain hopes, and idle fears, to

sink to final repose again, and forget the troubled dream
of life! . . . Ye armed men, knights templars, that sleep
in the stone aisles of that old Temple Church, where all is
silent above, and where a deeper silence reigns below (not
broken by the pealing organ), are ye not contented where
ye lie? Or would you come out of your long homes to go
to the Holy War? Or do ye complain that pain no longer
visits you, that sickness has done its worst, that you have
paid the last debt to nature, that you hear no more of the
thickening phalanx of the foe, or your lady's waning love;
and that while this ball of earth rolls its eternal round, no
sound shall ever pierce through to disturb your lasting
repose, fixed as the marble over your tombs, breathless
as the grave that holds you! And thou, oh! thou, to whom
my heart turns, and will turn while it has feeling left, who
didst love in vain, and whose first was thy last sigh, wilt
not thou too rest in peace?—or wilt thou cry to me complaining from thy clay-bed?—when that sad heart is no
longer sad, and that sorrow is dead which thou wert only
called into the world to feel!

It is certain that there is nothing in the idea of a pre-
existent state that excites our longing like the prospect
of a posthumous existence. We are satisfied to have
begun life when we did; we have no ambition to have set
out on our journey sooner; and feel that we have had quite
enough to do to battle our way through since. We cannot say:

> "The wars we well remember of King Nine,
>   Of old Assaracus and Inachus divine."

Neither have we any wish: we are contented to read of
them in story, and to stand and gaze at the vast sea of
time that separates us from them. It was early days then;
the world was not well-aired enough for us; we have no

inclination to have been up and stirring. We do not consider the six thousand years of the world before we were born as much time lost to us; we are perfectly indifferent about the matter. We do not grieve and lament that we did not happen to be in time to see the grand mask and pageant of human life going on in all that period; though we are mortified at being obliged to quit our stand before the rest of the procession passes.

It may be suggested in explanation of this difference, that we know from various records and traditions what happened in the time of Queen Anne, or even in the reigns of the Assyrian monarchs; but that we have no means of ascertaining what is to happen hereafter, but by awaiting the event, and that our eagerness and curiosity are sharpened in proportion as we are in the dark about it. This is not at all the case; for at that rate we should be constantly wishing to make a voyage of discovery to Greenland or to the Moon, neither of which we have, in general, the least desire to do. Neither, in truth, have we any particular solicitude to pry into the secrets of futurity, but as a pretext for prolonging our own existence. It is not so much that we care to be alive a hundred or a thousand years hence, any more than to have been alive a hundred or a thousand years ago; but the thing lies here, that we would all of us wish the present moment to last forever. We would be as we are, and would have the world remain just as it is, to please us.

"The present eye catches the present object"—to have and to hold while it may; and abhors, on any terms, to have it torn from us, and nothing left in its room. It is the pang of parting, the unloosing our grasp, the breaking asunder some strong tie, the leaving some cherished purpose unfulfilled, that creates the repugnance to go, and "makes calamity of so long life," as it often is.

> ". . . Oh! thou strong heart!
> There's such a covenant 'twixt the world and thee,
> They're loth to break!"

The love of life, then, is an habitual attachment, not an abstract principle. Simply *to be* does not "content man's natural desire": we long to be in a certain time, place, and circumstance. We would much rather be now, "on this bank and shoal of time," than have our choice of any future period, than take a slice of fifty or sixty years out of the Millenium, for instance. This shows that our attachment is not confined either to *being* or to *well-being;* but that we have an inveterate prejudice in favour of our immediate existence, such as it is. The mountaineer will not leave his rock, nor the savage his hut; neither are we willing to give up our present mode of life, with all its advantages and disadvantages, for any other that could be substituted for it. No man would, I think, exchange his existence with any other man, however fortunate. We had as lief *not be*, as *not be ourselves.* There are some persons of that reach of soul that they would like to live two hundred and fifty years hence, to see to what height of empire America will have grown up in that period, or whether the English constitution will last so long. These are points beyond me. But I confess I should like to live to see the downfall of the Bourbons. That is a vital question with me; and I shall like it the better, the sooner it happens!

No young man ever thinks he shall die. He may believe that others will, or assent to the doctrine that "all men are mortal" as an abstract proposition, but he is far enough from bringing it home to himself individually.[1] Youth, buoyant activity, and animal spirits, hold absolute antip-

---

[1] All men think all men mortal but themselves.—YOUNG.

athy with old age as well as with death; nor have we, in the heyday of life, any more than in the thoughtlessness of childhood, the remotest conception how

> "This sensible warm motion can become
>   A kneaded clod,"

nor how sanguine, florid health and vigour, shall "turn to withered, weak, and grey." Or if in a moment of idle speculation we indulge in this notion of the close of life as a theory, it is amazing at what a distance it seems; what a long leisurely interval there is between; what a contrast its slow and solemn approach affords to our present gay dreams of existence! We eye the farthest verge of the horizon, and think what a way we shall have to look back upon, ere we arrive at our journey's end; and without our in the least suspecting it, the mists are at our feet, and the shadows of age encompass us. The two divisions of our lives have melted into each other; the extreme points close and meet with none of that romantic interval stretching out between them, that we had reckoned upon; and for the rich, melancholy, solemn hues of age, "the sear, the yellow leaf," the deepening shadows of an autumnal evening, we only feel a dank, cold mist, encircling all objects, after the spirit of youth is fled. There is no inducement to look forward; and what is worse, little interest in looking back to what has become so trite and common. The pleasures of our existence have worn themselves out, are "gone into the wastes of time," or have turned their indifferent side to us; the pains by their repeated blows have worn us out, and have left us neither spirit nor inclination to encounter them again in retrospect. We do not want to rip up old grievances, nor to renew our youth like the phœnix, nor to live our lives twice over. Once is enough.

As the tree falls, so let it lie. Shut up the book and close the account once for all!

It has been thought by some that life is like the exploring of a passage that grows narrower and darker the farther we advance, without a possibility of ever turning back, and where we are stifled for want of breath at last. For myself, I do not complain of the greater thickness of the atmosphere as I approach the narrow house. I felt it more, formerly, when the idea alone seemed to suppress a thousand rising hopes, and weighed upon the pulses of the blood. At present I rather feel a thinness and want of support, I stretch out my hand to some object and find none, I am too much in a world of abstraction; the naked map of life is spread out before me, and in the emptiness and desolation I see Death coming to meet me. In my youth I could not behold him for the crowd of objects and feelings, and Hope stood always between us, saying— "Never mind that old fellow!" But I do not like a contract of pleasure broken off unfulfilled, a marriage with joy unconsummated, a promise of happiness rescinded. My public and private hopes have been left a ruin, or remain only to mock me. I would wish them to be re-edified. I should like to see some prospect of good to mankind, such as my life began with. I should like to leave some sterling work behind me. I should like to have some friendly hand to consign me to the grave. On these conditions I am ready, if not willing, to depart. I shall then write on my tomb—GRATEFUL AND CONTENTED! But I have thought and suffered too much to be willing to have thought and suffered in vain. In looking back, it sometimes appears to me as if I had in a manner slept out my life in a dream or shadow on the side of the hill of knowledge, where I have fed on books, on thoughts, on pictures, and only heard in half-murmurs the trampling of busy feet,

or the noises of the throng below.   Waked out of this dim,
twilight existence, and startled with the passing scene,
I have felt a wish to descend to the world of realities, and
join in the chase.   But I fear too late, and that I had better
return to my bookish chimeras and indolence once more!
Zanetto, lascia le donne, et studia la matematica.   I will
think of it.[1]

It is not wonderful that the contemplation and fear[2] of
death become more familiar to us as we approach nearer
to it; that life seems to ebb with the decay of blood and
youthful spirits; and that as we find everything about us
subject to chance and change, as our strength and beauty
die, as our hopes and passions, our friends and our affections leave us,[3] we begin to feel ourselves mortal!

I have never seen death but once, and that was in an
infant.   It is years ago.   The look was calm and placid,
and the face was fair and firm.   It was as if a waxen image
had been laid out in the coffin, and strewed with innocent
flowers.   It was not like death, but more like an image
of life!   No breath moved the lips,[4] no pulse stirred, no
sight or sound would enter those eyes or ears more.   While
I looked at it, I saw no pain there; it seemed to smile at the
short pang of life which was over; but I could not bear the
coffin-lid to be closed—it seemed to stifle me; and still as
the nettles wave in a corner of the churchyard over his little
grave, the welcome breeze helps to refresh me, and ease the
tightness at my breast.

I did not see my father after he was dead, but I saw
Death shake him by the palsied hand, and stare him in the
face.   He made as good an end as Falstaff; though dif-

[1] This sentence was added in proof.

[2] *Image.*—MS.

[3] *Affections are dead.*—MS.

[4] No breath moved, the lips did not breathe.—MS.   Compare
Memoirs of W. H., 1867, i, 170.

ferent, as became him. After repeating the name of his (Redeemer) often, he took my mother's hand, and looking up, put it in my sister's and so expired. There was something graceful and gracious in his nature, which showed itself in his last act. . . .

There is usually one pang added voluntarily and unnecessarily to the fear of death, by our affecting to compassionate the loss which others will have in us. If that were all, we might reasonably set our minds at rest. The pathetic exhortation on country tombstones, "Grieve not for me, my wife and children dear," etc., is for the most part speedily followed to the letter. We do not leave so great a void in society as we are inclined to imagine, partly to magnify our own importance, and partly to console ourselves by sympathy. Even in the same family the gap is not so great; the wound closes up sooner than we should expect. Nay, *our room* is not unfrequently thought better than *our company*. People walk along the streets the day after our deaths just as they did before, and the crowd is not diminished. While we were living, the world seemed in a manner to exist only for us, for our delight and amusement, because it contributed to them. But our hearts cease to beat, and it goes on as usual, and thinks no more about us than it did in our lifetime. The million are devoid of sentiment, and care as little for you or me as if we belonged to the moon. We live the week over in the Sunday's paper, or are decently interred in some obituary at the month's end! It is not surprising that we are forgotten so soon after we quit this mortal stage; we are scarcely noticed while we are on it. It is not merely that our names are not known in China—they have hardly been heard of in the next street. We are hand and glove with the universe, and think the obligation is mutual. This is an evident fallacy. If this, however, does not trouble us

now, it will not hereafter. A handful of dust can have no
quarrel to pick with its neighbours, or complaint to make
against Providence, and might well exclaim, if it had but
an understanding and a tongue, "Go thy ways, old world,
swing round in blue ether, voluble to every age, you and I
shall no more jostle!" . . .

A life of action and danger moderates the dread of death.
It not only gives us fortitude to bear pain, but teaches us
at every step the precarious tenure on which we hold our
present being. Sedentary and studious men are the most
apprehensive on this score. Doctor Johnson was an instance
in point. A few years seemed to him soon over, compared
with those sweeping contemplations on time and infinity with which he had been used to pose himself. In the
still-life of a man of letters, there was no obvious reason
for a change. He might sit in an arm-chair and pour out
cups of tea to all eternity. Would it had been possible
for him to do so! The most rational cure after all for the
inordinate fear of death is to set a just value on life. If we
merely wish to continue on the scene to indulge our head-
strong humours and tormenting passions, we had better
begone at once; and if we only cherish a fondness for
existence according to the good we derive from it, the pang
we feel at parting with it will not be very severe!

DEATHS OF LITTLE CHILDREN

Leigh Hunt

A Grecian philosopher being asked why he wept for the
death of his son, since the sorrow was in vain, replied, "I
weep on that account." And his answer became his
wisdom. It is only for sophists to contend, that we, whose
eyes contain the fountains of tears, need never give way

to them. It would be unwise not to do so on some occasions. Sorrow unlocks them in her balmy moods. The first bursts may be bitter and overwhelming; but the soil on which they pour, would be worse without them. They refresh the fever of the soul—the dry misery which parches the countenance into furrows, and renders us liable to our most terrible "flesh-quakes."

There are sorrows, it is true, so great, that to give them some of the ordinary vents is to run a hazard of being overthrown. These we must rather strengthen ourselves to resist, or bow quietly and drily down, in order to let them pass over us, as the traveller does the wind of the desert. But where we feel that tears would relieve us, it is false philosophy to deny ourselves at least that first refreshment; and it is always false consolation to tell people that because they cannot help a thing, they are not to mind it. The true way is, to let them grapple with the unavoidable sorrow, and try to win it into gentleness by a reasonable yielding. There are griefs so gentle in their very nature, that it would be worse than false heroism to refuse them a tear. Of this kind are the deaths of infants. Particular circumstances may render it more or less advisable to indulge in grief for the loss of a little child; but, in general, parents should be no more advised to repress their first tears on such an occasion, than to repress their smiles toward a child surviving, or to indulge in any other sympathy. It is an appeal to the same gentle tenderness: and such appeals are never made in vain. The end of them is an acquittal from the harsher bonds of affliction—from the tying down of the spirit to one melancholy idea.

It is the nature of tears of this kind, however strongly they may gush forth, to run into quiet waters at last. We cannot easily, for the whole course of our lives, think with pain of any good and kind person whom we have lost. It

is the divine nature of their qualities to conquer pain and
death itself: to turn the memory of them into pleasure; to
survive with a placid aspect in our imaginations. We are
writing at this moment just opposite a spot which contains
the grave of one inexpressibly dear to us. We see from our
windows the trees about it, and the church-spire. The
green fields lie around. The clouds are travelling overhead, alternately taking away the sunshine and restoring
it. The vernal winds, piping of the flowery summer-time
are nevertheless calling to mind the far-distant and dangerous ocean, which the heart that lies in that grave had
many reasons to think of. And yet the sight of this spot
does not give us pain. So far from it, it is the existence of
that grave which doubles every charm of the spot; which
links the pleasures of our childhood and manhood together;
which puts a hushing tenderness in the winds, and a patient
joy upon the landscape; which seems to unite heaven and
earth, mortality and immortality, the grass of the tomb
and the grass of the green field: and gives a more maternal
aspect to the whole kindness of nature. It does not hinder
gaiety itself. Happiness was what its tenant, through all
her troubles, would have diffused. To diffuse happiness,
and to enjoy it, is not only carrying on her wishes, but
realising her hopes; and gaiety, freed from its only pollu-
tions, malignity and want of sympathy, is but a child playing about the knees of its mother.

The remembered innocence and endearments of a child
stand us instead of virtues that have died older. Children
have not exercised the voluntary offices of friendship; they
have not chosen to be kind and good to us; nor stood by
us, from conscious will, in the hour of adversity. But they
have shared their pleasures and pains with us as well as they
could; the interchange of good offices between us has, of
necessity, been less mingled with the troubles of the world;

the sorrow arising from their death is the only one which
we can associate with their memories. These are happy
thoughts that cannot die. Our loss may always render
them pensive; but they will not always be painful. It is a
part of the benignity of Nature that pain does not survive
like pleasure, at any time, much less where the cause of it
is an innocent one. The smile will remain reflected by
memory, as the moon reflects the light upon us when the
sun has gone into heaven.

When writers like ourselves quarrel with earthly pain
(we mean writers of the same intentions, without implying,
of course, anything about abilities or otherwise), they are
misunderstood if they are supposed to quarrel with pains
of every sort. This would be idle and effeminate. They
do not pretend, indeed, that humanity might not wish, if it
could, to be entirely free from pain: for it endeavours, at all
times, to turn pain into pleasure: or at least to set off the
one with the other, to make the former a zest and the latter
a refreshment. The most unaffected dignity of suffering
does this, and, if wise, acknowledges it. The greatest
benevolence toward others, the most unselfish relish of their
pleasures, even at its own expense, does but look to increasing the general stock of happiness, though content, if it
could, to have its identity swallowed up in that splendid
contemplation. We are far from meaning that this is to
be called selfishness. We are far, indeed, from thinking so,
or of so confounding words. But neither is it to be called
pain when most unselfish, if disinterestedness be truly understood. The pain that is in it softens into pleasure, as the
darker hue of the rainbow melts into the brighter. Yet
even if a harsher line is to be drawn between the pain and
pleasure of the most unselfish mind (and ill-health, for instance, may draw it), we should not quarrel with it if it
contributed to the general mass of comfort, and were of a

6

nature which general kindliness could not avoid. Made
as we are, there are certain pains without which it would
be difficult to conceive certain great and overbalancing
pleasures. We may conceive it possible for beings to be
made entirely happy; but in our composition something of
pain seems to be a necessary ingredient, in order that the
materials may turn to as fine account as possible, though
our clay, in the course of ages and experience, may be refined more and more. We may get rid of the worst earth,
though not of earth itself.

Now, the liability to the loss of children—or rather what
renders us sensible of it, the occasional loss itself—seems to
be one of these necessary bitters thrown into the cup of
humanity. We do not mean that every one must lose one
of his children in order to enjoy the rest, or that every individual loss afflicts us in the same proportion. We allude
to the deaths of infants in general. These might be as
few as we could render them. But if none at all ever took
place, we should regard every little child as a man or a
woman secured; and it will easily be conceived what a
world of endearing cares and hopes this security would endanger. The very idea of infancy would lose its continuity with us. Girls and boys would be future men and
women, not present children. They would have attained
their full gowth in our imaginations, and might as well
have been men and women at once. On the other hand,
those who have lost an infant, are never, as it were, without
an infant child. They are the only persons who, in one
sense, retain it always, and they furnish their neighbours
with the same idea.[1] The other children grow up to manhood and womanhood, and suffer all the changes of mor-

---

[1] "I sighed," says old Captain Dalton, "when I envied you the
two bonnie children; but I sigh not now to call either the monk or
the soldier mine own."—*Monastery*, vol. iii, p. 341.

tality.   This one alone is rendered an immortal child.
Death has arrested it with his kindly harshness, and blessed
it into an eternal image of youth and innocence.

Of such as these are the pleasantest shapes that visit our
fancy and our hopes.   They are the ever-smiling emblems
of joy; the prettiest pages that wait upon imagination.
Lastly, "Of these is the kingdom of heaven."   Wherever
there is a province of that benevolent and all-accessible
empire, whether on earth or elsewhere, such are the gentle
spirits that must inhabit it.   To such simplicity, or the resemblance of it, must they come.   Such must be the
ready confidence of their hearts and creativeness of their
fancy.   And so ignorant must they be of the "knowledge
of good and evil," losing their discernment of that self-
created trouble, by enjoying the garden before them, and
not being ashamed of what is kindly and innocent.

II

The Letter Essay

THE LETTER ESSAY

THIS kind of essay-writing was the earliest of all divergences from the classic model established by Bacon. Nor did it derive itself from the essay form, but, having had an independent origin, when it had reached a certain stage in its growth, was grafted on to and made a part of the essay's development. The history of the letter essay and of the English published letter are the same until we come to James Howell (1594?–1666) (*vide The Great English Letter-Writers*, vol. i, pp. 1–25). The letter essay, as is obvious, was in its beginning no more than the ordinary form of private written communication, although intended for publication. Curiously enough, the didactic essay of Francis Bacon and the published letter, purporting to be private, of Bishop Hall made their first appearance in our language almost simultaneously. Technically, Bishop Hall holds premier claim to the earliest publication of English epistles, only his do not appear to have been genuine letters which were ever sent to any individual correspondent. Therefore, though in result they are identical with the letter essay of Daniel Defoe and Jonathan Swift, historically they differ in this, that they were meant to be mistaken for genuine, whereas the epistolary essay of later years was acknowledged by its writer and understood by its reader to be only a new way of saying things— a literary contrivance. To a modern man these pioneer deceptions of Bishop Hall proclaim themselves by their

internal evidence to be no real letters. They are cramped
both in thought and expression by the writer's knowledge
that his auditor is no one man, like-minded to himself,
but the hydra-headed public. Wherefore, being a man in
holy orders, he feels that he is expected to moralise; and
when he does so, it is not in the voice of a comrade friend,
going forward with loosened rein unwatchfully, but in the
authoritative tones of the pulpiteer. His aim is precisely
the same as Bacon's—to instruct; yet, by virtue of his
literary device, he allows himself a wider liberty than
Bacon, for he *must* be immediate and direct in his utterance,
and, though he may will otherwise, is continually compelled to stoop to the immodesty of naming himself.
James Howell, in publishing his *Familiar Letters*, at once
advanced and retarded the progress of the letter essay:
advanced it by his more generous friendliness and wider
range of topics; retarded it by the claim which he set up
that his letters were really genuine. Probably they were
only almost genuine, being compiled from his old correspondence, dated from various places at home and abroad,
which he over-wrote and made suitable for the public
when his time hung heavy on his hands, while he lay a
Royalist prisoner in the Fleet. For vividness they are
vastly superior to Bishop Hall's, and the incidents which
they relate, whether he actually witnessed them or only
learned them from hearsay, are worthy of Daniel Defoe,
that great father of so much that is modern in our literature,
of whom it is said that he surpassed all men in knowing
how "to lie like the truth." Very much of that which
Howell relates in the first person as his own experiences—
for example, our selection from him concerning the death of
Buckingham—appears likely to be fiction, but he possesses
the novelist's faculty for making every event that he
narrates seem actual. This genius for the momentary

deception of others and self—though the assumption of the first person, the dated address at the head and the signature at the end, and the supposition of that privacy which secures the letter-writer to his correspondent, are well known to be nothing but a form—has come to be the great prerequisite of the letter essayist. Though he is a public person writing for publication about something which perhaps never happened, he must appear to be a private person who scribbles leisurely to a friend concerning things which have occurred.

The history of the letter essay is closely connected with that of journalism; journalism began with the *news-letter*. The germ idea of the newspaper came into existence when accounts of the imperial armies of Rome were sent to generals serving in the provinces. These *Acta Diurna* were passed on by the generals to the officers under their command, and by the officers to their next inferiors, and so on, thus laying the foundation of a newspaper circulation. In Germany in the fifteenth century small news-sheets in the form of letters were issued in Augsburg, Vienna, Ratisbon, and Nuremburg. These are the earliest traces as yet found of journalism in Europe. Not until 1566, however, when the official *Notizie Scritte* were established at Venice by order of the Venetian Government, do we find a news-sheet at all answering to our present conception of the newspaper. Venice was at war with the Turks, and it was thus, by means of written sheets of limited number, that the Government communicated to the public the latest military and commercial information which it had received. About the same time, offices were set up in France, at the suggestion of the father of Montaigne, for making the wants of individuals known to one another. The advertisements received at these offices were sometimes pasted on walls in public places, in order to attract

more attention. This led in time to a systematic and
periodical publication of advertisements in sheets. In
the reign of James I. packets of news of extraordinary
interest were occasionally published in pamphlet form;
these were entitled *News from Italy, Hungary, France*, etc.,
according to the country from which the tidings were
supposed to come. Often they purported to be translations from the Low Dutch. In 1622, when the Thirty
Years' War of Gustavus Adolphus had excited curiosity,
these irregular pamphlets were converted into a regular
weekly issue, having for editor Nathaniel Butter. The
weekly pamphlet arose out of the exigencies of a crisis,
conveyed news concerning that crisis, and when the
necessity which had given it birth was at an end, de-
generated into an uninteresting, meagre chronicle. If a
squire in the country desired to keep in touch with town
happenings, he hired a professional correspondent—*a man
who sent him news-letters.* "In the capital," writes Lord
Macaulay, "the coffee-houses supplied in some measure
the place of a journal. Thither the Londoners flocked,
as the Athenians of old flocked to the market-place, to
hear whether there was any news. There men might learn
how brutally a Whig had been treated the day before in
Westminster Hall, what horrible accounts the letters from
Edinburgh gave of the torturing of Covenanters, how
grossly the Navy Board had cheated the crown in the
victualling of the fleet, and what grave charges the Lord
Privy Seal had brought against the Treasury in the matter
of the hearth money. But people who lived at a distance
from the great theatre of political contention could be kept
regularly informed of what was passing there only by
means of news-letters. To prepare such letters became a
calling in London, as it now is among the natives of India.
The news-writer rambled from coffee-room to coffee-room,

collecting reports, squeezed himself into the Sessions House at Old Bailey if there was an interesting trial, nay, perhaps obtained admission to the gallery of Whitehall, and noticed how the King and Duke looked. In this way he gathered materials for weekly epistles destined to enlighten some country town or some bench of rustic magistrates. Such were the sources from which inhabitants of the largest provincial cities, and the great body of the gentry and clergy, learned almost all that they knew of the history of their own time." During the civil war in the reign of Charles I. many new papers sprang into existence, called forth by the crisis. The differences of opinion which prevailed, clamouring for some public mode of expression, helped to make them more numerous. Another significant development was that many of them were published in the provinces; such were *News from Hull*, *Truths from York*, and *Warranted Tidings from Ireland*. We find in one of these newspapers a notice of the death of Captain Oliver, Cromwell's son, who had died of smallpox in his quarters at Newport. "He was a civil young gentleman," says the writer, "and the joy of his father." As the war proceeded, desire on the part of the country for early intelligence became more eager, consequently the intervals between publication were shortened and the papers began to be issued twice and thrice weekly. So important an auxiliary was the press considered, that each of the rival armies carried a printer along with it. During the Protectorate the newspaper press enjoyed the luxury of freedom, and there was a considerable increase in the number of political journals; but with the restoration of a monarchy which was not entirely popular with every section of the country, the press was put under a licenser. The newspaper censorship was established in 1662, and was continued down to 1695, when the press licensing law was abolished. "While the Licensing Act was in force," says Lord Macaulay, "there was no newspaper in England except the *London Gazette*, which was edited by a clerk in the office of the Secretary of State, and which contained nothing but what the Secretary of State wished the nation to know. There were indeed many periodical papers; but none of those papers could be called a newspaper." The way in which this attitude toward the press operated at a time when any man who did not fully approve of each separate action of Majesty, and of Majesty's office-bearers, was likely to be attacked as a traitor, is seen in the case of L'Estrange, editor of the *Observator*, who procured to be issued "a proclamation for suppressing the printing and publishing unlicensed books and pamphlets of news, because it has become a common practice for evil-disposed persons to vend to his majesty's people all the idle and malicious reports that they could collect or invent, contrary to law; the continuance whereof would in a short time endanger the peace of the kingdom." Another instance of this sensitiveness of government men in authority to any shadow of criticism is absurdly illustrated in the case of John Milton, who experienced very great difficulty in procuring a license for the publishing of *Paradise Lost*, because the censor imagined that in the noble simile of the sun in an eclipse he had discovered veiled treason. In an age when the papers contained nothing but *what the Secretary of State wished the nation to know*, when a suspicious, crabbed official played paterfamilias to a great people, the value of the news-letter is self-evident; the things which the Secretary of State did not wish to tell the nation were precisely the gossipy items which the nation was most eager to know. These tidings the professional news-monger conveyed to his provincial correspondent, together with countless delectable titbits of scandal, in his news-letter. Such weekly or fortnightly epistles must sometimes have approximated to the standard of excellence soon to be established by the letter essay when it dealt with a topic of contemporary interest,— *i.e.*, gave or discussed *news*. In 1695 the press licensing law was abolished, the immediate result of which was the fusion of the newspaper and the news - letter, which produced the letter essay, usually in the character of a leading article, and ultimately modern journalism. In 1695 the *Flying Post* announced that "if any gentleman has a mind to oblige his country friend or correspondent with this account of public affairs, he may have it for two pence of J. Salisbury, at the Rising Sun in Cornhill, on a sheet of fine paper; *half of which being blank*, he may thereon write his own private business, or the material news of the day." Still more inviting is the announcement published in *Dawkes's News-Letter*, that "this letter will be done up on good writing-paper, and blank space left, that any gentleman may write his own private business. *It will be useful to improve the younger sort in writing a curious hand!*" So, at the start, one-half of the newspaper was still a newsletter, only now the friend in town, and not the professional, might write the news-letter. This provision was probably made for the expression, on the part of the sender, of current criticism of the ungarnished facts stated in the paper, which criticism, if included in the printed portion, would have been actionable as seditious libel, although the licensing law had been withdrawn; and, if too freely indulged in, might have had the effect of bringing the law into force again. For the first few years after its abolition the press was on its good behaviour. On March 8, 1702, the *Daily Courant* appeared, the first regular daily paper, "giving all the Material News as every Post arrived." But Defoe was the earliest of his age to take proper advantage of the opportunity for *thinking in public* which this

new freedom afforded.   From Newgate, where he was confined for the seditious libel supposed to be contained in *The
Shortest Way with the Dissenters*, he issued the first copies of
The Review of the Affairs of France in 1704.   At first the
issue was weekly; after four numbers it became bi-weekly,
and so remained for a year.   It was really a news-letter
addressed to the nation.   This, when developed in later
years by Defoe himself and subsequent journalists, grew
into the letter essay.   This form of essay-writing persists
to this day, and will probably never die so long as the
newspaper continues to flourish.   It affords a convenient
way of anonymously satirising and accusing the contemporary world.   For this purpose it was used by Swift
and by the author of *The Letters of "Junius,"* which were
published in 1752 in the columns of the *Public Advertiser*.
It is the most flexible of all essay methods for the rambling
essayist, who writes to be friendly rather than to bestow
moral information.   It is thus applied to-day by one of the
most influential of English weeklies; the letter essay which
this publication contains is universally conceded to be the
most important feature of the paper, upon whose excellence
depends its sale, and in which the editor can give his
personality the fullest anonymous expression.   It affords
the most direct of all methods for the conveyance of intelligence, and is for this purpose very generally adopted
by the foreign correspondent of the modern newspaper.
The most important fact to remember about the letter
essay is that it grew up with journalism.   Its prime object
in its early stages was, and is in its most frequent form to
this day, to give news of whatever sort and to give it in-
terestingly—not to preach and moralise as did Bacon,
though perchance to advise in the undogmatic easy manner
of one who sits down to write to his friend.   In the giving
of news and the writing of a good letter, one of the most

delightful of asides is the relation of anecdote; the anecdote leads on to the truthful short story, told at greater length, and, in the absence of occurrences, the short story which is true gives place to the short story which is imagined and contrived. Hence, we arrive at the *short-story essay* of Steele, Addison, Swift, and Goldsmith. Therefore, the history of the letter essay, as most intimately concerns the early eighteenth-century writers, is best dealt with under *The Short-Story Essay.*

A GOOD MAN'S DAY

AN EPISTLE TO LORD DENNY

Bishop Hall

Every day is a little life: and our whole life is but a day repeated; whence it is that old Jacob numbers his life by days; and Moses desires to be taught this point of holy arithmetic, to number not his years, but his days. Those, therefore, that dare lose a day, are dangerously prodigal; those that dare mis-spend it, desperate. We can best teach others by ourselves; let me tell your lordship, how I would pass my days, whether common or sacred, that you (or whosoever others, overhearing me), may either approve my thriftiness, or correct my errors: to whom is the account of my hours either more due, or more known. All days are His, who gave time a beginning and continuance; yet some He hath made ours, not to command, but to use.

In none may we forget Him; in some we must forget all, besides Him. First, therefore, I desire to awake at those hours, not when I will, but when I must; pleasure is not a fit rule for rest, but health; neither do I consult so much with the sun, as mine own necessity, whether of body or in that of the mind. If this vassal could well serve me wak-

ing, it should never sleep; but now it must be pleased, that
it may be serviceable.   Now when sleep is rather driven
away than leaves me, I would ever awake with God; my
first thoughts are for Him, who hath made the night for
rest, and the day for travel; and as He gives, so blesses both.
If my heart be early seasoned with His presence, it will
savour of Him all day after.   While my body is dressing, not
with an effeminate curiosity, nor yet with rude neglect,
my mind addresses itself to her ensuing task, bethinking
what is to be done, and in what order, and marshalling
(as it may) my hours with my work; that done, after some
whiles meditation, I walk up to my masters and companions, my books, and, sitting down amongst them with
the best contentment, I dare not reach forth my hand to
salute any of them, till I have first looked up to heaven, and
craved favour of Him to whom all my studies are duly re-
ferred: without whom, I can neither profit nor labour.
After this, out of no over great variety, I call forth those
which may best fit my occasions, wherein I am not too
scrupulous of age; sometimes I put myself to school to
one of those ancients whom the Church hath honoured with
the name of Fathers; whose volumes I confess not to open
without a secret reverence of their holiness and gravity;
sometimes to those later doctors, which want nothing but
age to make them classical; always to God's Book.   That
day is lost, whereof some hours are not improved in those
divine monuments: others I turn over out of choice; these
out of duty.   Ere I can have sat unto weariness, my family,
having now overcome all household distractions, invites
me to our common devotions; not without some short preparation.   These, heartily performed, send me up with a
more strong and cheerful appetite to my former work,
which I find made easy to me by intermission and variety;
now, therefore, can I deceive the hours with change of

pleasures, that is, of labours. One while mine eyes are
busied, another while my hand, and sometimes my mind
takes the burthen from them both; wherein I would
imitate the skilfulest cooks, which make the best dishes
with manifold mixtures; one hour is spent in textual
divinity, another in controversy; histories relieve them
both. Now, when the mind is weary of others' labours, it
begins to undertake her own; sometimes, it meditates and
winds up for future use; sometimes it lays forth her conceits into present discourse; sometimes for itself, after for
others. Neither know I whether it works or plays in these
thoughts; I am sure no sport hath more pleasure, no work
more use; only the decay of a weak body makes me think
these delights insensibly laborious. Thus could I all day
(as ringers use) make myself music with changes, and
complain sooner of the day for shortness than of the business for toil, were it not that this faint monitor interrupts
me still in the midst of my busy pleasures, and enforces me
both to respite and repast; I must yield to both; while my
body and mind are joined together in these unequal couples,
the better must follow the weaker. Before my meals,
therefore, and after, I let myself loose from all thoughts,
and now would forget that I ever studied; a full mind takes
away the body's appetite no less than a full body makes a
dull and unwieldy mind; company, discourse, recreations,
are now seasonable and welcome: these prepare me for a
diet, not gluttonous, but medicinal; the palate may not be
pleased, but the stomach, nor that for its own sake; neither
would I think any of these comforts worth respect in themselves but in their use, in their end, so far as they may
enable me to better things. If I see any dish to tempt my
palate, I fear a serpent in that apple, and would please
myself in a wilful denial; I rise capable of more, not desirous;
not now immediately from my trencher to my book, but

7

after some intermission. Moderate speed is a sure help to all proceedings; where those things which are prosecuted with violence of endeavour or desire, either succeed not, or continue not.

After my later meal, my thoughts are slight; only my memory may be charged with her task, of recalling what was committed to her custody in the day; and my heart is busy in examining my hands and mouth, and all other senses, of that day's behaviour. And now the evening is come, no tradesman doth more carefully take in his wares, clear his shopboard, and shut his window, than I would shut up my thoughts, and clear my mind. That student shall live miserably, which like a camel lies down under his burden. All this done, calling together my family, we end the day with God. Thus do we rather drive the time away before us, than follow it. I grant neither is my practice worthy to be exemplary, neither are our callings proportionable. The lives of a nobleman, of a courtier, of a scholar, of a citizen, of a countryman, differ no less than their dispositions; yet must all conspire in honest labour.

Sweet is the destiny of all trades, whether of the brows or of the mind. God never allowed any man to do nothing. How miserable is the condition of those men, which spend the time as if it were given them, and not lent; as if hours were waste creatures, and such as should never be accounted for; as if God would take this for a good bill of reckoning: *Item*—spent upon my pleasures, forty years! These men shall once find that no blood can privilege idleness, and that nothing is more precious to God, than that which they desire to cast away—time. Such are my common days; but God's day calls for another respect. The same sun arises on this day and enlightens it; yet because that Sun of Righteousness arose upon it, and gave a new life unto the world in it, and drew the strength of God's moral precept unto it, therefore, justly do we sing with the psalmist: This is the day which the Lord hath made. Now I forget the world, and in a sort myself; and deal with my wonted thoughts, as great men use, who, at sometimes of their privacy, forbid the access of all suitors. Prayer, meditation, reading, hearing, preaching, singing, good conference, are the businesses of this day, which I dare not bestow on any work, or pleasure, but heavenly.

I hate superstition on the one side, and looseness on the other, but I find it hard to offend in too much devotion, easy in profaneness. The whole week is sanctified by this day; and according to my care of this, is my blessing on the rest. I show your lordship what I would do, and what I ought; I commit my desires to the imitation of the weak, my actions to the censures of the wise and holy, my weaknesses to the pardon and redress of my merciful God.

The Murder of Buckingham [1]

James Howell

(TO THE RIGHT HONOURABLE THE LADY SCROOP, COUNTESS OF SUNDERLAND: FROM STAMFORD)

MADAM,—I lay yesternight at the post-house at Stilton, and this morning betimes the post-master came to my bed's head and told me the Duke of Buckingham was slain: my faith was not then strong enough to believe it, till an hour ago I met in the way with my Lord of Rutland (your brother), riding post towards London; it pleased him to alight, and show me a letter wherein there was an exact relation of all the circumstances of this sad tragedy.

Upon Saturday last, which was but next before yester-

---

[1] From the *Familiar Letters.*

day, being Bartholomew Eve, the Duke did rise up in a well-disposed humour out of his bed, and cut a caper or two, and being ready, and having been under the barber's hands (when the murderer had thought to have done the deed, for he was leaning upon the window all the while), he went to breakfast attended by a great company of Commanders, where Monsieur Soubize came unto him, and whispered him in the ear that Rochelle was relieved, the Duke seemed to slight the news, which made some think that Soubize went away discontented: after breakfast the Duke going out, Colonel Fryer stepped before him, and stopping him upon some business, and Lieutenant Felton being behind, made a thrust with a common tenpenny knife over Fryer's arm at the Duke, which lighted so fatally, that he slit his heart in two, leaving the knife sticking in the body; the Duke took out the knife, and threw it away, and laying his hand on his sword, and drawing it half out said, "The villain hath killed me" (meaning, as some think, Colonel Fryer), for there had been some difference betwixt them, so reeling against a chimney, he fell down dead: the Duchess being with child, hearing the noise below, came in her nightgears from her bed-chamber, which was in an upper room, to a kind of rail, and thence beheld him weltering in his own blood. Felton had lost his hat in the crowd, wherein there was a paper sewed, wherein he declared that the reason which moved him to this act was no grudge of his own, though he had been far behind for his pay, and had been put by his Captain's place twice, but in regard he thought the Duke an enemy to the state, because he was branded in Parliament, therefore what he did was for the public good of his country. Yet he got clearly down, and so might have gone to his horse, which was tied to a hedge hard by; but he was so amazed that he missed his way, and so struck into the *pastry*, where although the cry went that some Frenchman had done it, he thinking the word was Felton, he boldly confessed, 'twas he that had done the deed, and so he was in their hands. Jack Stamford would have run at him, but he was kept off by Mr. Nicholas, so, being carried up to a tower, Captain Mince tore off his spurs, and asking how he durst attempt such an act, making him believe the Duke was not dead, he answered boldly that he knew he was dispatched, for 'twas not he, but the hand of Heaven that gave the stroke, and though his whole body had been covered over with armour of proof he could not have avoided it. Captain Charles Price went post presently to the King four miles off, who being at prayers on his knees, when it was told him, yet he never stirred, nor was he disturbed a whit till all divine service was done. This was the relation, as far as my memory could bear, in my Lord of Rutland's letter, who willed me to remember him unto your Ladyship, and tell you that he was going to comfort your niece (the Duchess) as fast as he could: and so I have sent the truth of this sad story to your Ladyship, as fast as I could by this post, because I cannot make that speed myself, in regard of some business I have to dispatch for my Lord in the way; so I humbly take my leave, and rest,

Your Ladyship's most dutiful servant,

J. H.

THE INSTABILITY OF HUMAN GLORY

Daniel Defoe

July 21, 1722.

SIR,—I have employ'd myself of late pretty much in the study of history, and have been reading the stories of the great men of past ages, Alexander the Great, Julius Cæsar, the great Augustus, and many more down, down, down, to the still greater Louis XIV., and even to the still greatest *John, Duke of Marlborough*. In my way I met with Tamerlane the Scythian, Tomornbejus the Egyptian, Solyman the Magnificent, and others of the Mahometan or Ottoman race; and after all the great things they have done, I find it said of them all, one after another, AND THEN HE DIED, all dead, dead! *hic jacet* is the finishing part of their history. Some lie in the bed of honour, and some in honour's truckle-bed; some were bravely slain in battle on the field of honour, some in the storm of a counterscarp, and died in the ditch of honour; some here, some there;—the bones of the bold and the brave, the cowardly and the base, the hero and the scoundrel, are heap'd up together;—there they lie in oblivion, and under the ruins of the earth, undistinguish'd from one another, nay, even from the common earth.

> "Huddled in dirt the blust'ring engine lies,
> That was so great, and thought himself so wise."

How many hundreds of thousands of the bravest fellows then in the world lie on heaps in the ground, whose bones are to this day plowed up by the rustics, or dug up by the labourer, and the earth their more noble vital parts are converted to, has been perhaps applied to the meanest uses!

How have we screen'd the ashes of heroes to make our mortar, and mingl'd the remains of a Roman general to make a hog-sty! Where are the ashes of a Cæsar, and the remains of a Pompey, a Scipio, or a Hannibal? All are vanish'd,—they and their very monuments are moulder'd into earth—their dust is lost, and their place knows them no more. They live only in the immortal writings of their historians, and poets, the renown'd flatterers of the age they liv'd in, and who have made us think of the persons, not as they really were, but as they were pleased to represent them.

As the greatest men, so even the longest-liv'd, — the *Methusalems* of the antediluvian world—the accounts of them all end with the same: Methusalem lived nine hundred sixty and nine years and begat sons and daughters; and what then? AND THEN HE DIED.

> "Death like an overflowing stream
> Sweeps us away; our life's a dream."

We are now solemnising the obsequies of the great Marlborough; all his victories, all his glories, his great projected schemes of war, his uninterrupted series of conquests, which are call'd his, as if he alone had fought, and conquer'd by his arm, what so many men obtain'd for him with their blood. All is ended, where other men, and, indeed, where all men ended: HE IS DEAD.

Not all his immense wealth, the spoils and trophies of his enemies, the bounty of his grateful mistress, and the treasure amass'd in war and peace; not all that mighty bulk of gold,—which some suggest is such, and so great, as I care not to mention,—could either give him life, or continue it one moment, but HE IS DEAD; and some say the great treasure he was possess'd of here had one strange particular quality attending it—which might have been very dissatisfying to him if he had consider'd much on it,— namely, that he could not carry much of it WITH HIM.

We have now nothing left us of this great man that we can converse with, but his monument and his history. He is now number'd among things pass'd. The funeral as well as the battles of the Duke of Marlborough are like to adorn our houses in sculpture, as things equally gay, and to be look'd on with pleasure. Such is the end of human glory, and so little is the world able to do—for the greatest men that come into it, and for the greatest merit those men can arrive to.

What then is the work of life? What the business of great men, that pass the stage of the world in seeming triumph, as these men, we call heroes, have done? Is it to grow great in the mouth of fame, and take up many pages in history? Alas! that is no more than making a tale for the reading of posterity, till it turns into fable and romance. Is it to furnish subject to the poets, and live in their immortal rhymes, as they call them? That is, in short, no more than to be hereafter turn'd into ballad and song, and be sung by old women to quiet children; or at the corner of a street, to gather crowds in aid of the pick-pocket and the whore. Or is their business rather to add virtue and piety to their glory, which alone will pass them into eternity, and make them truly immortal? What is glory without virtue? A great man without religion is no more than a great beast without a soul. What is honour without merit? And what can be call'd true merit, but that which makes a person be a good man, as well as a great man?

If we believe in a future state of life, a place for the reward of good men and for the punishment of the haters of virtue, how many heroes and famous men will crowd in among the last? How few crown'd heads wear the crowns of immortal felicity!

Let no man envy the great and glorious men, as we call them! Could we see them now, how many of them would move our pity rather than call for our congratulations! These few thoughts, sir, I send to prepare your readers' minds when they go to see the Magnificent Funeral of the late Duke of Marlborough.

Your humble servant, etc.

To a Very Young Lady on Her Marriage

Jonathan Swift

MADAME,—The Hurry and Impertinence of receiving
and paying Visits on account of your Marriage being now
over, you are beginning to enter into a Course of life, where
you will want much advice to divert you from falling into
many Errors, Fopperies, and Follies to which your Sex
is subject. I have always born an entire friendship to
your father and mother; and the person they have chosen
for your Husband, hath been for some years past my particular Favourite; I have long wished you might come
together, because I hoped, that from the goodness of your
Disposition, and by following the Counsel of wise Friends,
you might in time make yourself worthy of him. Your
Parents were so far in the right, that they did not produce
you into the World, whereby you avoided many wrong
steps which others have taken, and have fewer ill Impressions to be removed. But they failed, as it is generally
the case, in too much neglecting to cultivate your Mind;
without which it is impossible to acquire or preserve the
Friendship and Esteem of a wise man, who soon grows
weary of acting the Lover and treating his wife like a
mistress, but wants a reasonable Companion, and a true
Friend, through every stage of his life. It must be therefore your Business to qualify yourself for those offices;
wherein I will not fail to be your Director, as long as I shall
think you deserve it, by letting you know how you are to
act, and what you ought to avoid.

And beware of despising or neglecting Instructions,
whereon will depend not only your making a good Figure
in the World, but your own real Happiness, as well as that
of the person who ought to be the dearest to you.

I must therefore desire you, in the first place, to be **very** slow in changing the *modest behaviour of a Virgin*. It is usual in young Wives, before they have been many weeks married, to assume a bold forward Look and manner of talking, as if they intended to signify in all companies, that they were no longer Girls, and consequently that their whole Demeanor, before they got a Husband, was all but a Countenance and Constraint upon their Nature; whereas, I suppose, if the Votes of wise men were gathered, a very great Majority would be in favour of those Ladies, who, after they were entered into that state, rather chose to double their portion of Modesty and Reservedness.

I must likewise warn you strictly against the least degree of *Fondness* to your Husband before any Witness whatsoever, even before your nearest Relations, or the very Maids of your chamber. This Proceeding is so exceeding odious and disgustful to all who have either good Breeding or good Sense, that they assign two very unamiable reasons for it; the one is gross Hypocrisy, and the other has too bad a name to mention. . . . Conceal your Esteem and Love in your own breast, and reserve your kind looks and language for private Hours, which are so many in the four and twenty, that they will afford Time to employ a passion as exalted as any that was ever described in a *French* Romance.

Upon this head, I should likewise advise you to differ in practice from those Ladies who affect abundance of *Uneasiness* while their Husbands are abroad; start with every knock at the door, and ring the bell incessantly for the servants to let in their master; will not eat a bit at dinner or supper, if the Husband happens to stay out; and receive him at his return with such a medley of Chiding and Kindness, and catechising him where he has been, that a Shrew from *Billingsgate* would be a more easy and eligible companion.

Of the same leaven are those Wives, who, when their Husbands are gone a Journey, must have a Letter every post, upon pain of Fits and Hystericks; and a Day must be fixed for their return home, without the least Allowance for business, or sickness, or accidents, or weather; upon which, I can only say, that in my observation, those Ladies who are apt to make the greatest Clutter on such occasions, would liberally have paid a messenger for bringing them news, that their Husbands had broke their necks on the road.

You will perhaps be offended, when I advise you to abate a little of that violent Passion for *fine Cloaths*, so predominant in your Sex. It is a little hard, that ours, for whose Sake you wear them, are not admitted to be of your council. I may venture to assure you, that we will make an abatement at any time of four pounds a yard in a Brocade, if the Ladies will but allow a suitable addition of care in the *Cleanliness* and Sweetness of their Persons. For the satyrical part of Mankind will needs believe, that it is not impossible to be very fine and very filthy; and that the Capacities of a lady are sometimes apt to fall short in cultivating Cleanliness and Finery together. . . .

I am wholly at a loss how to advise you in the choice of *Company*, which, however, is a point of as great importance as any in your life. If your general Acquaintance be among Ladies who are your equals or superiors, provided they have nothing of what is commonly call'd an ill Reputation, you think you are safe; and this in the Style of the world will pass for good Company. Whereas I am afraid it will be hard for you to pick out one Female Acquaintance in this town, from whom you will not be in manifest danger of contracting some Foppery, Affectation, Vanity, Folly, or Vice. Your only safe way of conversing with them, is by a firm resolution to proceed in your Practice and Behaviour directly contrary to whatever they shall say or do. And this I take to be a good general rule, with very few exceptions. For instance, in the doctrines they usually deliver to young married Women in managing their Husbands; their several Accounts of their own Conduct in that particular, to recommend it to your imitation; the Reflections they make upon others of their sex for acting differently; their Directions how to come off with Victory upon any Dispute or Quarrel you may have with your husband; the Arts by which you may discover and practise upon his weak side; when to work by Flattery and Insinuation, when to melt him with Tears, and when to engage with a high Hand. In these, and a thousand other cases, it will be prudent to retain as many of their lectures in your memory as you can, and then determine to act in full Opposition to them all.

I hope your Husband will interpose his Authority to limit you in the trade of *Visiting:* half a dozen Fools are in all conscience as many as you should require; and it will be sufficient for you to see them twice a year. For I think, the Fashion does not exact, that Visits would be paid to Friends.

I advise, that your Company at home should consist of Men, rather than Women. To say the truth, I never yet knew a tolerable Woman to be fond of her own Sex. I confess, when both are mixed and well chosen, and put their best Qualities forward, there may be an Intercourse of civility and good-will; which, with the addition of some degree of Sense, can make conversation or any amusement agreeable. But a knot of Ladies, got together by themselves, is a very school of Impertinence and Detraction, and it is well if those be the worst.

Let your Men-Acquaintance be of your Husband's choice, and not recommended to you by any she-companions; because they will certainly fix a Coxcomb upon you, and it will cost you some time and pains, before you can arrive at the knowledge of distinguishing such a one from a Man of Sense.

Never take a *favourite Waiting-Maid* into your cabinet-council, to entertain you with Histories of those ladies, whom she hath formerly served, of their Diversions and their Dresses; to insinuate how great a Fortune you brought, and how little you are allowed to squander; to appeal to her from your husband, and to be determined by her judgment, because you are sure it will be always for you; to receive and discard Servants by her approbation, or dislike; to engage you, by her Insinuations, into Misunderstandings with your best Friends; to represent all things in false colours, and to be the common Emissary of Scandal.

But the grand Affair of your Life will be to gain and preserve the Friendship and Esteem of your *Husband*. You are married to a man of good Education and Learning, of an excellent understanding, and an exact Taste. It is true, and it is happy for you, that these qualities in him are adorned with great Modesty, a most amiable Sweetness of Temper, and an unusual disposition to Sobriety and Virtue. But neither good-nature nor virtue will suffer him to *esteem* you against his Judgment; and although he is not capable of using you ill, yet you will in time grow a thing indifferent and perhaps contemptible; unless you can supply the loss of Youth and Beauty with more durable qualities. You have but a very few Years to be young and handsome in the eyes of the World; and as few Months to be so in the eyes of a Husband, who is not a Fool; for I hope you do not still dream of Charms and Raptures, which Marriage ever did, and ever will, put a sudden end to. Besides, yours was a match of Prudence and common good-liking, without any mixture of that ridiculous Passion, which has no Being but in Play-books and Romances. . . .

As little Respect as I have for the generality of your Sex, it hath sometimes moved me with Pity, to see the Lady of the house forced to withdraw immediately after dinner, and this in Families where there is not much drinking; as if it were an established maxim, that Women are uncapable of all Conversation. In a room where both sexes meet, if the Men are discoursing upon any general subject, the Ladies never think it their business to partake in what passes, but in a separate club entertain each other with the Price and Choice of Lace, and Silk, and what Dresses they liked or disapproved at the Church or the Play-house. And when you are among yourselves, how naturally, after the first compliments, do you apply your hands to each others Lappets and Ruffles and Mantua's, as if the whole Business of your lives, and the publick Concern of the World, depended upon the Cut or Colour of your dresses. As Divines say, that some people take more pains to be damned, than it would cost them to be saved; so your Sex employs more Thought, Memory, and Application to be fools, than would serve to make them wise and useful. When I reflect on this, I cannot conceive you to be human Creatures, but a sort of Species hardly a degree above a Monkey; who has more diverting Tricks than any of you, is an animal less mischievous and expensive, might in time be a tolerable critick in Velvet and Brocade, and, for ought I know, would equally become them.

I would have you look upon Finery as a necessary Folly, as all great Ladies did, whom I have ever known. I do not desire you to be out of the Fashion, but to be the last and least in it. I expect that your Dress shall be one degree lower than your fortune can afford; and in your own heart I would wish you to be an utter Contemner of all Distinctions which a finer Petticoat can give you; because it will neither make you richer, handsomer, younger, better-natured, more virtuous, or wise, than if it hung upon a Peg.

If you are in company with men of learning, though they happen to discourse of Arts and Sciences out of your compass, yet you will gather more Advantage by listening to them, than from all the Nonsense and Frippery of your own Sex; but if they be Men of Breeding as well as Learning, they will seldom engage in any conversation where you ought not to be a Hearer, and in time have your part. If they talk of the Manners and Customs of the several Kingdoms of *Europe*, of Travels into remoter Nations, of the State of their own Country, or of the great men and actions of *Greece* and *Rome;* if they give their judgment upon *English* and *French* Writers, either in Verse or Prose, or of the nature and limits of Virtue and Vice, it is a shame for an *English* Lady not to relish such discourses, not to improve by them, and endeavour, by reading and information, to have her Share in those entertainments, rather than turn aside, as is the usual custom, and consult with the Woman, who sits next her, about a new cargo of Fans.

It is a little hard, that not one Gentleman's Daughter in a thousand should be brought to read or understand her own natural Tongue, or be judge of the easiest Books that are written in it, as any one may find, who can have the Patience to hear them, when they are disposed to mangle a Play or a Novel, where the least Word out of the common road is sure to disconcert them. It is no wonder, when they are not so much as taught to spell in their childhood, nor can ever attain to it in their whole lives. I advise you therefore to read aloud, more or less, every day to your Husband, if he will permit you, or to any other Friend (but not a female one), who is able to set you right; and as for spelling, you may compass it in time, by making collections from the books you read.

I know very well, that those who are commonly called Learned Women, have lost all manner of credit by their impertinent Talkativeness and Conceit of themselves: but there is an easy Remedy for this, if you once consider, that after all the pains you may be at, you never can arrive in point of learning to the perfection of a School-boy. The Reading I would advise you to, is only for improvement of your own good Sense, which will never fail of being mended by Discretion. It is a wrong method, and ill Choice of Books, that makes those learned ladies just so much worse for what they have read. And therefore it shall be my Care to direct you better, a Task for which I take myself to be not ill qualified; because I have spent more time, and have had more opportunities than many others, to observe and discover from what Sources the various Follies of Women are derived. . . .

There is never wanting in this Town a Tribe of bold, swaggering, rattling Ladies, whose Talents pass among Coxcombs for Wit and Humour; their Excellency lies in rude choquing Expressions, and what they call *running a Man down*. If a Gentleman in their company happens to have any Blemish in his birth or person, if any Misfortune hath befallen his Family or himself for which he is ashamed, they will be sure to give him broad Hints of it without any provocation. I would recommend you to the acquaintance of a common Prostitute, rather than to that of such Termagants as these. I have often thought that no man is obliged to suppose such Creatures to be Women; but to treat them like insolent Rascals disguised in female habits, who ought to be stript and kickt down stairs. . . .

I desire you will keep this Letter in your cabinet, and often examine impartially your whole Conduct by it. And so God bless you and make you a fair Example to your Sex,

and a perpetual Comfort to your Husband, and your Parents. I am with great Truth and Affection

MADAM

Your most faithful Friend, and humble Servant.

REFLECTIONS ON THE REVOLUTION IN FRANCE

Edmund Burke

(A LETTER INTENDED TO HAVE BEEN SENT TO A GENTLEMAN
IN PARIS.)

But among the revolutions in France must be reckoned
a considerable revolution in their ideas of politeness.   In
England we are said to learn manners at second-hand from
your side of the water, and that we dress our behaviour
in the frippery of France.   If so, we are still in the old cut;
and have not so far conformed to the new Parisian mode
of good breeding, as to think it quite in the most refined
strain of delicate compliment (whether in condolence or
congratulation) to say, to the most humiliated creature
that crawls upon the earth, that great public benefits are
derived from the murder of his servants, the attempted
assassination of himself and of his wife, and the mortification, disgrace, and degradation that he has personally
suffered.   It is a topic of consolation which our ordinary
of Newgate would be too humane to use to a criminal at the
foot of the gallows.   I should have thought that the hang-
man of Paris, now that he is liberalised by the vote of the
National Assembly, and is allowed his rank and arms in
the heralds' college of the rights of men, would be too
generous, too gallant a man, too full of the sense of his new
dignity, to employ that cutting consolation to any of the
persons whom the *leze nation* might bring under the ad-
ministration of his *executive power*.

8

A man is fallen indeed when he is thus flattered. The anodyne draught of oblivion, thus drugged, is well calculated to preserve a galling wakefulness, and to feed the living ulcer of a corroding memory. Thus to administer the opiate potion of amnesty, powdered with all the ingredients of scorn and contempt, is to hold to his lips, instead of "the balm of hurt minds," the cup of human misery full to the brim, and to force him to drink it to the dregs.

Yielding to reasons, at least as forcible as those which were so delicately urged in the compliment on the new year, the King of France will probably endeavour to forget these events and that compliment. But history, who keeps a durable record of all our acts, and exercises her awful censure over the proceedings of all sorts of sovereigns, will not forget either those events, or the era of this liberal refinement in the intercourse of mankind. History will record that on the morning of the 6th October, 1789, the King and Queen of France, after a day of confusion, alarm, dismay, and slaughter, lay down, under the pledged security of public faith, to indulge nature in a few hours of respite, and troubled, melancholy repose. From this sleep the Queen was first startled by the voice of the sentinel at her door, who cried out to her to save herself by flight—that this was the last proof of fidelity he could give—that they were upon him, and he was dead. Instantly he was cut down. A band of cruel ruffians and assassins, reeking with his blood, rushed into the chamber of the Queen, and pierced with a hundred strokes of bayonets and poniards the bed, from whence this persecuted woman had but just time to fly almost naked, and, through ways unknown to the murderers, had escaped to seek refuge at the feet of a king and husband, not secure of his own life for a moment.

This king, to say no more of him, and this queen, and their infant children (who once would have been the pride and hope of a great and generous people), were then forced to abandon the sanctuary of the most splendid palace in the world, which they left swimming in blood, polluted by massacre, and strewed with scattered limbs and mutilated carcases. Thence they were conducted into the capital of their kingdom. Two had been selected from the unprovoked, unresisted, promiscuous slaughter which was made of the gentlemen of birth and family who composed the king's body guard. These two gentlemen, with all the parade of an execution of justice, were cruelly and publicly dragged to the block, and beheaded in the great court of the palace. Their heads were stuck upon spears, and led the procession; whilst the royal captives who followed in the train were slowly moved along, amidst the horrid yells, and shrilling screams, and frantic dances, and infamous contumelies, and all the unutterable abominations of the furies of hell, in the abused shape of the vilest of women. After they had been made to taste, drop by drop, more than the bitterness of death, in the slow torture of a journey of twelve miles, protracted to six hours, they were, under a guard, composed of those very soldiers who had thus conducted them through this famous triumph, lodged in one of the old palaces of Paris, now converted into a bastile for kings.

Is this a triumph to be consecrated at altars? to be commemorated with grateful thanksgiving? to be offered to the divine humanity with fervent prayer and enthusiastic ejaculation?

. . . I hear that the august person, though he supported himself, felt much on that shameful occasion. As a man, it became him to feel for his wife and his children, and the faithful guards of his person, that were massacred in cold blood about him; as a prince, it became him to feel for the strange and frightful transformation of his civilised subjects, and to be more grieved for them than solicitous for himself. It derogates little from his fortitude, while it adds infinitely to the honour of his humanity. I am very sorry to say it, very sorry indeed, that such personages are in a situation in which it is not becoming in us to praise the virtues of the great.

I hear, and I rejoice to hear, that the great lady, the other object of the triumph, has borne that day (one is interested that beings made for suffering should suffer well), and that she bears all the succeeding days, that she bears the imprisonment of her husband, and her own captivity, and the exile of her friends, and the insulting adulation of addresses, and the whole weight of her accumulated wrongs, with a serene patience, in a manner suited to her rank and race, and becoming the offspring of a sovereign distinguished for her piety and her courage; that, like her, she has lofty sentiments; that she feels with the dignity of a Roman matron; that in the last extremity she will save herself from the last disgrace; and that, if she must fall, she will fall by no ignoble hand.

It is now sixteen or seventeen years since I saw the Queen of France, then the dauphiness, at Versailles; and surely never lighted on this orb, which she hardly seemed to touch, a more delightful vision. I saw her just above the horizon, decorating and cheering the elevated sphere she just began to move in — glittering like the morning-star, full of life, and splendour, and joy. Oh! what a revolution! and what a heart must I have to contemplate without emotion that elevation and that fall! Little did I dream when she added titles of veneration to those of enthusiastic, distant, respectful love, that she should ever be obliged to carry the sharp antidote against disgrace concealed in that bosom; little did I dream that I should have lived to see such disasters fallen upon her in a nation of gallant men, in a nation of men of honour, and of cavaliers. I thought ten thousand swords must have leaped from their scabbards to avenge even a look that threatened her with insult. But the age of chivalry is gone. That of sophisters, economists, and calculators has succeeded; and the glory of Europe is extinguished for ever. Never, never more shall we behold that generous loyalty to rank and sex, that proud submission, that dignified obedience, that subordination of the heart, which kept alive, even in servitude itself, the spirit of an exalted freedom. The unbought grace of life, the cheap defence of nations, the nurse of manly sentiment and heroic enterprise, is gone! It is gone, that sensibility of principle, that chastity of honour, which felt a stain like a wound, which inspired courage whilst it mitigated ferocity, which ennobled whatever it touched, and under which vice itself lost half its evil, by losing all its grossness.

The Repudiation of the Pennsylvanian Debt

Sydney Smith

To the Editor of the " Morning Chronicle " :

Sir,—You did me the favour, some time since, to insert in your valuable journal a petition of mine to the American Congress, for the repayment of a loan made by me, in common with many other unwise people, to the State of Pennsylvania. For that petition I have been abused in the grossest manner by many of the American papers. After some weeks' reflection, I see no reason to alter my opinions, or to retract my expressions. What I then said was not wild declamation, but measured truth. I repeat again, that no conduct was ever more profligate than that of the State of Pennsylvania. History cannot pattern it: and let no deluded being imagine that they will ever repay a single farthing—their people have tasted of the dangerous

luxury of dishonesty, and they will never be brought back
to the homely rule of right.   The money transactions of
the Americans are become a by-word among the nations
of Europe.   In every grammar school of the old world
ad Græcas Calendas is translated — the American dividends.

I am no enemy to America.   I loved and admired honest
America when she respected the laws of pounds, shillings,
and pence; and I thought the United States the most
magnificent picture of human happiness: I meddle now in
these matters because I hate fraud—because I pity the
misery it has occasioned—because I mourn over the hatred
it has excited against free institutions.

Among the discussions to which the moral lubricities
of this insolvent people have given birth, they have arrogat-
ed to themselves the right of sitting in judgment upon the
property of their creditors—of deciding who among them
is rich, and who poor, and who are proper objects of compassionate payment; but in the name of Mercury, the great
god of thieves, did any man ever hear of debtors alleging
the wealth of the lender as a reason for eluding the payment
of the loan?   Is the Stock Exchange a place for the tables
of the money-lenders; or is it a school of moralists, who may
amerce the rich, exalt the poor, and correct the inequalities
of fortune?   Is *Biddle* an instrument in the hand of
Providence to exalt the humble, and send the rich empty
away?   Does American Providence work with such instruments as *Biddle?*

But the only good part of this bad morality is not acted
upon.   The rich are robbed, but the poor are not paid:
they growl against the dividends of Dives, and don't lick
the sores of Lazarus.   They seize, with loud acclamations,
on the money bags of Jones Loyd, Rothschild, and Baring,
but they do not give back the pittance of the widow, and

the bread of the child. Those knaves of the setting sun
may call me rich, for I have a twentieth part of the income
of the Archbishop of Canterbury; but the curate of the next
parish is a wretched soul, bruised by adversity; and the
three hundred pounds for his children, which it has taken
his life to save, is eaten and drunken by the mean men of
Pennsylvania—by men who are always talking of the virtue
and honour of the United States—by men who soar above
others in what they say, and sink below all nations in what
they do—who, after floating on the heaven of declamation,
fall down to feed on the offal and garbage of the earth.

Persons who are not in the secret are inclined to consider
the abominable conduct of the repudiating States to proceed from exhaustion—"They don't pay because they
cannot pay"; whereas, from estimates which have just
now reached this country, this is the picture of the finances
of the insolvent states. Their debts may be about 200
millions of dollars; at an interest of 6 per cent., this makes
an annual charge of 12 millions of dollars, which is little
more than 1 per cent. of their income in 1840, and may be
presumed to be less than 1 per cent. of their present income;
but if they were all to provide funds for the punctual payment of interest, the debt could readily be converted into a
4 or 5 per cent. stock, and the excess, converted into a
sinking fund, would discharge the debt in less than thirty
years. The debt of Pennsylvania, estimated at 40 millions
of dollars, bears, at 5 per cent., an annual interest of 2
millions. The income of this State was, in 1840, 131
millions of dollars, and is probably at this time not less than
150 millions: a net revenue of only $1\frac{1}{2}$ per cent. would
produce the two millions required. So that the price of
national character in Pennsylvania is $1\frac{1}{2}$ per cent. on
the net income; and if this market price of morals were
established here, a gentleman of a thousand a year would

deliberately and publicly submit to infamy for £15 per annum; and a poor man who by laborious industry had saved one hundred a year, would incur general disgrace and opprobrium for thirty shillings by the year. There really should be lunatic asylums for nations as well as for individuals.

But they begin to feel all this: their tone is changed; they talk with bated breath and whispering apology, and allay with some cold drops of modesty their skipping spirit. They strutted into this miserable history, and begin to think of sneaking out.

And then the subdolous press of America contends that the English under similar circumstances would act with their own debt in the same manner; but there are many English constituencies where are thousands not worth a shilling, and no such idea has been broached among them, nor has any petition to such effect been presented to the legislature. But what if they did act in such a manner, would it be a conduct less wicked than that of the Americans? Is there not one immutable law of justice—is it not written in the book? Does it not beat in the heart?— are the great guidemarks of life to be concealed by such nonsense as this? I deny the fact on which the reasoning is founded; and if the facts were true, the reasoning would be false.

I never meet a Pennsylvanian at a London dinner without feeling a disposition to seize and divide him— to allot his beaver to one sufferer and his coat to another —to appropriate his pocket-handkerchief to the orphan, and to comfort the widow with his silver watch, Broadway rings, and the *London Guide*, which he always carries in his pockets. How such a man can set himself down at an English table without feeling that he owes two or three pounds to every man in company I am at a loss to conceive:

he has no more right to eat with honest men than a leper
has to eat with clean men.   If he have a particle of honour
in his composition he should shut himself up, and say, "I
cannot mingle with you, I belong to a degraded people—
I must hide myself—I am a plunderer from Pennsylvania."

Figure to yourself a Pennsylvanian receiving foreigners
in his own country, walking over the public works with
them, and showing them Larcenous Lake, Swindling
Swamp, Crafty Canal, and Rogues' Railway, and other
dishonest works. "This swamp we gained" (says the
patriotic borrower) "by the repudiated loan of 1828. Our
canal robbery was in 1830; we pocketed your good people's
money for the railroad only last year." All this may seem
very smart to the Americans; but if I had the misfortune
to be born among such a people, the land of my fathers
should not retain me a single moment after the act of repudiation. I would appeal from my fathers to my forefathers. I would fly to Newgate for greater purity of
thought, and seek in the prisons of England for better rules
of life.

This new and vain people can never forgive us for having
preceded them 300 years in civilisation. They are prepared
to enter into the most bloody wars in England, not on account of Oregon, or boundaries, or right of search, but
because our clothes and carriages are better made, and
because Bond Street beats Broadway. Wise Webster
does all he can to convince the people that these are not
lawful causes of war; but wars, and long wars, they will one
day or another produce; and this, perhaps, is the only advantage of repudiation. The Americans cannot gratify
their avarice and ambition at once; they cannot cheat and
conquer at the same time. The warlike power of every
country depends on their Three per Cents. If Cæsar were

to reappear upon earth, Wettenhall's list would be more important than his Commentaries; Rothschild would open and shut the temple of Janus; Thomas Baring, or Bates, would probably command the Tenth Legion, and the soldiers would march to battle with loud cries of Scrip and Omnium reduced, Consols, and Cæsar! Now the Americans have cut themselves off from all resources of credit. Having been as dishonest as they can be, they are prevented from being as foolish as they wish to be. In the whole habitable globe they cannot borrow a guinea, and they cannot draw the sword because they have not money to buy it.

If I were an American of any of the honest States, I would never rest till I had compelled Pennsylvania to be as honest as myself. The bad faith of that State brings disgrace on all; just as common snakes are killed because vipers are dangerous. I have a general feeling, that by that breed of men I have been robbed and ruined, and I shudder and keep aloof. The pecuniary credit of every State is affected by Pennsylvania. Ohio pays; but with such a bold bankruptcy before their eyes, how long will Ohio pay? The truth is, that the eyes of all capitalists are averted from the United States. The finest commercial understandings will have nothing to do with them. Men rigidly just, who penetrate boldly into the dealings of nations, and work with vigour and virtue for honourable wealth—great and high-minded merchants—will loathe, and are now loathing, the name of America: it is becoming, since its fall, the common-sewer of Europe, and the native home of the needy villain.

And now, drab-coloured men of Pennsylvania, there is yet a moment left: the eyes of all Europe are anchored upon you—

"Surrexit mundus justis furiis:"

start up from that trance of dishonesty into which you are plunged; don't think of the flesh which walls about your life, but of that sin which has hurled you from the heaven of character, which hangs over you like a devouring pestilence, and makes good men sad, and ruffians dance and sing. It is not for Gin Sling and Sherry Cobler alone that man is to live, but for those great principles against which no argument can be listened to—principles which give to every power a double power above their functions and their offices, which are the books, the arts, the academies that teach, lift up, and nourish the world—principles (I am quite serious in what I say) above cash, superior to cotton, higher than currency—principles, without which it is better to die than to live, which every servant of God, over every sea and in all lands, should cherish—*usque ad abdita spiramenta animæ.*

Yours, &c.

SYDNEY SMITH.

November 3, 1843.

ON THE ACCESSION OF A LIBERAL POPE

Walter Savage Landor

DEDICATION OF THE FIRST EDITION OF THE "HELLENICS"
(1847) TO THE NEWLY ELECTED POPE PIUS IX

Never until now, most Holy Father! did I hope or desire to offer my homage to any potentate on earth; and now I offer it only to the highest of them all.

There was a time when the cultivators of literature were permitted and expected to bring the fruit of their labour to the Vatican. Not only was incense welcome there, but even the humblest produce of the poorest soil.

Verbenam, pueri, ponite Thuraque.

If those better days are returning, without what was bad
or exceptionable in them, the glory is due entirely to your
Holiness. You have restored to Italy hope and happiness; to the rest of the world hope only. But a single
word from your prophetic lips, a single motion of your
earth-embracing arm, will overturn the firmest seats of
iniquity and oppression. The word must be spoken; the
arm must wave. What do we see before us? If we take
the best of rulers under our survey, we find selfishness and
frivolity; if we extend the view, ingratitude, disregard of
honour, contempt of honesty, breach of promises; one step
yet beyond, and there is cold-blooded idiocy, stabbing the
nobles at home, spurning the people everywhere, and
voiding its corrosive slaver in the fair face of Italy. It is
better to look no farther, else our eyes must be riveted on
frozen seas of blood superfused with blood fresh flowing.
The same ferocious animal leaves the impression of its
broad and heavy foot on the snow of the Arctic Circle and
of the Caucasus. And is this indeed all that Europe has
brought forth, after such long and painful throes? Has
she endured her Marats, her Robespierres, her Buonapartes,
for this? God inflicted on the latter of these wretches his
two greatest curses—uncontrolled power and perverted
intellect; and they were twisted together to make a scourge
for a nation which revelled in every crime, but above all
in cruelty. It was insufficient. She is now undergoing
from a weaker hand a more ignominious punishment,
pursued by the derision of Europe. To save her honour,
she pretended to admire the courage that decimated her
children: to save her honour, she now pretends to admire the
wisdom that imprisons them. Cunning is not wisdom;
prevarication is not policy; and (novel as the notion is, it is
equally true) armies are not strength: Acre and Waterloo
show it, and the flames of the Kremlin and the solitudes of

Fontainebleau. One honest man, one wise man, one peaceful man, commands a hundred millions, without a baton and without a charger. He wants no fortress to protect him; he stands higher than any citadel can raise him, brightly conspicuous to the most distant nations, God's servant by election, God's image by beneficence.

III

The Short-Story Essay

THE SHORT-STORY ESSAY

ONE of the reasons why the essay, as a periodic production, was led aside into the realm of fiction may have been that it was dangerous to deal with vital topics, and to write the ungarnished truth concerning contemporary men and manners, in a day when libel had a very liberal interpretation—a lesson which Daniel Defoe learnt to his cost on more than one occasion. It was safer and wiser to take a nom-de-plume and to invent your own characters in the early eighteenth century. A second reason may be found in the natural instinct of men, when writing or talking freely, to drift into the narration of anecdote, for the genius for story-telling is as old as speech itself, it has found expression in every form of written utterance which in any way allows of it, in poetry, theology, history, and private correspondence.

It has been seen that Francis Bacon derived his method largely from Montaigne, Machiavelli, and Philip de Comines, who derived theirs from the Greek and Latin authors. His essays often read like excerpts from reflections upon men and nations wherewith the classic historian was accustomed to interlard his relation of incidents. It was inevitable that the essay, when once it had freed itself from the Baconian restraint, should one day evolve itself into fiction; and what day was more fitting for this development than a time when it was rapidly becoming the most popular form of current literature through its attachment to the newspaper? Sir William Temple (1628–1699) was one of the earliest to foreshadow the evolution, of which his essay on *Health and Long Life*, wherein he draws upon his memory for facts and incidents which he himself has experienced, is a proof and illustration. But to Daniel Defoe is due the credit for first introducing in popular form the short-story essay, often through the medium of the *letter-essay*—a practice which was continued by many of his successors. It is not too much to say that he struck the new note chiefly because he was unhampered by a knowledge of the classics—wherewith his predecessors had been overladen. He was a modern type—the irrepressible journalist, keen and unscrupulous in his pursuit of copy. There is a spice of adventure about the man and inquisitiveness concerning the ways of life of all classes of society, which make him robust and refreshing. With the lower orders he is most at his ease; but he can also gossip about lords and ladies, though, it is true, very much in the hushed tones of a butler repeating scandal, which he had overheard in the dining-hall, to the serving-maid in the kitchen. His most vital characteristic is that he has a point of view from which, no matter what he relates, he watches life curiously. On this account he stands out in marked contrast to the many shallow and tired gentlemen of his age, who seem to have written their books in bed, babbling insincerely of the country while they gazed on a city thoroughfare; and even then to have written only to pass the time of day, because it did not happen to be the fashionable hour for going to the coffee-tavern, where they could sit with others of their kind, interminably discussing pedantries. Defoe was a trifle vulgar, perhaps; but vulgarity in him meant realism, and was an outstanding virtue, for the tendency of the Restoration had been to emasculate literature with over-elegance. And even before that period Bacon had been careful to tell his readers, as if it were a convincing claim to worthiness, that his essays were *not vulgar*. It was just this taint of the common people which writers of the seventeenth century lacked, and most required to make themselves comprehensible to the great majority of their fellow-men. Their absence of sturdiness and limitation of range is largely to be accounted for by the fact that they despised all men of classes lower than themselves. Though he often hated, Defoe despised no man who dwelt within the boundaries of his own land. Yet, because he was reputed vulgar, a mere Grub Street hack, he received no applause or recognition from his contemporaries. Alexander Pope could see nothing admirable in him. Referring to the occasion when he was pilloried for the libel contained in *The Shortest Way with the Dissenters*, he numbers him among the foolish ones and pillories him a second time in his *Dunciad* with the line, "Earless on high stood unabashed Defoe." Shut out from clubland and the coffee-tavern, because of his imperfect gentility, quite out of touch with the cultured and literary communities of his day, lacking a patron and never certain of a friend, harassed throughout life by political enemies, encountering repeated failures, with his religion for a jeer and a drawback, coming out of Newgate haunted by the fear that he would soon go in again, he went courageously on his way, doing his work, unsustained by any sense of greatness or heroism, still spiritful and unashamed. He is in many respects the bravest figure in all our English literature.

Sir William Temple tells us of himself that he "never wrote anything for the public without the intention of some public good." Defoe's purpose is different, as we might expect from a man the first copies of whose *Review* were issued from a prison-house. His real purpose was to make a livelihood, and to do this by literature, since he was no scholar, he was forced to interest the populace. Primarily the object of the *Review* was political, but it soon occurred to him that the inclusion of society scandal might increase its sale; to this end he added the *"Mercure Scandale"; or, Advices from the Scandalous Club.* It was probably from this venture of Defoe that Steele borrowed the idea of using club-life as a background for his essays. Defoe himself declares his intention as a man of letters, and it may be taken as the highest moral aim of any of his literary endeavours, when he writes, "and thus we *wheedle them into* the knowledge of the world, who, rather than take more pains, would be content with their ignorance, and search into nothing." One of the easiest ways of *wheedling* the simple or the obstinate into a knowledge of something concerning which they are not naturally curious is to tell them tales; this Defoe does in his short-story essays, which he often writes in letter form. Thus, when it is his desire *to wheedle* the public out of a belief in quack medicines, he sits down and feigns to write an unsolicited letter to Nathaniel Mist's *Journal*, descriptive of one such impostor whom he pretends to have seen "the other day" dispensing his wares in a little village through which he happened to be passing. The result is a short-story essay.

Steele, in his dedication of the first collected volume of the *Tatler*, states frankly his ambition. He resolved, he says, "to publish a paper which should observe upon the manners of the pleasurable, as well as the busy part of mankind." He did not propose to instruct, nor even to wheedle, but simply to observe and report to the world the results of his observation. Such reports consisted of news interwoven with reflection; they partook of the wide charity of Defoe in so far as they observed upon not only the pleasurable classes of society, but also upon the busy part of mankind. The *Tatler* was started on April 12, 1709, at the first mainly as a "letter of intelligence." At this time, as during the two previous years, Steele held the position of gazetteer, which made him the only authorised dispenser of government news. In 1711 the *Tatler* was abandoned and the *Spectator* commenced its career. In the *Tatler* the separate papers had borne slight relation one to another, the little continuity which the work as a whole possessed being derived from the personality of the supposed author, who styled himself Isaac Bickerstaff. The *Spectator* was an attempt to give unity to the miscellaneous daily issues of the paper; for this purpose Defoe's idea of the club was taken as a basis, and characters were invented who, as members of the club, were available to appear in every essay. If Defoe by his training was not a purely literary man, neither was Steele. Defoe in his time had served as a soldier in the Duke of Monmouth's insurrection, had been a hosier, tile-maker, and woollen-merchant, and in his boyhood had been trained for the dissenting ministry. Steele had been sent to Oxford, and almost before his university career was begun had enlisted in the Horse Guards. While still in the army, he had "commenced author" and, having turned dramatist, was in 1707 appointed to the post of gazetteer. He was always much more of a man about town than of letters. Hence he brought to his task, as did Defoe, a thorough knowledge of men, which made him charitable; with him also literature was very much an affair of livelihood, as the following story will prove, which Johnson relates of him in his *Life of Savage*:

"He (Savage) was once desired by Sir Richard, with an air of the utmost importance, to come very early to his house the next morning. Mr. Savage came as he had promised, found the chariot at the door, and Sir Richard waiting for him, and ready to go out. What was intended,

and whither they were to go, Savage would not con-
jecture, and was not willing to inquire; but immediately
seated himself with Sir Richard; the coachman was ordered
to drive, and they hurried with the utmost expedition to
Hyde Park Corner, where they stopped at a petty tavern,
and retired to a private room. Sir Richard then informed
him that he intended to publish a pamphlet, and that he
had desired him to come thither that he might write for
him. They soon sat down to the work. Sir Richard
dictated, and Savage wrote, till the dinner that had been
ordered was put upon the table. Savage was surprised
at the meanness of the entertainment, and after some
hesitation, ventured to ask for wine, which Sir Richard
ordered to be brought. They then finished their dinner,
and proceeded in their pamphlet, which they concluded in
the afternoon.

" Mr. Savage then imagined his task over, and expected
that Sir Richard would call for the reckoning, and return
home; but his expectations deceived him, for Sir Richard
told him that he was without money, and that the pamphlet
must be sold before the dinner could be paid for, and Savage
was therefore obliged to go and offer their new production
to sale for two guineas, which with some difficulty he obtained. Sir Richard then returned home, having retired
that day only to avoid his creditors, and composed the
pamphlet only to discharge his reckoning."

The purpose of Steele's contributions to the *Spectator*
was manifestly to entertain, and he brought to his work a
delicacy of humour of which Defoe was never capable.
Addison's share very often had for its motive the purpose
of the older essayists—to moralise and instruct. He was
at no time so far in advance of his age as were Defoe and
Steele. Yet out of this blending of the old with the new
he contrived a fresh form of story-essay which, however,

save in the case of Swift who utilised it on a larger scale, was rarely followed up—the fable-essay, the finest and unsurpassed example of which is *The Vision of Mirza*. Charles Lamb has wisely pointed out the affinity between Temple and Addison as writers of "genteel" English; and genteel is the adjective which best describes him. His gentility on separate occasions was accountable for both his perfection and shortcoming; it caused him to be high-minded and stainless, but it also caused him to be unduly reticent, so that he fears to discover his emotions. Where Lamb uses his scholarship and classics to enhance the merriment or pathos, Addison repeatedly uses them as instruments of restraint. Perhaps this reticence helps to make his work more truly national, since reticence is a dominant characteristic of his nation; certainly it serves to keep his humour pure, and that in a day when grossness passed currency as wit. Whatever may be the just estimate, and it has yet to be arrived at, of the permanent value of the work done by Steele and Addison in the *Spectator*, its final worth to English literature must forever remain unshaken. It is to be judged by the fact that it succeeded in establishing a standard of humour which was taintless, in a day when humour was too much dependent on licentiousness for its zest, and that, though the *Spectator* essays were issued through the daily press, they proved themselves superior to their means of conveyance and, in so doing, rescued the essay from the sole possession of the journalist. When the *Spectator* commenced its career, the essay was bidding fair to deteriorate into a merely fugitive form of writing; but before the last copy was published, at the end of the twenty-first month, the collaboration of these two men had lifted the essay-form beyond reach of the threatened oblivion, and had restored it to a permanent place in literature. What Thackeray has said of the *Tatler* may be said with equal truth of the *Spectator*, that when its publication began, "our great-great-grandfathers must have seized upon that new and delightful paper with much such eagerness as lovers of light literature in a later day exhibited when the Waverley novels appeared, upon which the public rushed, forsaking that feeble entertainment of which the Miss Porters, the Anne of Swanseas, and worthy Mrs. Radcliffe herself, with her dreary castles and exploded old ghosts, had had pretty much the monopoly." Scott rescued the novel from profane and palsied hands by contriving a new development and so establishing a new tradition, and this was the service which Steele and Addison wrought for the essay in an earlier day. Their new development, which they first borrowed from Defoe and then established, was the *short-story essay*. Defoe had not the reputation to achieve this for himself, for, as we have seen, he was everywhere regarded as only a Grub Street hack.

Swift, by reason of his originality in choice of subject and carelessness of public opinion in method of handling it, may almost be classed with George Borrow as one of the daring amateurs. No literary professional, however august, could have written as he did; the education of his atmosphere would have restrained him, as it did Addison, and have made him too timid for such temerarious assaults upon convention. Even Swift ruined his clerical career by his writing. The chief end which he proposed to himself in all his labours, so he wrote to Pope, was *to vex the world*, and no man will deny that he amply fulfilled his purpose. He vexes the world very frequently by accusing it through the medium of fable. He accuses it as a satirist of everything that emanates from man, not as Milton did politically and in the guise of a prophet, but as a monstrous jester, with Gargantuan volleys of ribaldry and the cruelty of thundrous laughter.

Goldsmith also accuses the world, but he does so with a humour gentle as that of Steele or Addison. He does not desire to make men angry, but rather to make them friends—*his* friends if possible. He moulds his short-story essay in the form of a letter, and so attains the intimacy of the first person. He outrides Defoe and Steele in his charity, for while they were only interested in all men of whatsoever class of their own nation, he is entirely lacking in national prejudice and takes for his theme all men—the world.

Charles Lamb is the last of the short-story essayists. As such, he fittingly gathers up into himself many of the merits which had gradually accumulated throughout the past age. He adopts the archaic phraseology of the seventeenth-century writers of the classic essay, but he does so only to be quaint and stately. He uses his scholarship lavishly and, as we have seen, not to restrain, as did Addison, but to spur on his fancy. He possesses all the quiet humour of Steele, and some of the uproar of Swift—without his bitterness. Like Goldsmith, his aim is to be companionable and friendly: he uses the first person, and the larger portion of his writing is scarcely veiled autobiography. In *Rejoicings Upon the New Year's Coming of Age*, which is here included as his specimen, he attempts the fable-essay, adapting it to humour simply and omitting the grave moral of Addison's *Vision of Mirza*. He is the ultimate of his race, and, in many ways, the most perfect.

With the growth of technique, the path of the short story diverged from that of the essay, and the short story became a separate department in literature—perhaps, a novel in miniature. But the influence of the short-story essay remained, and was directed from the channels of fiction and absorbed into those of truthful narration, out of which sprung the most unique contribution of the nineteenth century to the essay-form — the biographic essay.

HEALTH AND LONG LIFE

Sir William Temple

For the honour of our climate, it has been observed by ancient authors, that the Britons were longer-lived than any other nation to them known. And in modern times there have been more and greater examples of this kind than in any other countries of Europe. The story of old Parr is too late to be forgotten by many now alive, who was brought out of Derbyshire to the court in King Charles the First's time, and lived to a hundred and fifty-three years old; and might have, as was thought, gone further, if the change of country air and diet for that of the town, had not carried him off untimely at that very age. The late Robert Earl of Leicester, who was a person of great learning and observation, as well as of truth, told me several stories very extraordinary upon this subject; one of a Countess Desmond, married out of England in Edward the Fourth's time, and who lived far in King James's reign, and was counted to have died some years above a hundred and forty; at which age she came from Bristol to London to beg some relief at court, having long been very poor by the ruin of that Irish family into which she was married.

Another he told me was of a beggar at a bookseller's shop, where he was some weeks after the death of Prince Henry; and, observing those that passed by, he was saying to his company, that never such a mourning had been seen in England; this beggar, said, "No, never since the death of Prince Arthur." My Lord Leicester, surprised, asked what she meant, and whether she remembered it; she said, "Very well"; and upon his more curious inquiry, told him that her name was Rainsford, of a good family in Oxford-shire; that when she was about twenty years old, upon the falseness of a lover, she fell distracted; how long she had been so, nor what passed in that time, she knew not; that when she was thought well enough to go abroad, she was fain to beg for her living; that she was some time at this trade before she recovered any memory of what she had been, or where bred; that when this memory returned, she went down into her country, but hardly found the memory of any of her friends she had left there; and so returned to a parish in Southwark, where she had some small allowance among other poor, and had been for many years; and once a week walked into the city, and took what alms were given.   My Lord Leicester told me he sent to inquire at the parish, and found their account agree with the woman's; upon which he ordered her to call at his house once a week, which she did for some time; after which he heard no more of her.   This story raised some discourse upon a remark of some in the company, that mad people are apt to live long.   They alleged examples of their own knowledge; but the result was that if it were true, it must proceed from the natural vigour of their tempers, which disposed them to passions so violent as end in frenzies; and from the great abstinence and hardships of diet they are forced upon by the methods of their cure, and severity of those who had them in care; no other drink but water being allowed them, and very little meat.

The last story I shall mention from that noble person, upon this subject, was of a morris-dance in Herefordshire; whereof he said, he had a pamphlet still in his library, written by a very ingenious gentleman of that country; and which gave an account how, such a year of King James, his reign, there went about the country, a set of morris-dancers composed of ten men who danced a Maid Marian, and a tabor and pipe; and how these twelve, one with another made up twelve hundred years. 'Tis not so much that so many in one small county should live to that age, as that they should be in vigour and in humour to travel and to dance.

I have in my life met with two of above a hundred and twelve whereof the woman had passed her life in service, and the man in common labour till he grew old and fell upon the parish. But I met with one who had gone a much greater length, which made me more curious in my inquiries. 'Twas an old man who begged usually at a lonely inn upon the road in Staffordshire, who told me he was a hundred and twenty-four years old; that he had been a soldier in the Cadiz voyage under the Earl of Essex, of which he gave me a sensible account. That after his return, he fell to labour in his own parish, which was about a mile from the place where I met him. That he continued to work till a hundred and twelve, when he broke one of his ribs by a fall from a cart, and being thereby disabled he fell to beg. This agreeing with what the master of the house told me was reported and believed by all his neighbours. I asked him what his usual food was; he said, milk, bread, and cheese, and flesh when it was given him. I asked what he used to drink; he said, "Oh, sir, we have the best water in our parish that is in all the neighbourhood." Wherefore he never drank any thing else. He said, yes, if anybody gave it him, but not otherwise; and the host told me, he had got many a pound in his house, but never spent one penny. I asked if he had any neighbours as old as he, and he told me but one, who had been his fellow-soldier at Cadiz, and was three years older; but he had been most of his time in a good service, and had something to live on now he was old.

I have heard, and very credibly, of many in my life above

a hundred years old, brought as witnesses upon trials of titles, and bounds of land; but have observed most of them to have been of Derbyshire, Staffordshire, or Yorkshire, and none above the rank of common farmers. The oldest I ever knew any persons of quality, or indeed, any gentleman, either at home or abroad, was four-score and twelve. This added to all the former recites or observations, either of long-lived races or persons in any age or country, makes it easy to conclude that health and long life are usually blessings of the poor, not of the rich; and the fruits of temperance, rather than of luxury and excess. And indeed if a rich man does not in many things live like a poor, he will certainly be the worse for his riches; if he does not use exercise, which is but voluntary labour; if he does not restrain appetite by choice as the other does by necessity. If he does not practise sometimes even abstinence and fasting, which is the last extreme of want and poverty; if his cares and his troubles increase with his riches, or his passions with his pleasures; he will certainly impair in health, whilst he improves his fortunes, and lose more than he gains by the bargain; since health is the best of all human possessions, and without which the rest are not relished or not kindly enjoyed.

DESCRIPTION OF A QUACK DOCTOR[1]

Daniel Defoe

December 5, 1719.

M. MIST,—Passing occasionally the other day through a little village, at some distance from town, I was entertained with the view of a very handsome equipage moving toward me. The gravity of the gentleman who sat in it, and the

---

[1] This same theme is treated of by William Clowes (1540–1604), in his *Proved Practise for All Young Chirurgeons*. Clowes, in his early life, served in the navy, and was present with the fleet

eagerness wherewith the coachman drove along, engaged my whole attention; and I immediately concluded, that it could be nothing less than some Minister of State, who was posting this way, upon some very important affair. They were now got about the middle of the place, when making a full stand, the footman deserting his station be-

at the defeat of The Armada. He afterward became surgeon to Queen Elizabeth. His description of a quack occurs in the following passage: "Then riseth out of his chair, fleering and jeering, this miraculous surgeon, gloriously glittering like the man in the moon, with his bracelets about his arms, therein many precious jewels and stones of Saint Vincent his rocks, his fingers full of rings, a silver case with instruments hanging at his girdle, and a gilt *spatula* sticking in his hat, with a rose and crown fixed on the same, standing upon his comparisons, and said unto me that he would open the wound, and if it were before my face: for (said he) my business lieth not in London, but abroad in the country, and with such persons that I cannot nor will not tarry for you, nor for no other whatsoever. And now here he did begin to brag and boast as though all the keys of knowledge did hang at his girdle. For he said he had attained unto the deep knowledge of the making of a certain quintessence which he learned beyond the seas of his master Bornelius, a great magician. This shameless beast letted not to say that if a man did drink of his quintessence continually every day a certain quantity, the virtue thereof was such that a man should not die before the day of the great Judgement, and that it would preserve him in that state he was in at thirty years of age, and in the same strength and force of will, although a man were a hundred or six score years of age. Moreover his plaster was answerable unto this, and forsooth he called it the only plaster of the world, and that he attained unto it by his great travail, cost, and charge, and that it was first sent from God by an angel unto a red hill in Almayne, where was in times past a holy man which wrought great marvels only with this plaster, and he never used any other medicine but only this. His precious balm or oil he said no man had, but only he, and that it was as rare a thing to be had or found, as to see a black swan or a winter swallow, and he called it the secret of the world, which is his common vaunting phrase: but God knows the medicines were no such things, but only shadowed under the vizard of deceit, and a bait to steal fame and credit, and to catch or scrape up money or ware, for all is fish that cometh unto his net. Then this gaudy fellow with his peerless speeches, said that he had done more good hind, and making up abreast of his master, gave us a very fine blast with a trumpet. I was surprised to see a skip transformed so speedily into a trumpeter, and began to wonder what should be the meaning of such an unusual phenomenon; when the coachman, jumping from his box, laying by his whip, and slipping off his great coat, in an instant rose up a complete Merry Andrew. My surprise was now heightened, and, though honest pickle, with a world of grimace and gesticulation endeavoured to move my gaiety, I began to be very fearful where the metamorphosis might end. I looked very earnestly first at the horse, and then at the wheels, and expected every minute to have seen them take their turn in the farce, and, laying aside their present appearances, assume other shapes. By this time the gentleman, who had hitherto appeared wonderfully sedate and composed, began to throw off his disguise; and having pocketed all his former modesty and demureness, and flushed his forehead with all the impudence of a thorough-paced quack, I immediately discovered him to be a very eminent and learned *mountebank*.

This discovery raised my curiosity as much as it abated my surprise, so that being very desirous to hear what new proposal the doctor had to make, or what new arcanum in physic he had found out, I quitted my former station, and joined myself to the crowd that incompassed him. After a short preamble, he began to open the design of his

cures with his said quintessence, his only plaster, and his precious balm than any one surgeon in England had done or could do with all the best medicines and remedies they have. And moreover said that he had spoken nothing but that which he would stand to and prove it. And that he did know that it was not necessary for us common surgeons (as it pleased the bragger to call us) to use such a number of medicines as we do." (For a further example of William Clowes' work, *vide* vol. i, p. 593, of Mr. Henry Craik's scholarly *English Prose Selections*.)

embassy, setting forth, at large, the great affection which he bore, in particular, to the people of that place; amplifying on his own merits and qualifications, specifying great numbers of cures which he had wrought on incurable distempers, expatiating on the extreme danger of being without his physic, and offering health and immortality to sale, for the price of a tester.

You'd have burst your sides, Mr. Mist, had you but heard the foolish allusions, quaint expressions, and inconsistent metaphors, which fell from the mouth of this eloquent declaimer. For my part, I should have wondered where he could have raked up nonsense enough to furnish out such a wordy harangue, but that I am told he has studied the *Flying Post* with a great deal of application; and, that most of the silly things in his speech are borrowed from that excellent author. Sometimes he'd creep, in the most vulgar phrases imaginable; by and by he'd soar out of sight and traverse the spacious *realms of fustian and bombast.* He was, indeed, very sparing of his Latin and Greek, as (God knows) having a very slender stock of those commodities; but then, for hard words and terms, which neither he, nor you, nor I, nor any one else understand, he poured them out in such abundance, that you'd have sworn he had been rehearsing some of the occult philosophy of Agrippa or Rosicrusius, or reading a lecture out of Cabala.

After the doctor had given such ample indications of the greatest humanity, skill, and erudition, who d' ye think would be so incredulous as not to believe him, or so uncourteous as to refuse to purchase one of his packets? Lest any of us, however, should be too tenacious of our money to part with it on these considerations, he had one other motive which did not fail to do the business; this was, by persuading us that there were the seeds of *some malignant distemper* lurking in every one of our bodies; and, that there was nothing in Nature could save us, but some one or other of his medicines. He threaten'd us with death in case of refusal, and assured us, with a prophetic air, that without his physic every mother's son of us would be in our graves by that day twelve-month. The poor people were infinitely terrified, with the imminent danger they found themselves under, but were as much pleased to find how easy it was to be evaded; so that, without more ado, every man bought his packet, and turned the doctor adrift to pursue further adventures.

The scene being now removed, I was at leisure to reflect on what had passed, and could really have either cry'd or laugh'd very heartily, at what I had seen. The arrogance of the *doctor* and the silliness of his *patients* were each of them ridiculous enough to have set a person of more gravity than myself laughing; but then to consider the tragical issue to which these things tended, and the fatal effect so many murthering medicines might have on several of his Majesty's good subjects, wou'd have made the merriest *buffoon* alive serious. I have not often observed a more hale, robust crowd of people than that which incircled this doughty doctor; methinks one might have read health in their very faces, and there was not a countenance among them which did not give the lie to the doctor's suggestions. Cou'd but one see a little into futurity, and observe the condition they will be in, a few months hence, what an alteration wou'd one find! How many of those brawny youths are already puking in chimney corners? And how many rosy complexioned girls are by this time reduced to the paleness of a *cockney* ?

I propose in a little time to make a second journey to this place, in order to see how the doctor's physic has *operated*. By searching the parish register, and comparing the number of funerals made weekly before the doctor's visit, with those which have followed, it will be easy to form an estimate of the havoc which this *itinerant man-slayer* made in the space of two hours. I shall then proceed to compute the number of *quacks* in the three kingdoms, from which it will be no hard matter to determine the number of people carried off *per annum* by the whole fraternity. Lastly, I shall calculate the loss which the government sustains by the death of every subject; from all of which, the immense damages accruing to his Majesty will evidently appear, and the public will be fully convinced of the truth of what I had heretofore asserted, *viz. that the quacks contribute more toward keeping us poor, than all our national debts; and that to suppress the former, would be an infallible means of redeeming the latter*. The whole scheme shall be drawn up in due form and presented to the Parliament in the ensuing session, and that august assembly, I don't doubt, will pay all regard thereto, which the importance of the subject and the weight of my argument shall require.

Methinks the course of justice, which has hitherto obtained among us, is chargeable with great absurdities. *Petty* villains are hanged or transported, while *great* ones are suffered to pass *impune*. A man cannot take a purse upon the highway, or cut a single throat, but he must presently be called to answer for it at the Old Bailey, and perhaps to suffer for it at Tyburn; and yet, here are wretches suffered to commit murthers by wholesale, and to plunder, not only private persons and pockets, but even the King and the Exchequer, without having any questions asked! Pray, Mr. Mist, what were gibbets, gallows, and whipping-posts made for?

But to return to Doctor Thornhill. I have had the curiosity to examine several of his medicines in a reverberatory, reducing compounds into their simples by a chymical

analysis, and have constantly found a considerable proportion of some poisonous plant or mineral in every one
of them. Arsenic, mercury, and hemlock are *sine quibus
non;* and he could no more take up a medicament
without some of these than remove a mountain. Accordingly as they are variously mix'd and disposed among
other drugs, he gives them various names, calling them
pills, electuaries, etc. His pills I would prescribe as a
succedaneum to a halter; so that such persons as are
weary of this troublesome world, and wou'd willingly quit
it for a better, but are too squeamish to take up with that
queer old-fashioned recipe called hanging, may have their
business done as securely, and more decently by some of
these excellent pills. His bolus, too, is very good in its
kind; I have made experiments with it on several animals,
and find that it poisons to a miracle. A moderate dose of
it has perfectly silenced a bawling dog that used to disturb
my morning slumbers; and a like quantity of it has quieted
several other snarling curs in my neighbourhood. And
then, if you be troubled with rats, Mr. Mist, there's the
doctor's electuary is an infallible remedy, as I myself have
experienced. I have effectually cleared my house of those
troublesome animals, by disposing little parcels of it in the
places they frequent; and do recommend it to you and
your readers, as the most powerful ratsbane in the world.
It would be needless to enumerate all the virtues of the
doctor's several medicines; but I dare affirm that what the
ancients fabulously reported of *Pandora's box* is strictly
true of the *doctor's packet*, and, that it contains in it the
seeds and principles of all diseases.

I must ask your pardon, Mr. Mist, for being so grave on
so ludicrous a subject, and, spending so many words on an
empty quack.

The Fates of Clergymen

Jonathan Swift

There is no *Talent* so useful toward rising in the World, or which puts men more out of the Reach of Fortune, than that Quality generally possessed by the dullest sort of People, and is in common Speech called *Discretion*, a Species of lower Prudence, by the Assistance of which People of the meanest Intellectuals, without any other Qualification, pass through the World in great Tranquillity, and with universal good Treatment, neither giving nor taking Offence. *Courts* are seldom unprovided of Persons under this Character, on whom, if they happen to be of great Quality, most Employments, even the greatest, naturally fall, when Competitors will not agree; and in such Promotions nobody rejoices or grieves. The Truth of this I could prove by several Instances within my own Memory (for I say nothing of the present Times). . . .

This Talent of *Discretion* is no where so serviceable as to the *Clergy*, to whose Preferment nothing is so fatal as the Character of Wit, Politeness in Reading, or Manners, or that kind of Behaviour, which we contract by having too much conversed with Persons of high Stations and Eminency; these Qualifications being reckoned by the *Vulgar* of all *Ranks* to be Marks of *Levity*, which is the last Crime the World will pardon in a *Clergyman :* to this I may add a free Manner of speaking in mixt Company, and too frequent an Appearance in Places of much Resort, which are equally noxious to spiritual Promotions. . . .

I will here give the Reader a short History of two *Clergymen* in *England*, the Characters of each, and the Progress of their Fortunes in the World; by which the Force of

Worldly Discretion, and the bad Consequences from the Want of that Virtue will strongly appear.

Corusodes, an *Oxford* Student, and a Farmer's son, was never absent from Prayers or Lecture, nor once out of his *College* after *Tom* had toll'd. He spent every day ten Hours in his Closet, in reading his Courses, Dozing, clipping Papers, or darning his Stockings, which last he performed to Admiration. He could be soberly drunk at the Expence of others with *College* Ale, and at those seasons was always most devout. He wore the same Gown five years, without draggling or tearing. He never once look'd into a Play-book or a Poem. He read *Virgil* and *Ramus* in the same Cadence, but with a very different Taste. He never understood a Jest, or had the least Conception of Wit.

For one Saying he stands in Renown to this day. Being with some other Students over a Pot of Ale, one of the Company said so many pleasant Things, that the rest were much diverted, only *Corusodes* was silent and unmoved. When they parted, he called this merry Companion aside, and said, *Sir, I perceive by your often speaking, and our Friends Laughing, that you spoke many Jests, and you could not but observe my Silence. But, Sir, this is my Humour; I never make a Jest myself, nor ever laugh at another Man's.*

Corusodes thus endowed got into Holy Orders, having by the most extreme Parsimony saved thirty-four pounds out of a beggarly Fellowship; went up to *London*, where his Sister was Waiting-Woman to a Lady, and so good a Sollicitor, that by her means he was admitted to read Prayers in the Family twice a day, at fourteen shillings a Month. He had now acquired a low, obsequious, awkward Bow and a Talent of gross Flattery both in and out of season; he would shake the Butler by the Hand; he taught the Page his *Catechism*, and was sometimes admitted to dine at the Steward's Table. In short, he got the good

Word of the whole Family, and was recommended by my Lady for Chaplain to some other Noble House, by which his Revenue (besides Vales) amounted to about thirty pounds a Year; his Sister procured him a Scarf from my Lord (who had a small Design of Gallantry upon her); and by his Lordship's sollicitations he got a Lectureship in Town of sixty Pounds a Year; where he preached constantly in Person, in a grave Manner, with an audible Voice, a Style Ecclesiastick, and the Matter (such as it was) well suited to the Intellectuals of his Hearers. Some time after a Country Living fell into my Lord's Disposal, and his Lordship, who had now some Encouragement given him of Success in his Amour, bestow'd the Living on *Corusodes*, who still kept his Lectureship and Residence in Town, where he was a constant Attendant at all Meetings relating to Charity, without ever contributing further than his frequent pious Exhortations. If any Woman of better Fashion in the Parish happened to be absent from Church, they were sure of a Visit from him in a Day or two, to chide and to dine with them.

He had a select Number of Poor constantly attending at the Street Door of his Lodgings, for whom he was a common Sollicitor to his former Patroness, dropping in his own half-Crown among the Collections, and taking it out when he disposed of the Money. At a Person of Quality's House, he would never sit down till he was thrice bid, and then upon the Corner of the most distant Chair. His whole Demeanor was formal and starched, which adhered so close, that he could never shake it off in his highest Promotion.

His Lord was now in high Employment at Court, and attended by him with the most abject Assiduity, and his Sister being gone with Child to a private Lodging, my Lord continued his Graces to *Corusodes*, got him to be a Chaplain in Ordinary, and in due Time a Parish in Town, and a *Dignity in the Church.*

He paid his *Curates* punctually, at the lowest Salary. and partly out of the Communion-Money; but gave them good Advice in Abundance. He married a Citizen's Widow, who taught him to put out small Sums at *Ten per Cent.*, and brought him acquainted with Jobbers in *Change-Alley.* By her Dexterity he sold the Clarkship of his Parish, when it became vacant.

He kept a miserable House, but the Blame was laid wholly upon *Madam;* for the good Doctor was always at his *Books,* or visiting the sick, or doing other Offices of Charity and Piety in his Parish.

He treated all his Inferiors of the Clergy with a most sanctified Pride; was rigorously and universally censorious upon all his Brethren of the Gown on their first appearance in the World, or while they continued meanly preferred, but gave large Allowance to the Laity of high Rank or great Riches, using neither Eyes nor Ears for their Faults; He was never sensible of the least Corruption in *Courts, Parliaments,* or *Ministries,* but made the most favourable constructions of all publick proceedings; and Power, in whatever Hands, or whatever Party, was always secure of his most charitable Opinion. He had many wholesome Maxims ready to excuse all Miscarriages of State; *Men are but Men; Erunt vitia donec homines;* and *Quod Supra nos, nil ad nos;* with several others of equal Weight.

It would lengthen my Paper beyond measure to trace out the whole System of his Conduct; his dreadful Apprehensions of *Popery;* his great Moderation toward Dissenters of all Denominations; with hearty Wishes, that by yielding somewhat on both sides, there might be a general Union among Protestants; in short, inoffensive Sermons in his Turns at Court, and the Matter exactly suited to the present

Juncture of prevailing Opinions; the Arts he used to obtain a Mitre, by writing against Episcopacy; and the Proofs he gave of his Loyalty, by palliating or defending the Murder of a martyr'd Prince.

Endowed with all these Accomplishments, we leave him in the full Career of Success, mounting fast toward the top of the Ladder Ecclesiastical, which he hath a fair probability to reach, without the merit of one single Virtue, moderately stocked with the least valuable parts of Erudition, utterly devoid of all *Taste, Judgment*, or *Genius*, and in his Grandeur naturally chusing to hawl up others after him, whose Accomplishments most resemble his own, except his beloved Sons, Nephews, or other Kindred, be not in Competition; or lastly, except his Inclinations be diverted by those, who have power to mortify or further advance him.

Eugenio set out from the same University, and about the same Time with *Corusodes;* he had the Reputation of an arch Lad at school, and was unfortunately possessed with a *Talent* for *Poetry*, on which Account he received many chiding Letters from his Father, and grave Advice from his Tutor. He did not neglect his College Learning, but his chief Study was the Authors of Antiquity, with a perfect Knowledge in the *Greek* and *Roman Tongues*. He could never procure himself to be chosen Fellow, for it was objected against him, that he had written Verses, and particularly some, wherein he glanced at a certain Reverend Doctor famous for Dulness; that he had been seen bowing to Ladies, as he met them in the streets; and it was proved, that once he had been found dancing in a private Family with half a dozen of both Sexes.

He was the younger Son to a Gentleman of a good Birth, but small Fortune; and his Father dying, he was driven to *London* to seek his Fortune; He got into Orders, and became

Reader in a Parish Church at twenty pounds a Year, was carried by an *Oxford* Friend to *Will's Coffee-House* frequented in those days by Men of Wit, where in some Time he had the bad Luck to be distinguished. His scanty Salary compelled him to run deep in Debt for a new Gown and Cassock, and now and then forced him to write some Paper of Wit or Humour, or preach a Sermon for ten shillings, to supply his Necessities. He was a thousand times recommended by his political Friends to great Persons, as a young Man of excellent Parts, who deserved Encouragement; and received a thousand promises; but his Modesty, and a generous Spirit, which disdained the slavery of continual Applications and Attendance, always disappointed him, making room for vigilant Dunces, who were sure to be never out of sight.

He had an excellent Faculty in preaching, if he were not sometimes a little too refined, and apt to trust too much to his own Way of thinking and reasoning.

When upon the Vacancy of Preferment he was hardly drawn to attend upon some promising Lord, he received the usual Answer, that he came too late, for it had been given to another, the very Day before. And he had only this Comfort left, that every Body said, it was a thousand Pities, something could not be done for poor Mr. *Eugenio*.

The remainder of his Story will be dispatched in a few Words: Wearied with weak Hopes, and weaker Pursuits, he accepted a Curacy in *Derbyshire* of thirty pounds a Year, and when he was five and forty, had the great Felicity to be preferred by a Friend of his Father's to a Vicaridge worth annually sixty pounds in the most desart Parts of *Lincolnshire*, where his Spirit quite sunk with those Reflections that Solitude and disappointments bring, he married a Farmer's Widow, and is still alive, utterly undistinguished, and forgotten, only some of the Neighbours have accidentally heard, *that he had been a notable Man in his Youth.*

SCENE OF DOMESTIC FELICITY

Sir Richard Steele

From my own Apartment, November 16.

There are several persons who have many pleasures and entertainments in their possession, which they do not enjoy. It is, therefore, a kind and good office to acquaint them with their own happiness, and turn their attention to such instances of their good fortune as they are apt to overlook. Persons in the married state often want such a monitor; and pine away their days, by looking upon the same condition in anguish and murmur, which carries with it, in the opinion of others, a complication of all the pleasures of life, and a retreat from its inquietudes.

I am led into this thought by a visit I made an old friend, who was formerly my schoolfellow. He came to town last week with his family for the winter, and yesterday morning sent me word his wife expected me to dinner. I am, as it were at home at that house, and every member of it knows me for their well - wisher. I cannot indeed express the pleasure it is, to be met by the children with so much joy as I am when I go thither. The boys and girls strive who shall come first, when they think it is I that am knocking at the door; and that child which loses the race to me runs back again to tell the father it is Mr. Bickerstaffe. This day I was led in by a pretty girl, that we all thought must have forgot me; for the family has been out of town these two years. Her knowing me again was a mighty subject with us, and took up our discourse at the first entrance. After which, they began to rally me upon a thousand little stories they heard in the country, about my marriage to one of my neighbour's daughters.   Upon which the gentleman, my friend, said, "Nay, if Mr. Bickerstaffe marries a child of any of his old companions, I hope mine shall have the preference; there is Mrs. Mary, now sixteen, and would make him as fine a widow as the best of them.   But I know him too well; he is so enamoured with the very memory of those who flourished in our youth, that he will not so much as look upon the modern beauties.   I remember, old gentleman, how often you went home in a day to refresh your countenance and dress when Teraminta reigned in your heart.   As we came up in the coach, I repeated to my wife some of your verses on her."   With such reflections on little passages which happened long ago, we passed our time, during a cheerful and elegant meal. After dinner, his lady left the room, as did also the children. As soon as we were alone, he took me by the hand; "Well, my good friend," said he, "I am heartily glad to see thee; I was afraid you would never have seen all the company that dined with you to-day again.   Do not you think the good woman of the house a little altered since you followed her from the play-house, to find out who she was, for me?" I perceived a tear fall down his cheek as he spoke, which moved me not a little.   But to turn the discourse, I said, "She is not indeed quite that creature she was, when she returned me the letter I carried from you; and told me, 'she hoped, as I was a gentleman, I would be employed no more to trouble her, who had never offended me; but would be so much the gentleman's friend, as to dissuade him from a pursuit, which he could never succeed in.' You may remember, I thought her in earnest; and you were forced to employ your cousin Will, who made his sister get acquainted with her, for you.   You cannot expect her to be forever fifteen."   "Fifteen!" replied my good friend: "Ah, you little understand, you that have lived a bachelor, how great, how exquisite a pleasure there is, in being really beloved! It is impossible, that the most beauteous face in nature should raise in me such pleasing ideas, as when I look upon that excellent woman. That fading in her countenance is chiefly caused by her watching with me, in my fever. This was followed by a fit of sickness, which had like to have carried her off last winter. I tell you sincerely, I have so many obligations to her, that I cannot, with any sort of moderation, think of her present state of health. But as to what you say of fifteen, she gives me every day pleasures beyond what I ever knew in the possession of her beauty, when I was in the vigour of youth. Every moment of her life brings me fresh instances of her complacency to my inclinations, and her prudence in regard to my fortune. Her face is to me much more beautiful than when I first saw it; there is no decay in any feature, which I cannot trace, from the very instant it was occasioned by some anxious concern for my welfare and interests. Thus, at the same time, methinks, the love I conceived towards her for what she was, is heightened by my gratitude for what she is. The love of a wife is as much above the idle passion, commonly called by that name, as the loud laughter of buffoons is inferior to the elegant mirth of gentlemen. Oh! she is an inestimable jewel. In her examination of her household affairs, she shows a certain fearfulness to find a fault, which makes her servants obey her like children; and the meanest we have has an ingenuous shame for an offence, not always to be seen in children in other families. I speak freely to you, my old friend; ever since her sickness, things that gave me the quickest joy before, turn now to a certain anxiety. As the children play in the next room, I know the poor things by their steps, and am considering what they must do, should they lose their mother in their tender years. The pleasure I used to take in telling my boy stories of battles, and asking my girl questions about the disposal of her baby, and the gossiping of it, is turned into inward reflection and melancholy."

He would have gone on in this tender way, when the good lady entered, and with an inexpressible sweetness in her countenance told us, "she had been searching her closet for something very good to treat such an old friend as I was." Her husband's eye sparkled with pleasure at the cheerfulness of her countenance; and I saw all his fears vanish in an instant. The lady observing something in our looks which showed we had been more serious than ordinary, and seeing her husband receive her with great concern under a forced cheerfulness, immediately guessed at what we had been talking of; and applying herself to me, said with a smile, "Mr. Bickerstaffe, do not believe a word of what he tells you, I shall still live to have you for my second, as I have often promised you, unless he takes more care of himself than he has done since his coming to town. You must know, he tells me he finds London is a much more healthy place than the country; for he sees several of his old acquaintances and schoolfellows are here, *young fellows with fair full-bottomed periwigs*. I could scarce keep him this morning from going out *open-breasted*." My friend, who is always extremely delighted with her agreeable humours, made her sit down with us. She did it with that easiness which is peculiar to women of sense; and to keep up the good-humor she had brought in with her, turned her raillery upon me. "Mr. Bickerstaffe, you remember you followed me one night from the play-house; suppose you should carry me thither to-morrow night, and lead me into the front box." This put us into a long field of discourse about the beauties who were mothers to the present, and shined in the boxes twenty years ago. I told her, "I was glad she had transferred so many of her charms, and I did not question but her eldest daughter was within half a year of being a toast."

We were pleasing ourselves with this fantastical preferment of the young lady, when on a sudden we were alarmed with the noise of a drum, and immediately entered my little godson to give me a point of war. His mother, between laughing and chiding, would have put him out of the room; but I would not part with him so. I found, upon conversation with him, though he was a little noisy in his mirth, that the child had excellent parts, and was a great master of all the learning on the other side eight years old. I perceived him a very great historian in Æsop's Fables: but he frankly declared to me his mind, "that he did not delight in that learning, because he did not believe they were true"; for which reason I found he had very much turned his studies, for about a twelvemonth past, into the lives and adventures of Don Bellianis of Greece, Guy of Warwick, the Seven Champions, and other historians of that age. I could not but observe the satisfaction the father took in the forwardness of his son; and that these diversions might turn to some profit, I found the boy had made remarks, which might be of service to him during the course of his whole life. He would tell you the mismanagements of John Hickerthrift, find fault with the passionate temper in Bevis of Southampton, and loved Saint George for being the champion of England; and by this means had his thoughts insensibly moulded into the notions of discretion, virtue, and honour. I was extolling his accomplishments, when his mother told me that, "The little girl who led me in this morning, was in her way a better scholar than he. Betty," said she, "deals chiefly in fairies and sprights; and sometimes in a winter-night will terrify the maids with her accounts, until they are afraid to go up to bed."

I sat with them until it was very late, sometimes in merry, sometimes in serious discourse, with this particular pleasure, which gives the only true relish to all conversation, a sense that every one liked each other. I went home considering the different conditions of a married life and that of a bachelor; and I must confess it struck me with a secret concern, to reflect, that whenever I go off, I shall leave no traces behind me. In this pensive mood I return to my family; that is to say, to my maid, my dog, and my cat, who only can be better or worse for what happens to me.

NED SOFTLY'S POETRY

Joseph Addison

Will's Coffee-house, April 24.

I yesterday came hither about two hours before the company generally make their appearance, with a design to read over all the newspapers; but upon my sitting down, I was accosted by Ned Softly, who saw me from a corner in the other end of the room, where I found he had been writing something. "Mr. Bickerstaffe, (says he,) I observe by a late paper of yours, that you and I are just of a humour; for you must know, of all impertinencies, there is nothing which I so much hate as news. I never read a Gazette in my life; and never trouble my head about our armies, whether they win or lose, or in what part of the world they lie encamped." Without giving me time to reply, he drew a paper of verses out of his pocket, telling me that he had something which would entertain me more agreeably, and that he would desire my judgment upon every line, for that we had time enough before us until the company came in.

Ned Softly is a very pretty poet, and a great admirer of easy lines. Waller is his favourite: and as that admirable writer has the best and worst verses of any among our great English poets, Ned Softly has got all the bad ones without book, which he repeats upon occasion, to show his reading, and garnish his conversation. Ned is indeed a true English reader, incapable of relishing the great and masterly strokes of this art; but wonderfully pleased with the little Gothic ornaments of epigrammatical conceits, turns, points, and quibbles, which are so frequent in the most admired of our English poets, and practised by those who want genius and strength to represent, after the manner of the ancients, simplicity in its natural beauty and perfection.

Finding myself unavoidably engaged in such a conversation, I was resolved to turn my pain into a pleasure, and to divert myself as well as I could with so very odd a fellow. " You must understand, (says Ned,) that the sonnet I am going to read to you was written upon a lady, who showed me some verses of her own making, and is, perhaps, the best poet of our age. But you shall hear it." Upon which he began to read as follows:

" 'TO MIRA, ON HER INCOMPARABLE POEMS.

I

" ' When dress'd in laurel wreaths you shine,
    And tune your soft melodious notes,
You seem a sister of the Nine,
    Or Phœbus' self in petticoats.

II

" ' I fancy, when your song you sing,
    (Your song you sing with so much art)
Your pen was pluck'd from Cupid's wing;
    For ah! it wounds me like his dart.' "

"Why, (says I,) this is a little nosegay of conceits, a very lump of salt: every verse hath something in it that piques; and then the dart in the last line is certainly as pretty a sting in the tail of an epigram, (for so I think you critics call it,) as ever entered into the thought of a poet." "Dear Mr. Bickerstaffe, (says he, shaking me by the hand,) everybody knows you to be a judge of these things; and to tell you truly, I read over Roscommon's translation of Horace's Art of Poetry three several times, before I sat down to write the sonnet which I have shown you. But you shall hear it again, and pray observe every line of it; for not one of them shall pass without your approbation.

"'When dress'd in laurel wreaths you shine.'

"That is, (says he,) when you have your garland on; when you are writing verses." To which I replied, "I know your meaning; a metaphor!" "The same," said he, and went on.

"'And tune your soft melodious notes.'

"Pray observe the gliding of that verse; there is scarce a consonant in it: I took care to make it run upon liquids. Give me your opinion of it." "Truly, (said I,) I think it as good as the former." "I am very glad to hear you say so, (says he:) but mind the next.

"'You seem a sister of the Nine.'

"That is, (says he,) you seem a sister of the Muses; for, if you look into ancient authors, you will find it was their opinion that there were nine of them." "I remember it very well, (said I;) but pray proceed."

11   "'Or Phœbus' self in petticoats.'

"Phœbus, (says he,) was the god of poetry. These little
instances, Mr. Bickerstaffe, show a gentleman's reading.
Then to take off from the air of learning, which Phœbus
and the Muses had given to this first stanza, you may
observe, how it falls all of a sudden into the familiar, 'in
petticoats'!

"'Or Phœbus' self in petticoats.'"

"Let us now, (says I,) enter upon the second stanza.
I find the first line is still a continuation of the metaphor.

"'I fancy when your song you sing.'"

"It is very right, (says he;) but pray observe the turn of
words in those two lines. I was a whole hour in adjusting
of them, and have still a doubt upon me whether in the
second line it should be, 'Your song you sing'; or, 'You
sing your song.' You shall hear them both:

"'I fancy when your song you sing,'
(Your song you sing with so much art);

or,

"'I fancy when your song you sing,'
(You sing your song with so much art)."

"Truly, (said I,) the turn is so natural either way, that
you have made me almost giddy with it."   "Dear sir,
(said he, grasping me by the hand,) you have a great deal
of patience; but pray what do you think of the next verse?

"'Your pen was pluck'd from Cupid's wing.'"

"Think! (says I;) I think you have made Cupid look
like a little goose."   "That was my meaning, (says he,)

I think the ridicule is well enough hit off. But we come now to the last, which sums up the whole matter.

"'For ah! it wounds me like his dart.'

"Pray how do you like that *ah ?* doth it not make a pretty figure in that place? *Ah!* it looks as if I felt the dart, and cried out as being pricked with it.

"'For ah! it wounds me like his dart.'

"My friend, Dick Easy, (continued he,) assured me, he would rather have written that *ah!* than to have been the author of the Æneid. He indeed objected, that I made Mira's pen like a quill in one of the lines, and like a dart in the other. But as to that—" "Oh! as to that, (says I,) it is but supposing Cupid to be like a porcupine, and his quills and darts will be the same thing." He was going to embrace me for the hint; but half a dozen critics coming into the room, whose faces he did not like, he conveyed the sonnet into his pocket, and whispered me in the ear, he would show it me again as soon as his man had written it over fair.

PROCEEDINGS OF A CLUB OF AUTHORS

Oliver Goldsmith

By my last advices from Moscow I find the caravan has not yet departed for China. I still continue to write, expecting that you may receive a large number of my letters at once. In them you will find rather a minute detail of English peculiarities, than a general picture of their manners or disposition. Happy it were for mankind if all travellers would thus, instead of characterising a people in general terms, lead us into a detail of those minute circumstances which first influenced their opinion. The genius of a country should be investigated with a kind of experimental inquiry; by this means we should have more precise and just notions of foreign nations, and detect travellers themselves when they happened to form wrong conclusions.

My friend and I repeated our visit to the club of authors; where, upon our entrance, we found the members all assembled and engaged in a loud debate.

The poet, in shabby finery, holding a manuscript in his hand, was earnestly endeavouring to persuade the company to hear him read the first book of an heroic poem which he had composed the day before. But against this all the members very warmly objected. They knew no reason why any member of the club should be indulged with a particular hearing, when many of them had published whole volumes which had never been looked in. They insisted that the law should be observed, where reading in company was expressly noticed. It was in vain that the plaintiff pleaded the peculiar merit of his piece: he spoke to an assembly insensible to all his remonstrances: the book of laws was opened, and read by the secretary, where it was expressly enacted, "That whatsoever poet, speech-maker, critic, or historian should presume to engage the company by reading his own works, he was to lay down sixpence previous to opening the manuscript, and should be charged one shilling an hour while he continued reading: the said shilling to be equally distributed among the company as a recompense for their trouble."

Our poet seemed at first to shrink at the penalty, hesitating for some time whether he should deposit the fine, or shut up the poem; but looking round, and perceiving two strangers in the room, his love of fame outweighed his prudence, and laying down the sum by law established, he insisted on his prerogative.

A profound silence ensuing, he began by explaining his design. "Gentlemen," says he, "the present piece is not one of your common epic poems, which come from the press like paper kites in summer; there are none of your Turnuses or Didos in it; it is an heroical description of Nature. I only beg you'll endeavour to make your souls unison with mine, and hear with the same enthusiasm with which I have written. The poem begins with the description of an author's bedchamber; the picture was sketched in my own apartment, for you must know, gentlemen, that I am myself the hero." Then putting himself into the attitude of an orator, with all the emphasis of voice and action, he proceeded:

"'Where the Red Lion, flaring o'er the way
  Invites each passing stranger that can pay;
  Where Calvert's butt and Parson's black champagne,
  Regale the drabs and bloods of Drury Lane:
  There, in a lonely room, from bailiffs snug,
  The muse found Scroggen stretch'd beneath a rug.
  A window, patch'd with paper, lent a ray,
  That dimly show'd the state in which he lay:
  The sanded floor, that grits beneath the tread;
  The humid wall, with paltry pictures spread;
  The royal game of goose was there in view,
  And the twelve rules the royal martyr drew;
  The seasons, fram'd with listing, found a place,
  And brave Prince William show'd his lampblack face.
  The morn was cold: he views with keen desire
  The rusty grate, unconscious of a fire;
  With beer and milk arrears the frieze was scored,
  And five crack'd teacups dress'd the chimney-board,
  A night-cap deck'd his brows instead of bay;
  A cap by night—a stocking all the day!'"[1]

With this last line he seemed so much elated that he was

[1] The first draft of this poem was enclosed in a letter to his brother Henry, dated 1759.

unable to proceed. "There, gentlemen," cries he, "there is a description for you; Rabelais's bedchamber is but a fool to it.

"'A cap by night—a stocking all the day!'—

there is sound, and sense, and truth, and nature in the trifling compass of ten little syllables."

He was too much employed in self-admiration to observe the company, who, by nods, winks, shrugs, and stifled laughter, testified every mark of contempt. He turned severally to each for their opinion, and found all, however, ready to applaud. One swore it was inimitable; another said it was damn'd fine; and a third cried out in a rapture, "Carissimo!" At last, addressing himself to the president, "And pray, Mr. Squint," says he, "let us have your opinion." "Mine!" answered the president, taking the manuscript out of the author's hand; "may this glass suffocate me, but I think it equal to anything I have seen; and I fancy," continued he, doubling up the poem, and forcing it into the author's pocket, "that you will get great honour when it comes out; so I shall beg leave to put it in. We will not intrude upon your good nature, in desiring to hear more of it at present; *ex ungue Herculem*, we are satisfied, perfectly satisfied." The author made two or three attempts to pull it out a second time, and the president made as many to prevent him. Thus, though with reluctance, he was at last obliged to sit down, contented with the commendations for which he had paid.

When this tempest of poetry and praise was blown over, one of the company changed the subject, by wondering how any man could be so dull as to write poetry at present, since prose itself would hardly pay. "Would you think it, gentlemen?" continued he, "I have actually written last week sixteen prayers, twelve bawdy jests, and three sermons, all at the rate of sixpence apiece; and what is still more extraordinary, the bookseller had lost by the bargain. Such sermons would once have gained me a prebend's stall; but now, alas! we have neither piety, taste, nor humour among us. Positively, if this season does not turn out better than it has begun, unless the ministry commit some blunders to furnish us with a new topic of abuse, I shall resume my old business of working at the press, instead of finding it employment."

The whole club seemed to join in condemning the season, as one of the worst that had come for some time; a gentleman particularly observed that the nobility were never known to subscribe worse than at present. "I know not how it happens," said he, "though I follow them up as close as possible yet I can hardly get a single subscription in a week. The houses of the great are as inaccessible as a frontier garrison at midnight. I never see a nobleman's door half-opened that some surly porter or footman does not stand full in the breach. I was yesterday to wait with a subscription-proposal upon my Lord Squash, the creolian. I had posted myself at his door the whole morning, and just as he was getting into his coach thrust my proposal snug into his hand, folded up in the form of a letter from myself. He just glanced at the superscription, and not knowing the hand, consigned it to his valet-de-chambre; this respectable personage treated it as his master, and put it into the hands of the porter; the porter grasped my proposal frowning; and measuring my figure from top to toe, put it back in my own hands unopened."

"To the devil I pitch all the nobility!" cries a little man, in a peculiar accent; "I am sure they have of late used me most scurvily. You must know, gentlemen, some time ago, upon the arrival of a certain noble duke from his travels, I set myself down, and vamped up a fine flaunting

poetical panegyric, which I had written in such a strain
that I fancied it would have even wheedled milk from a
mouse. In this I represented the whole kingdom welcom-
ing his grace to his native soil, not forgetting the loss
France and Italy would sustain in their arts by his departure. I expected to touch for a bank-bill at least; so fold-
ing up my verses in gilt paper, I gave my last half-crown to
a genteel servant to be the bearer. My letter was safely
conveyed to his grace, and the servant, after four hours'
absence, during which time I led the life of a fiend, returned
with a letter four times as big as mine. Guess my ecstasy
at the prospect of so fine a return. I eagerly took the
packet into my hands, that trembled to receive it. I kept
it some time unopened before me, brooding over the expected treasure it contained; when, opening it, as I hope to
be saved, gentlemen, his grace had sent me, in payment
for my poem, no bank-bills, but six copies of verses, each
longer than mine, addressed to him upon the same occasion."

"A nobleman," cries a member who had hitherto been
silent, "is created as much for the confusion of us authors
as the catchpoll. I'll tell you a story, gentlemen, which
is as true as that this pipe is made of clay. When I was
delivered of my first book, I owed my tailor for a suit of
clothes; but that is nothing new, you know, and may be
any man's case as well as mine. Well, owing him for a suit
of clothes, and hearing that my book took very well, he
sent for his money, and insisted upon being paid immediately; though I was at that time rich in fame, for
my book ran like wild-fire, yet I was very short in money,
and being unable to satisfy his demand, prudently resolved
to keep my chamber, preferring a prison of my own choosing at home to one of my tailor's choosing abroad. In
vain the bailiffs used all their arts to decoy me from my

citadel; in vain they sent to let me know that a gentleman wanted to speak with me at the next tavern; in vain they came with an urgent message from my aunt in the country; in vain I was told that a particular friend was at the point of death, and desired to take his last farewell; I was deaf, insensible, rock, adamant; the bailiffs could make no impression on my hard heart, for I effectually kept my liberty by never stirring out of the room.

"This was very well for a fortnight; when one morning I received a most splendid message from the Earl of Doomsday, importing that he had read my book, and was in raptures with every line of it; he impatiently longed to see the author, and had some designs which might turn out greatly to my advantage. I paused upon the contents of this message, and found there could be no deceit, for the card was gilt at the edges, and the bearer, I was told, had quite the looks of a gentleman. Witness, ye powers, how my heart triumphed at my own importance! I saw a long perspective of felicity before me; I applauded the taste of the times, which never saw genius forsaken; I had prepared a set introductory speech for the occasion, five glaring compliments for his lordship, and two more modest for myself. The next morning, therefore, in order to be punctual to my appointment, I took coach, and ordered the fellow to drive to the street and house mentioned in his lordship's address. I had the precaution to pull up the window as I went along to keep off the busy part of mankind, and, big with expectation, fancied the coach never went fast enough. At length, however, the wished-for moment of its stopping arrived: this for some time I impatiently expected, and letting down the window in a transport, in order to take a previous view of his lordship's magnificent palace and situation, I found—poison to my sight! I found myself, not in an elegant street, but a paltry lane; not at a nobleman's door, but the door of a sponging-house; I found the coachman had all this while been driving me to jail, and I saw the bailiff, with a devil's face, coming out to secure me."

To a philosopher no circumstance, however trifling, is too minute; he finds instruction and entertainment in occurrences which are passed over by the rest of mankind as low, trite, and indifferent; it is from the number of these particulars, which to many appear insignificant, that he is at last enabled to form general conclusions. This, therefore, must be my excuse for sending so far as China accounts of manners and follies, which, though minute in their own nature, serve more truly to characterize this people than histories of their public treaties, courts, ministers, negotiations and ambassadors.   Adieu.

Rejoicings Upon the New Year's Coming of Age

Charles Lamb

The *Old Year* being dead, and the *New Year* coming of age, which he does, by Calendar Law, as soon as the breath is out of the old gentleman's body, nothing would serve the young spark but he must give a dinner upon the occasion, to which all the *Days* in the year were invited. The *Festivals*, whom he deputed as his stewards, were mightily taken with the notion.   They had been engaged time out of mind, they said, in providing mirth and good cheer for mortals below; and it was time they should have a taste of their own bounty.   It was stiffly debated among them whether the *Fasts* should be admitted.   Some said the appearance of such lean, starved guests, with their mortified faces, would pervert the ends of the meeting. But the objection was overruled by *Christmas-Day*, who had a design upon *Ash-Wednesday* (as you shall hear), and a mighty desire to see how the old Domine would behave himself in his cups. Only the *Vigils* were requested to come with their lanterns, to light the gentlefolks home at night.

All the *Days* came to their day. Covers were provided for three hundred and sixty-five guests at the principal table, with an occasional knife and fork at the side-board for the *Twenty-Ninth of February*.

I should have told you that cards of invitation had been issued. The carriers were the *Hours:* twelve little, merry, whirligig foot-pages, as you should desire to see, that went all round, and found out the persons invited well enough, with the exception of *Easter-Day, Shrove-Tuesday*, and a few such *Movables*, who had lately shifted their quarters.

Well, they all met at last—foul *Days*, fine *Days*, all sorts of *Days*, and a rare din they made of it. There was nothing but, Hail! fellow *Day*, well met—brother *Day*—sister *Day* —only *Lady-Day* kept a little on the aloof, and seemed somewhat scornful. Yet some said *Twelfth-Day* cut her out and out, for she came in a tiffany suit, white and gold, like a queen on a frostcake, all royal, glittering, and *Epiphanous*. The rest came, some in green, some in white —but old *Lent and his family* were not yet out of mourning. Rainy *Days* came in, dripping; and sunshiny *Days* helped them to change their stockings. *Wedding-Day* was there in his marriage finery, a little the worse for wear. *Pay-Day* came late, as he always does; and *Doomsday* sent word —he might be expected.

April Fool (as my young lord's jester) took upon himself to marshal the guests, and wild work he made with it. It would have posed old Erra Pater to have found out any given *Day* in the year to erect a scheme upon—good *Days*, bad *Days*, were so shuffled together, to the confounding of all sober horoscopy.

He had stuck the *Twenty-First of June* next to the *Twenty-Second of December*, and the former looked like a Maypole siding a marrow - bone. *Ash - Wednesday* got wedged in (as was concerted) betwixt *Christmas* and *Lord Mayor's Day*. Lord! how he laid about him! Nothing but barons of beef and turkeys would go down with him— to the great greasing and detriment of his new sackcloth bib and tucker. And still *Christmas-Day* was at his elbow, plying with him the wassail-bowl, till he roared and hic-cupp'd, and protested there was no faith in dried ling, but commended it to the devil for a sour, windy, acrimonious, censorious, hy-po-crit-crit—critical mess, and no dish for a gentleman. Then he dipt his fist into the middle of the great custard that stood before his *left-hand neighbour*, and daubed his hungry beard all over with it, till you would have taken him for the *Last Day in December*, it so hung in icicles.

At another part of the table *Shrove-Tuesday* was helping the *Second of September* to some cock broth, which courtesy the latter returned with the delicate thigh of a hen pheasant —so there was no love lost for that matter. The *Last of Lent* was spunging upon *Shrove-tide's* pancakes; which *April Fool* perceiving, told him that he did well, for pancakes were proper to a *good fry-day*.

In another part, a hubbub arose about the *Thirtieth of January*, who, it seems, being a sour, puritanic character, that thought nobody's meat good or sanctified enough for him, had smuggled into the room a calf's head, which he had had cooked at home for that purpose, thinking to feast thereon incontinently; but as it lay in the dish, *March Manyweathers*, who is a very fine lady, and subject to the meagrims, screamed out there was a "'human head' in the platter," and raved about Herodias' daughter to that degree that the obnoxious viand was obliged to be removed, nor did she recover her stomach till she had gulped down a *Restorative*, confected of *Oak Apple*, which the merry *Twenty-Ninth of May* always carries about with him for that purpose.

The King's Health being called for after this, a notable dispute arose between the *Twelfth of August* (a zealous old Whig gentlewoman) and the *Twenty-Third of April* (a new-fangled woman of the Tory stamp), as to which of them should have the honour to propose it. *August* grew hot upon the matter, affirming time out of mind the pre-scriptive right to have lain with her, till her rival had basely supplanted her; whom she represented as little better than a *kept* mistress who went about in *fine clothes*, while she (the legitimate Birthday) had scarcely a rag, etc.

April Fool, being made mediator, confirmed the right, in the strongest form of words, to the appellant, but de-cided for peace' sake that the exercise of it should remain with the present possessor. At the same time, he slyly rounded the first lady in the ear, that an action might lie against the Crown for *bi-geny*.

It beginning to grow a little duskish, *Candlemas* lustily bawled out for lights, which was opposed by all the *Days*, who protested against burning daylight. Then fair water was handed round in silver ewers, and the *same lady* was observed to take an unusual time in *Washing* herself.

May-Day, with that sweetness which is peculiar to her, in a neat speech proposing the health of the founder, crowned her goblet (and by her example the rest of the company) with garlands. This being done, the lordly *New Year*, from the upper end of the table, in a cordial but somewhat lofty tone, returned thanks. He felt proud on an occasion of meeting so many of his worthy father's late tenants, promised to improve their farms, and at the same time to abate (if anything was found unreasonable) in their rents.

At the mention of this, the four *Quarter Days* involuntarily looked at each other, and smiled; *April Fool* whistled to an old tune of "New Brooms"; and a surly old rebel at the farther end of the table (who was discovered to be no other than the *Fifth of November*) muttered out, distinctly enough to be heard by the whole company, words to this effect—that "when the old one is gone, he is a fool that looks for a better." Which rudeness of his, the guests resenting, unanimously voted his expulsion; and the malecontent was thrust out neck and heels into the cellar, as the properest place for such a *boutefeu* and firebrand as he had shown himself to be.

Order being restored, the young lord (who, to say truth, had been a little ruffled, and put beside his oratory) in as few and yet as obliging words as possible, assured them of entire welcome; and, with a graceful turn, singling out poor old *Twenty-Ninth of February*, that had sate all this while mumchance at the sideboard, begged to couple his health with that of the good company before him, which he drank accordingly; observing that he had not seen his honest face any time these four years, with a number of endearing expressions besides. At the same time removing the solitary *Day* from the forlorn seat which had been assigned him, he stationed him at his own board, somewhere between the *Greek Calends* and *Latter Lammas*.

Ash-Wednesday, being now called upon for a song, with his eyes fast stuck in his head, and as well as the Canary he had swallowed would give him leave, struck up a Carol, which *Christmas-Day* had taught him for the nonce; and was followed by the latter, who gave "Miserere" in fine style, hitting off the mumping notes and lengthened drawl of *Old Mortification* with infinite humour. *April Fool* swore they had exchanged conditions; but *Good Friday* was observed to look extremely grave, and *Sunday* held her fan before her face that she might not be seen to smile.

Shrove-tide, Lord Mayor's Day, and *April Fool* next joined in a glee—

'Which is the properest day to drink?'

in which all the Days chiming in, made a merry burden.

They next fell to quibbles and conundrums. The question being proposed, who had the greatest number of followers? The *Quarter Days* said there could be no question as to that; for they had all the creditors in the world dogging their heels. But *April Fool* gave it in favour of the *Forty Days before Easter;* because the debtors in all cases outnumbered the creditors, and they kept *Lent* all the year.

All this while *Valentine's Day* kept courting pretty *May,* who sate next him, slipping amorous *billets-doux* under the table, till the *Dog - Days* (who are naturally of a warm constitution) began to be jealous, and to bark and rage exceedingly. *April Fool,* who likes a bit of sport above measure, and had some pretensions to the lady besides, as being but a cousin once removed, clapped and halloo'd them on; and as fast as their indignation cooled, those mad wags, the *Ember-Days,* were at it with their bellows, to blow it into a flame; and all was in a ferment, till old Madam *Septuagesima* (who boasts herself the *Mother of the Days*) wisely diverted the conversation with a tedious tale of the lovers which she could reckon when she was young, and of one, Master *Rogation-Day,* in particular, who was for ever putting the *question* to her; but she kept him at a distance, as the chronicle would tell, by which I apprehend she meant the Almanac. Then she rambled on to the *Days that were gone*, the *good old Days*, and so to the *Days before the Flood*—which plainly showed her old head to be little better than crazed and doited.

Day being ended, the *Days* called for their cloaks and greatcoats, and took their leaves. *Lord Mayor's Day* went off in a mist as usual; *Shortest Day* in a deep black fog, that wrapt the little gentleman all round like a hedgehog. Two *Vigils*—so watchmen are called in heaven—saw *Christmas-Day* safe home — they had been used to the business before. Another *Vigil* — a stout, sturdy patrol, called the *Eve of St. Christopher* — seeing *Ash-Wednesday* in a condition little better than he should be, e'en whipt him over his shoulders, pick-a-back fashion; and *Old Mortification* went floating home singing:

"On the bat's back I do fly,"

and a number of old snatches besides, between drunk and sober; but very few Aves or Penitentiaries (you may believe me) were among them. *Longest Day* set off westward in beautiful crimson and gold; the rest, some in one fashion, some in another; but *Valentine* and pretty *May* took their departure together in one of the prettiest silvery twilights a Lover's Day could wish to set in.

IV

The Biographical and Critical Essay

The Place of Milton as a Poet.

Samuel Johnson (1709–1784)

The Functions of the Chorus in the Greek Tragic Drama.

Samuel Taylor Coleridge (1772–1834)

Hamlet.

William Hazlitt (1778–1830)

Joan of Arc.

Thomas De Quincey (1785–1859)

The Hero as a Man of Letters: Samuel Johnson.

Thomas Carlyle (1795–1881)

Doctor Johnson and His Times.

Thomas Babington Macaulay (1800–1859)

A Visit to Wordsworth.

Ralph Waldo Emerson (1803–1882)

The Loves of Stella and the Dean.

William Makepeace Thackeray (1811–1863)

The Great Armada's Home-Coming.

James Anthony Froude (1818–1894)

Emerson, the Lecturer.

James Russell Lowell (1819–1891)

The Death of Thomas Carlyle.

Walt Whitman (1819–1892)

Thomas Gray.

Matthew Arnold (1822–1888)

The First Expedition of Jean Ribaut.

Francis Parkman (1823–1893)

The Marquis of Montrose.

Sir John Skelton (1831–1897)

THE BIOGRAPHICAL AND CRITICAL ESSAY

THE biographical and critical essay may be accounted a modern development of the essay, although it had many forerunners. Among the forerunners may be named Dryden's *Essay on Dramatic Poesy*, and Isaak Walton's *Lives*. John Dryden (1631 – 1700) was scarcely less eminent as a prose-writer than as a poet, and his characterisations of Shakespeare, Ben Jonson, Beaumont, and Fletcher, are among the best pieces of critical writing of his generation. Isaak Walton (1593–1683), in his *Life of Dr. Donne*, written as a preface to Donne's sermons, and published in 1640, created a model of compressed biography only equalled by himself in his subsequent *Lives* of Sir Henry Wotton, Richard Hooker, and George Herbert. Dryden excels in stateliness, Walton in a certain inimitable quaintness and simplicity of style; yet, upon the whole, their work was solitary, and had no very wide influence on literary forms. It is not until we come to Samuel Johnson that we have the critical and biographical essay in what may be recognised as its modern form. When Johnson sat down to write his *Lives of the Poets*, the struggles of his laborious career were over, his authority was established, his powers were generally recognised, and the result is that he attains a frequent freedom of style not found in any other of his writings. It is true that he himself is not free from the turgidity of language which he attributes to Milton, that he writes with a certain pontifical air of omniscience, and allows his own prejudices to deflect the accuracy of his judgment, particularly in the case of Gray; but allowing for these faults, incident to habit and to his advanced age, and to the curious despotism which he exercised over his contemporaries, his essays on the lives of the poets are happily conceived, written with evident enjoyment, and are characterised by great acuteness, wisdom, and a wealth of suggestive illustration. Where Dryden is purely critical, and Walton purely biographic, Johnson succeeds in welding criticism with biographic detail, and it is in this respect that he may be said to be the first of a great school of critical and biographic essayists.

The critical and biographic essay thus initiated by Johnson was destined to attain great popularity. Its development was rapid and continuous. It becomes in the nineteenth century a distinct new branch of literature, of such importance that it may be justly considered the most striking feature in the literary development of the period. The multiplication of reviews and journals demanded a new race of essayists. Among the essayists there was slowly developed a scientific method of criticism. Johnson was content to express personal opinions, and indulge strong prejudices, and among the early critical essayists of the nineteenth century the same habit of thought was dominant. The critical essay was often an extended review of a book, in which the critic did not disguise his own personal rancour, and made little effort to interpret his author. In many instances a book was used merely as an excuse for the publication of the critic's own opinions. Matthew Arnold was the first man to lay down the principle that no criticism of an author ought to be attempted without sympathy in the critic; that, in fact, criticism was less a polemic than an interpretation.

Matthew Arnold, working in this spirit, did more than

any other writer to give dignity to the essay, and he stands easily first among pure critics. His essay upon Gray, included in this volume, marks the highest point of development in the critical essay, and it is difficult to imagine how it can be surpassed. Arnold excels in lucidity, insight, and a certain penetrating and comprehensive intellectual sympathy. Thus the secret of Gray, which was wholly hidden from Johnson, was entirely manifest to Arnold— "Gray never spoke out." Arnold can sometimes be a little finical in his distinctions, a little tedious in his reiterated definitions; but he never fails to get to the heart of his subject, and his patient search for the right word, which often appears the meticulous exactitude of the pedant, usually has its issue in the invention of some vital and illuminating phrase, which becomes the complete synonym of his meaning. Where Johnson writes with a garrulous freedom, which ignores details, Arnold toils over his task with the patience of a scientific discoverer. He is probably too near our own time for a just perception of his magnitude, either as poet or essayist. The touch of the pedant in him, the condescending air of the superior person, have done not a little to alienate his readers; yet these are defects so slight compared with his great qualities, that no sensible man resents them. What will become increasingly apparent is that Arnold has elevated the critical essay into the highest form of art, beyond which little can be achieved by any future writer.

Coleridge imparts to the critical essay a weight of thought rather than any new grace of style. Hazlitt adds rhetorical vivacity, De Quincey extraordinary eloquence. Of these three writers De Quincey ranks much the highest. He is the master of a peculiarly solemn and impassioned eloquence; he attains pictorial effects which no one else has rivalled; he writes prose, but it is in the spirit and method of a poet, who seizes the essential thing, moves in the company of high visions, and therefore exercises on the imaginations of his readers a power much more common in the great lyric and dramatic poet than in the essayist. His magnificent picture of Joan of Arc, included in this volume, is a masterpiece of emotional eloquence. It might justly be included in the specimens of impassioned prose; it might equally be ranked among the great orations, for it has all the qualities of spoken eloquence; it is only by virtue of its biographical importance that it finds its place where it does. De Quincey is not always eloquent or impassioned. Few writers are more uneven; few can sink so rapidly; and when the wing of his imagination tires De Quincey can become the most prolix and tedious of essayists. Nevertheless his best work constitutes a very large part of the whole, and is so individual, so wonderful in merit, that he will always rank among the greatest of the English essayists.

Carlyle and Macaulay stand in a class by themselves, though entirely opposed in quality. Carlyle's *Heroes and Hero-Worship*, from which the extract on Johnson is taken, is in reality a sermon, and Carlyle was at all times a preacher. But he is a critic also; a prophetic critic; a man with the keenest eye for character, and for the causes and motives which underlie character. His style may be admired or denounced, but it is not by style he lives. His true power lies in a kind of penetrating sagacity, an oracular wisdom, a vitalising imagination. He has an almost demoniac gift of illumination. He *sees* Johnson, sees the very heart of the man, "the pulse of the machine," and makes us see him. Macaulay has no touch of this demoniac power. He sees the outside of things, with an astounding accuracy, but into the depths of personality he cannot penetrate. He can infer much from the outside, but he has no gift of divination. When Carlyle speaks of Johnson, he gives us the man, the essential honest, bigoted, dogmatic, struggling, heroic man, whose inherent force of character made the greatest men of his time his grateful vassals. When Macaulay speaks of Johnson he gives us his clothes, his uncouth form, his disorderly habits, his grotesque superstitions, his painful defects; but almost all that lies beneath these habitudes is hidden from us. Yet both Carlyle and Macaulay are united in this, that they did much to make the critical and biographic essay one of the most popular forms of literature. They perceived its possibilities, and gave to it the full measure of their powers. In their hands the essay attained a new scope, and became what it has remained ever since, a permanent and pictorial form of literature, only second in value to biography and history.

Of the remaining writers included in this section, Thackeray and Froude stand highest. Thackeray is a stylist of the first order. With a sobriety of temper and a power of restraint impossible to De Quincey, he nevertheless comes near to De Quincey's note of passion in the concluding passages of his essay on Swift. He also, cynic as he was often and quite wrongly deemed, has the gift of sympathy, and it is by virtue of this interpretative sympathy that he reads so accurately the strange character of Swift. Froude writes with a delusive ease of style which is apt to hide from us its really great qualities. He does not deal in "purple patches," he is always limpid, lucid, engaging, and if he rises into eloquence it is by such delicate gradations that his intention is disguised from us. He also possesses a gift of quiet humour, the humour of the man of the world, at times inclining to cynicism, but never obtruded —the gentlemanly humour of the scholar. Emerson sometimes displays a similar humour, shrewd and dry, rather than opulent. Emerson, like Carlyle, is a preacher, and the preaching habit never quite leaves him. He has little

of Carlyle's keen insight into character, but he always
contrives to be suggestive, and often deeply so. Lowell's
essays are the essays of a scholar, and an accomplished
man of letters. Whitman, whose work as a prose writer
has never been recognised, shares with Carlyle the gift
of divination. In the fewest words, often rugged and
always touched with obvious spontaneity, he contrives
to get to the heart of his theme. His tribute to Carlyle,
among a thousand similar tributes from the whole realm
of literature, takes precedence of almost all by its vital
truth, its uncalculated and fine sincerity. Parkman is
another American writer to whom his country has done
scant justice. Living under physical conditions which for
a man less brave would have made a literary life impossible,
Parkman made himself the one great American historian,
who found in the development of civilisation in America,
a theme not less thrilling and romantic than that afforded
by the greatest episodes of European history. There is
certainly no historian of his own nation who has written
prose so pictorial, or so finely coloured; and the qualities
which make his histories so remarkable are found also in
his essays. In his essay on James Fenimore Cooper, he
says, "Of all American writers Cooper is the most original,
the most thoroughly national. His genius drew aliment
from the soil where God had planted it, and rose to a
vigorous growth, rough and gnarled, but strong as a mountain cedar. His volumes are a faithful mirror of that rude
Trans-Atlantic nature which, to European eyes, appears so
strange and new. The sea and the forest have been the
scenes of his countrymen's most conspicuous achieve-
ments; it is on the sea and in the forest that Cooper is most
thoroughly at home. Their spirit inspires him, their
images were graven on his heart; and the men whom their
embrace has nurtured, the sailor, the hunter, the pioneer,

move and act upon his pages with all the truth and energy of real life." This striking tribute to Cooper applies equally to Parkman. Alone among all American writers of history, Parkman owes nothing to European suggestion, and is the most loyal to his race and country.

Sir John Skelton, whose fine description of the trial and death of Montrose is included in this section, was a writer who never attained national fame. Under the nom-de-plume of *Shirley* he was a regular contributor of essays and reviews to *Frazer's Magazine* and the *Guardian*, a short-lived Edinburgh periodical. He was a Scotch advocate, a close friend of Froude's, and an authority upon the history of Mary Stuart; a man of wide culture and remarkable literary gifts. The inclusion of his essay on Montrose among the great examples of the biographic essay, is justified by its singular merit; but it serves also to illustrate the degree of excellence frequently attained by nineteenth-century writers who expected nothing from their exertions but the kind of reputation which is enjoyed by the able reviewer or magazine contributor. Such men frequently do work that in an earlier age would have won extended fame; if they are not found upon Parnassus it is only because they toiled in a crowded field, and that they contested for the prize with giants.

The Place of Milton as a Poet[1]

Samuel Johnson

Milton would not have excelled in dramatic writing; he knew human nature only in the gross, and had never studied the shades of character, nor the combinations of

---

[1] From *The Lives of the Most Eminent English Poets.*

concurring, nor the perplexity of contending passions. He had read much, and knew what books could teach, but had mingled little in the world, and was deficient in the knowledge which experience must confer.

Through all his greater works there prevails a uniform peculiarity of *diction*, a mode and cast of expression which bears little resemblance to that of any former writer, and which is so far removed from common use, that an unlearned reader, when he first opens his book finds himself surprised by new language.

This novelty has been, by those who can find nothing wrong in Milton, imputed to his laborious endeavours after words suitable to the grandeur of his ideas. *Our language*, says Addison, *sunk under him*. But the truth is, that, both in prose and verse, he had formed his style by a perverse and pedantic principle. He was desirous to use English words with a foreign idiom. This in all his prose is discovered and condemned; for there judgment operates freely, neither softened by the beauty, nor awed by the dignity of his thoughts: but such is the power of his poetry, that his call is obeyed without resistance, the reader finds himself in captivity to a higher and a nobler mind, and criticism sinks in admiration.

Milton's style was modified by his subject; what is shown with greater extent in *Paradise Lost* may be found in *Comus*. One source of his peculiarity was his familiarity with the Tuscan poets: the disposition of his words is, I think, frequently Italian, perhaps sometimes combined with other tongues. Of him, at last, may be said what Jonson said of Spenser, that *he wrote no language*, but has formed what Butler calls a *Babylonish dialect*, in itself harsh and barbarous, but made, by exalted genius and extensive learning, the vehicle of so much instruction and so much pleasure, that, like other lovers, we find grace in its deformity.

Whatever be the faults of his diction, he cannot want the praise of copiousness and variety: he was master of his language in its full extent, and has selected the melodious words with such diligence, that from his book alone the Art of English Poetry might be learned.

After his diction, something must be said of his *versification. The measure,* he says, *is the English heroic verse without rhyme.* Of this mode he had many examples among the Italians, and some in his own country. The Earl of Surrey is said to have translated one of Virgil's books without rhyme; and, besides our tragedies, a few short poems had appeared in blank verse, particularly one tending to reconcile the nation to Raleigh's wild attempt upon Guiana, and probably written by Raleigh himself. These petty performances cannot be supposed to have much influenced Milton, who more probably took his hint from Trissino's *Italia Liberata,* and, finding blank verse easier than rhyme was desirous of persuading himself that it is better.

Rhyme, he says, and says truly, *is no necessary adjunct of true poetry* But, perhaps, of poetry as a mental operation, metre or music, is no necessary adjunct; it is, however, by the music of metre that poetry has been discriminated in all languages; and in languages melodiously constructed with a due proportion of long and short syllables, metre is sufficient. But one language cannot communicate its rules to another: where metre is scanty and imperfect, some help is necessary. The music of the English heroic line strikes the ear so faintly that it is easily lost, unless all the syllables of every line co-operate together: this co-operation can be only obtained by the preservation of every verse unmingled with another, as a distinct system of sounds and this distinctness is obtained and preserved by the artifice of rhyme. The variety of pauses, so much boasted

by the lovers of blank verse, changes the measures of an
English poet to the periods of a declaimer; and there are
only a few skilful and happy readers of Milton who enable
their audience to perceive where the lines end or begin.
Blank verse, said an ingenious critic, *seems to be verse only
to the eye.*

Poetry may subsist without rhyme, but English poetry
will not often please; nor can rhyme be safely spared but
where the subject is able to support itself. Blank verse
makes some approach to that which is called *lapidary
style;* has neither the easiness of prose, nor the melody of
numbers, and therefore tires by long continuance. Of
the Italian writers without rhyme, whom Milton alleges
as precedents, not one is popular; what reason could urge
in its defence has been confuted by the ear.

But, whatever be the advantage of rhyme, I cannot prevail on myself to wish that Milton had been a rhymer, for
I cannot wish his work to be other than it is; yet, like other
heroes, he is to be admired rather than imitated. He that
thinks himself capable of astonishing, may write blank
verse; but those that hope only to please, must condescend
to rhyme.

The highest praise of genius is original invention. Milton
cannot be said to have contrived the structure of an epic
poem, and therefore owes reverence to that vigour and
amplitude of mind to which all generations must be indebted for the art of poetical narration, for the texture of
the fable, the variation of incidents, the interposition of
dialogue, and all the stratagems that surprise and enchain
attention. But, of all the borrowers from Homer, Milton
is perhaps the least indebted. He was naturally a thinker
for himself, confident of his own abilities, and disdainful
of help or hindrance: he did not refuse admission to the
thoughts or images of his predecessors, but he did not seek

them. From his contemporaries he neither courted nor received support; there is in his writings nothing by which the pride of other authors might be gratified, or favour gained; no exchange of praise or solicitation of support. His great works were performed under discountenance, and in blindness, but difficulties vanished at his touch; he was born for whatever is arduous; and his work is not the greatest of heroic poems, only because it is not the first.

THE FUNCTIONS OF THE CHORUS IN THE GREEK TRAGIC DRAMA

Samuel Taylor Coleridge

It will not be improper, in this place, to make a few remarks on the remarkable character and functions of the chorus in the Greek tragic drama.

The chorus entered from below, close by the orchestra, and there, pacing to and fro during the choral odes, performed their solemn measured dance. In the centre of the *orchestra*, directly over against the middle of the *scene*, there stood an elevation with steps in the shape of a large altar, as high as the boards of the *logeion* or moveable stage. This elevation was named the *thymele* (θυμέλη), and served to recall the origin and original purpose of the chorus, as an altar-song in honour of the presiding deity. Here, and on these steps, the persons of the chorus sate collectively, when they were not singing; attending to the dialogue as spectators, and acting as (what in truth they were), the ideal representatives of the real audience, and of the poet himself in his own character, assuming the supposed impressions made by the drama, in order to direct and rule them. But when the chorus itself formed part of the dialogue, then the leader of the band, the foreman or *coryphæus*, ascended, as some think, the level summit of the *thymele* in order to command the stage, or, perhaps, the whole chorus advanced to the front of the orchestra, and thus put themselves in ideal connection, as it were, with the *dramatis personæ* there acting. This *thymele* was in the centre of the whole edifice; all the measurements were calculated, and the semi-circle of the amphitheatre was drawn, from this point. It had a double use, a twofold purpose; it constantly reminded the spectators of the origin of tragedy, as a religious service, and declared itself as the ideal representative of the audience by having its place exactly in the point, to which all the radii from the different seats or benches converged.

In this double character, as constituent parts, and yet at the same time as spectators of the drama, the chorus could not but tend to enforce the unity of place;—not on the score of any supposed improbability, which the understanding or common sense might detect in a change of place;—but because the senses themselves put it out of the power of any imagination to conceive a place coming to, and going away from the persons, instead of the persons changing their place. Yet there are instances, in which, during the silence of the chorus, the poets have hazarded this by a change in that part of the scenery which represented the more distant objects to the eye of the spectator—a demonstrative proof, that this alternately extolled and ridiculed unity (as ignorantly ridiculed as extolled) was grounded on no essential principle of reason, but arose out of circumstances which the poet could not remove, and therefore took up into the form of the drama, and co-organized it with all the other parts into a living whole.

The Greek tragedy may rather be compared to our serious opera than to the tragedies of Shakspere; nevertheless, the difference is far greater than the likeness. In the opera all is subordinated to the music, the dresses, and the scenery;— the poetry is a mere vehicle for articulation, and as little pleasure is lost by ignorance of the Italian language, so is little gained by the knowledge of it. But in the Greek drama all was but as instruments and accessories to the poetry; and hence we should form a better notion of the choral music from the solemn hymns and psalms of austere church music than from any species of theatrical singing. A single flute or pipe was the ordinary accompaniment; and it is not to be supposed, that any display of musical power was allowed to obscure the distinct hearing of the words. On the contrary, the evident purpose was to render the words more audible, and to secure by the elevations and pauses greater facility of understanding the poetry. For the choral songs are, and ever must have been, the most difficult part of the tragedy; there occur in them the most involved verbal compounds, the newest expressions, the boldest images, the most recondite allusions. Is it credible that the poets would, one and all, have been thus prodigal of the stores of art and genius, if they had known that in the representation, the whole must have been lost to the audience,—at a time too, when the means of after publication were so difficult, and expensive, and the copies of their works so slowly and narrowly circulated?

The masks also must be considered—their vast variety and admirable workmanship. Of this we retain proof by the marble masks which represented them; but to this in the real mask we must add the thinness of the substance and the exquisite fitting on to the head of the actor; so that not only were the very eyes painted with a single opening left for the pupil of the actor's eye, but in some instances, even the iris itself was painted, when the colour was a known characteristic of the divine or heroic personage represented.

Finally, I will note down those fundamental characteristics which contradistinguish the ancient literature from the modern generally, but which more especially appear in prominence in the tragic drama. The ancient was allied to statuary, the modern refers to painting. In the first there is a predominance of rhythm and melody, in the second of harmony and counterpoint. The Greeks idolized the finite, and therefore were the masters of all grace, elegance, proportion, fancy, dignity, majesty—of whatever, in short, is capable of being definitely conveyed by defined forms or thoughts: the moderns revere the infinite, and affect the indefinite as a vehicle of the infinite;—hence their passions, their obscure hopes and fears, their wandering through the unknown, their grander moral feelings, their more august conception of man as man, their future rather than their past—in a word, their sublimity.

HAMLET[1]

William Hazlitt

This is that Hamlet the Dane, whom we read of in our youth, and whom we may be said almost to remember in our after-years; he who made that famous soliloquy on life, who gave the advice to the players, who thought "this goodly frame, the earth, a steril promontory, and this brave o'er-hanging firmament, the air, this majestical roof fretted with golden fire, a foul and pestilent congregation of vapours"; whom "man delighted not, nor woman neither"; he who talked with the grave-diggers, and

---

[1] From *Characters of Shakespeare's Plays.*

moralised on Yorick's skull; the school-fellow of Rosencrantz and Guildenstern at Wittenberg; the friend of Horatio; the lover of Ophelia; he that was mad and sent to England; the slow avenger of his father's death; who lived at the court of Horwendillus five hundred years before we were born, but all whose thoughts we seem to know as well as we do our own, because we have read them in Shakespeare.

Hamlet is a name; his speeches and sayings but the idle coinage of the poet's brain. What, then, are they not real? They are as real as our own thoughts. Their reality is in the reader's mind. It is *we* who are Hamlet. This play has a prophetic truth, which is above that of history. Whoever has become thoughtful and melancholy through his own mishaps or those of others; whoever has borne about with him the clouded brow of reflection, and thought himself "too much i' the sun"; whoever has seen the golden lamp of day dimmed by envious mists rising in his own breast, and could find in the world before him only a dull blank with nothing left remarkable in it; whoever has known "the pangs of despised love, the insolence of office, or the spurns which patient merit of the unworthy takes"; he who has felt his mind sink within him, and sadness cling to his heart like a malady, who has had his hopes blighted and his youth staggered by the apparitions of strange things; who cannot be well at ease, while he sees evil hovering near him like a spectre; whose powers of action have been eaten up by thought, he to whom the universe seems infinite, and himself nothing; whose bitterness of soul makes him careless of consequences, and who goes to a play as his best resource to shove off, to a second remove, the evils of life by a mock representation of them— this is the true Hamlet.

We have been so used to this tragedy that we hardly

know how to criticise it any more than we should know how to describe our own faces. But we must make such observations as we can. It is the one of Shakespeare's plays that we think of the oftenest, because it abounds most in striking reflections on human life, and because the distresses of Hamlet are transferred, by the turn of his mind, to the general account of humanity. Whatever happens to him we apply to ourselves, because he applies it to himself as a means of general reasoning. He is a great moraliser; and what makes him worth attending to is, that he moralises on his own feelings and experience. He is not a commonplace pedant. If *Lear* is distinguished by the greatest depth of passion, HAMLET is the most re- markable for the ingenuity, originality, and unstudied development of character. Shakespeare had more mag- nanimity than any other poet, and he has shewn more of it in this play than in any other. There is no attempt to force an interest: everything is left for time and circum- stances to unfold. The attention is excited without effort, the incidents succeed each other as matters of course, the characters think and speak and act just as they might do, if left entirely to themselves. There is no set purpose, no straining at a point. The observations are suggested by the passing scene—the gusts of passion come and go like sounds of music borne on the wind. The whole play is an exact transcript of what might be supposed to have taken place at the court of Denmark, at the remote period of time fixed upon, before the modern refinements in morals and man- ners were heard of. It would have been interesting enough to have been admitted as a bystander in such a scene, at such a time, to have heard and witnessed some- thing of what was going on. But here we are more than spectators. We have not only "the outward pageants and the signs of grief"; but "we have that within which passes shew." We read the thoughts of the heart, we catch the passions living as they rise. Other dramatic writers give us very fine versions and paraphrases of nature; but Shakespeare, together with his own comments, gives us the original text, that we may judge for ourselves. This is a very great advantage.

The character of Hamlet stands quite by itself. It is not a character marked by strength of will or even of passion, but by refinement of thought and sentiment. Hamlet is as little of the hero as a man can well be: but he is a young and princely novice, full of high enthusiasm and quick sensibility—the sport of circumstances, questioning with fortune and refining on his own feelings, and forced from the natural bias of his disposition by the strangeness of his situation. He seems incapable of deliberate action, and is only hurried into extremities on the spur of the occasion, when he has no time to reflect, as in the scene where he kills Polonius, and again, where he alters the letters which Rosencrantz and Guildenstern are taking with them to England, purporting his death. At other times, when he is most bound to act, he remains puzzled, undecided, and sceptical, dallies with his purposes, till the occasion is lost, and finds out some pretence to relapse into indolence and thoughtfulness again. For this reason he refuses to kill the King when he is at his prayers, and by a refinement in malice, which is in truth only an excuse for his own want of resolution, defers his revenge to a more fatal opportunity, when he shall be engaged in some act "that has no relish of salvation in it."

> "He kneels and prays,
> And now I'll do't, and so he goes to heaven,
> And so am I reveng'd: *that would be scann'd.*
> He kill'd my father, and for that,

> I, his sole son, send him to heaven.
> Why this is reward, not revenge.
> Up sword and know thou a more horrid time,
> When he is drunk, asleep, or in a rage."

He is the prince of philosophical speculators; and because he cannot have his revenge perfect, according to the most refined idea his wish can form, he declines it altogether. So he scruples to trust the suggestions of the ghost, contrives the scene of the play to have surer proof of his uncle's guilt, and then rests satisfied with this confirmation of his suspicions, and the success of his experiment, instead of acting upon it. Yet he is sensible of his own weakness, taxes himself with it, and tries to reason himself out of it.

Still he does nothing; and this very speculation on his own infirmity only affords him another occasion for indulging it. It is not from any want of attachment to his father or of abhorrence of his murder that Hamlet is thus dilatory, but it is more to his taste to indulge his imagination in reflecting upon the enormity of the crime and refining on his schemes of vengeance, than to put them into immediate practice. His ruling passion is to think, not to act: and any vague pretext that flatters this propensity instantly diverts him from his previous purposes.

The moral perfection of this character has been called in question, we think, by those who did not understand it. It is more interesting than according to rules; amiable, though not faultless. The ethical delineations of "that noble and liberal casuist" (as Shakespeare has been well called) do not exhibit the drab-coloured quakerism of morality. His plays are not copied either from The Whole Duty of Man, or from The Academy of Compliments! We confess we are a little shocked at the want of refinement in those who are shocked at the want of refinement in Hamlet. The neglect of punctilious exactness in his behaviour either partakes of the "licence of the time," or else belongs to the very excess of intellectual refinement in the character, which makes the common rules of life, as well as his own purposes, sit loose upon him. He may be said to be amenable only to the tribunal of his own thoughts, and is too much taken up with the airy world of contemplation to lay as much stress as he ought on the practical consequences of things. His habitual principles of action are unhinged and out of joint with the time. His conduct to Ophelia is quite natural in his circumstances. It is that of assumed severity only. It is the effect of disappointed hope, of bitter regrets, of affection suspended, not obliterated, by the distractions of the scene around him! Amidst the natural and preternatural horrors of his situation, he might be excused in delicacy from carrying on a regular courtship. When "his father's spirit was in arms," it was not a time for the son to make love in. He could neither marry Ophelia, nor wound her mind by explaining the cause of his alienation, which he durst hardly trust himself to think of. It would have taken him years to have come to a direct explanation on the point. In the harassed state of his mind, he could not have done much otherwise than he did. His conduct does not contradict what he says when he sees her funeral,

> "I loved Ophelia: forty thousand brothers
> Could not with all their quantity of love
> Make up my sum."

Nothing can be more affecting or beautiful than the Queen's apostrophe to Ophelia on throwing the flowers into the grave.

> "Sweets to the sweet, farewell.
> I hop'd thou should'st have been my Hamlet's wife:
> I thought thy bride-bed to have deck'd, sweet maid,
> And not have strew'd thy grave."

Shakespeare was thoroughly a master of the mixed motives of human character, and he here shews us the Queen, who was so criminal in some respects, not without sensibility and affection in other relations of life. Ophelia is a character almost too exquisitely touching to be dwelt upon. Oh rose of May, oh flower too soon faded! Her love, her madness, her death, are described with the truest touches of tenderness and pathos. It is a character which nobody but Shakespear could have drawn in the way that he has done, and to the conception of which there is not even the smallest approach, except in some of the old romantic ballads.[1] Her brother, Laertes, is a character we do not like so well: he is too hot and choleric, and somewhat rhodomontade. Polonius is a perfect character in its kind; nor is there any foundation for the objections which have been made to the consistency of this part. It is said that he acts very foolishly and talks very sensibly. There is no inconsistency in that. Again, that he talks wisely at one time and foolishly at another; that his advice to Laertes is very excellent, and his advice to the King and Queen on the subject of Hamlet's madness very ridiculous. But he gives the one as a father, and is sincere in it; he gives the other as a mere courtier, a busy-body, and is accordingly officious, garrulous, and impertinent. In short, Shakespeare has been accused of inconsistency in this and other characters, only because he has kept up the distinction

---

[1] In the account of her death, a friend has pointed out an instance of the poet's exact observation of nature:

"There is a willow growing o'er a brook,
    That shews its hoary leaves i' th' glassy stream."

The inside of the leaves of the willow, next the water, is of a whitish colour, and the reflection would therefore be "hoary."

which there is in nature, between the understandings and the moral habits of men, between the absurdity of their ideas and the absurdity of their motives. Polonius is not a fool, but he makes himself so. His folly, whether in his actions or speeches, comes under the head of impropriety of intention.

We do not like to see our author's plays acted, and least of all, HAMLET. There is no play that suffers so much in being transferred to the stage. Hamlet himself seems hardly capable of being acted. Mr. Kemble unavoidably fails in this character from a want of ease and variety. The character of Hamlet is made up of undulating lines; it has the yielding flexibility of "a wave o' th' sea." Mr. Kemble plays it like a man in armour, with a determined inveteracy of purpose, in one undeviating straight line, which is as remote from the natural grace and refined susceptibility of the character, as the sharp angles and abrupt starts which Mr. Kean introduces into the part. Mr. Kean's Hamlet is as much too splenetic and rash as Mr. Kemble's is too deliberate and formal. His manner is too strong and pointed. He throws a severity, approaching to virulence, into the common observations and answers. There is nothing of this in Hamlet. He is, as it were, wrapped up in his reflections, and only *thinks aloud*. There should therefore be no attempt to impress what he says upon others by a studied exaggeration of emphasis or manner; no *talking at* his hearers. There should be as much of the gentleman and scholar as possible infused into the part, and as little of the actor. A pensive air of sadness should sit reluctantly upon his brow, but no appearance of fixed and sullen gloom. He is full of weakness and melancholy, but there is no harshness in his nature. He is the most amiable of misanthropes.

JOAN OF ARC

Thomas De Quincey

What is to be thought of *her?*   What is to be thought of the poor shepherd girl from the hills and forests of Lorraine, that—like the Hebrew shepherd boy from the hills and forests of Judea—rose suddenly out of the quiet, out of the safety, out of the religious inspiration, rooted in deep pastoral solitudes, to a station in the van of armies, and to the more perilous station at the right hand of kings?   The Hebrew boy inaugurated his patriotic mission by an *act*, by a victorious *act*, such as no man could deny.   But so did the girl of Lorraine, if we read her story as it was read by those who saw her nearest.   Adverse armies bore witness to the boy as no pretender; but so they did to the gentle girl.   Judged by the voices of all who saw them *from a station of good-will*, both were found true and loyal to any promises involved in their first acts.   Enemies it was that made the difference between their subsequent fortunes.   The boy rose to a splendour and a noonday prosperity, both personal and public, that rang through the records of his people, and became a by-word amongst his posterity for a thousand years, until the sceptre was departing from Judah.   The poor, forsaken girl, on the contrary, drank not herself from that cup of rest which she had secured for France.   She never sang together with the songs that rose in her native Domrémy as echoes to the departing steps of invaders.   She mingled not in the festal dances at Vancouleurs which celebrated in rapture the redemption of France.   No! for her voice was then silent; no! for her feet were dust.   Pure, innocent, noble-hearted girl! whom, from earliest youth, ever I believed in as full of truth and self-sacrifice, this was amongst the strongest pledges of *thy* truth, that never once—no, not for a moment of weakness—didst thou revel in the vision of coronets and honour from man. Coronets for thee! Oh no! Honours, if they come when all is over, are for those that share thy blood. Daughter of Domrémy, when the gratitude of thy king shall awaken, thou wilt be sleeping the sleep of the dead. Call her, King of France, but she will not hear thee. Cite her by the apparitors to come and receive a robe of honour, but she will be found *en contumace*. When the thunders of universal France, as even yet may happen, shall proclaim the grandeur of the poor shepherd girl that gave up all for her country, thy ear, young shepherd girl, will have been deaf five centuries. To suffer and to do, that was thy portion in this life; that was thy destiny; and not for a moment was it hidden from thyself. Life, thou saidst, is short; and the sleep which is in the grave is long; let me use that life, so transitory, for the glory of those heavenly dreams destined to comfort the sleep which is so long! This pure creature—pure from every suspicion of even a visionary self-interest, even as she was pure in senses more obvious—never once did this holy child, as regarded herself, relax from her belief in the darkness that was travelling to meet her. She might not prefigure the very manner of her death; she saw not in vision, perhaps, the aerial altitude of the fiery scaffold, the spectators without end on every road pouring into Rouen, as to a coronation, the surging smoke, the volleying flames, the hostile faces all around, the pitying eye that lurked but here and there, until nature and imperishable truth broke loose from artificial restraints; these might not be apparent through the mists of the hurrying future. But the voice that called her to death, *that* she heard forever.

Great was the throne of France even in those days, and great was he that sat upon it: but well Joanna knew that not the throne, nor he that sat upon it, was for *her;* but, on the contrary, that she was for *them;* not she by them, but they by her, should rise from the dust. Gorgeous were the lilies of France, and for centuries had the privilege to spread their beauty over land and sea, until, in another century, the wrath of God and man combined to wither them; but well Joanna knew, early at Domrémy she had read that bitter truth, that the lilies of France would decorate no garland for *her*. Flower nor bud, bell nor blossom, would ever bloom for *her!*

The education of this poor girl was mean according to the present standard: was ineffably grand, according to purer philosophic standard: and only not good for our age, because for us it would be unattainable.   She read nothing, for she could not read; but she had heard others read parts of the Roman martyrology. She wept in sympathy with the sad *Misereres* of the Romish Church; she rose to heaven with the glad triumphant *Te Deums* of Rome; she drew her comfort and her vital strength from the rites of the same Church. But, next after these spiritual advantages, she owed most to the advantages of her situation. The fountain of Domrémy was on the brink of a boundless forest; and it was haunted to that degree by fairies that the parish priest (*curé*) was obliged to read mass there once a year, in order to keep them in any decent bounds. Fairies are important, even in a statistical view: certain weeds mark poverty in the soil; fairies mark its solitude. As surely as the wolf retires before cities does the fairy sequester herself from the haunts of the licensed victualler. A village is too much for her nervous delicacy: at most, she can tolerate a distant view of a hamlet. We may judge, therefore, by the uneasiness and extra trouble which they gave to the parson, in what strength the fairies mustered at Domrémy, and, by a satisfactory consequence, how thinly sown with men and women must have been that region even in its inhabited spots. But the forests of Domrémy—those were the glories of the land: for in them abode mysterious powers and ancient secrets that towered into tragic strength. "Abbeys there were, and abbey windows,"—"like Moorish temples of the Hindoos,"—that exercised even princely power both in Lorraine and in the German Diets. These had their sweet bells that pierced the forests for many a league at matins or vespers, and each its own dreamy legend. Few enough, and scattered enough were these abbeys, so as in no degree to disturb the deep solitude of the region; yet many enough to spread a network or awning of Christian sanctity over what else might have seemed a heathen wilderness.

Joanna was a girl of natural piety, that saw God in forests, and hills, and fountains, but did not the less seek him in chapels and consecrated oratories.

This peasant girl was self-educated through her own natural meditativeness. If the reader turns to that divine passage in *Paradise Regained*, which Milton has put into the mouth of our Saviour when first entering the wilderness, and musing upon the tendency of those great impulses growing within himself—

> "Oh, what a multitude of thoughts at once
> Awakened in me swarm, while I consider
> What from within I feel myself, and hear
> What from without comes often to my ears,
> Ill sorting with my present state compared!
> When I was yet a child, no childish play
> To me was pleasing; all my mind was set
> Serious to learn and know, and thence to do,
> What might be public good; myself I thought
> Born to that end—"

he will have some notion of the vast reveries which brooded over the heart of Joanna in early girlhood, when the wings were budding that should carry her from Orleans to Rheims; when the golden chariot was dimly revealing itself that should carry her from the kingdom of *France Delivered* to the Eternal Kingdom.

France had become a province of England, and for the ruin of both, if such a yoke could be maintained. Dreadful pecuniary exhaustion caused the English energy to droop; and that critical opening *La Pucelle* used with a corresponding felicity of audacity and suddenness (that were in themselves portentous), for introducing the wedge of French native resources, for rekindling the national pride, and for planting the dauphin once more upon his feet. When Joanna appeared, he had been on the point of giving up the struggle with the English, distressed as they were, and of flying to the south of France. She taught him to blush for such abject counsels. She liberated Orleans, that great city, so decisive by its fate for the issue of the war, and then beleaguered by the English with an elaborate application of engineering skill unprecedented in Europe. Entering the city after sunset on the 29th of April, she sang mass on Sunday, May 8th, for the entire disappearance of the besieging force. On the 29th of June she fought and gained over the English the decisive battle of Patay; on the 9th of July she took Troyes by a coup-de-main from a mixed garrison of English and Burgundians; on the 15th of that month she carried the dauphin into Rheims; on Sunday, the 17th, she crowned him; and there she rested from her labour of triumph. All that was to be *done* she had now accomplished: what remained was—to *suffer*.

On the day when she had finished her work, she wept; for she knew that, when her *triumphal* task was done, her end must be approaching. Her aspirations pointed only to a place which seemed to her more than usually full of natural piety, as one in which it would give her pleasure to die. And she uttered, between smiles and tears, as a wish that inexpressibly fascinated her heart, and yet was half-fantastic, a broken prayer that God would return her to the solitudes from which he had drawn her, and suffer her to become a shepherdess once more. It was a natural prayer, because nature has laid a necessity upon every human heart to seek for rest and to shrink from torment. Yet, again, it was a half-fantastic prayer, because from childhood upwards, visions that she had no power to mistrust, and the voices which sounded in her ear forever, had long since persuaded her mind that for *her* no such prayer could be granted. Too well she felt that her mission must be worked out to the end, and that the end was now at hand. All went wrong from this time. She herself had created the *funds* out of which the French restoration should grow; but she was not suffered to witness their development, or their prosperous application. More than one military plan was entered upon which she did not approve. But she still continued to expose her person as before. Severe wounds had not taught her caution. And at length, in a sortie from Compiègne (whether through treacherous collusion on the part of her own friends is doubtful to this day), she was made prisoner by the Burgundians, and finally surrendered to the English.

Now came her trial. This trial, moving of course under English influence, was conducted in chief by the Bishop of Beauvais. He was a Frenchman, sold to English interests, and hoping, by favour of the English leaders, to reach the highest preferment. *Bishop that art, Archbishop that shalt be, Cardinal that mayest be,* were the words that sounded continually in his ear; and doubtless a whisper of visions still higher, of a triple crown, and feet upon the necks of kings, sometimes stole into his heart. M. Michelet is anxious to keep us in mind that this bishop was but an agent of the English. True. But it does not better the case for his countrymen that, being an accomplice in the crime, making himself the leader in the persecution against the helpless girl, he was willing to be all this in the spirit, and with the conscious vileness of a cat's-paw. Never from the foundations of the earth was there such a trial as this, if it were laid open in all its beauty of defence, and all its hellishness of attack. Oh, child of France! shepherdess, peasant girl! trodden under foot by all around thee, how I honour thy flashing intellect, quick as God's lightning, and true as God's lightning to its mark, that ran before France and laggard Europe by many a century, confounding the malice of the ensnarer, and making dumb the oracles of falsehood!

On the Wednesday after Trinity Sunday in 1431, being then about nineteen years of age, the Maid of Arc underwent her martyrdom.

Bishop of Beauvais! thy victim died in fire upon a scaffold —thou upon a down bed. But, for the departing minutes of life, both are oftentimes alike. At the farewell crisis, when the gates of death are opening, and flesh is resting from its struggles, oftentimes the tortured and the torturer have the same truce from carnal torment; both sink together into sleep; together both sometimes kindle into dreams. When the mortal mists were gathering fast upon you two, bishop and shepherd girl—when the pavilions of life were closing up their shadowy curtains about you—let us try, through the gigantic glooms, to decipher the flying features of your separate visions.

The shepherd girl that had delivered France—she, from her dungeon, she, from her baiting at the stake, she, from her duel with fire, as she entered her last dream—saw Domrémy, saw the fountain of Domrémy, saw the pomp of forests in which her childhood had wandered. That Easter festival which man had denied to her languishing heart—that resurrection of spring-time, which the darkness of dungeons had intercepted from *her*, hungering after the glorious liberty of forests—were by God given back into her hands, as jewels that had been stolen from her by robbers. With those, perhaps (for the minutes of dreams can stretch into ages), was given back to her by God the bliss of childhood. By special privilege for *her* might be created, in this farewell dream, a second childhood, innocent as the first; but not, like *that*, sad with the gloom of a fearful mission in the rear. This mission had now been fulfilled. The storm was weathered; the skirts even of that mighty storm were drawing off. The blood that she was to reckon for had been paid to the last. The hatred to herself in all eyes had been faced steadily, had been suffered, had been survived. And in her last fight upon the scaffold she had triumphed gloriously; victoriously she had tasted the stings of death. For all, except this comfort from her farewell dream, she had died—died, amidst the tears of ten thousand enemies—died, amidst the drums and trumpets of armies — died, amidst peals redoubling upon peals, volleys upon volleys, from the saluting clarions of martyrs.

Bishop of Beauvais! because the guilt-burdened man is in dreams haunted and waylaid by the most frightful of his crimes, and because upon that fluctuating mirror—rising (like the mocking mirrors of *mirage* in Arabian deserts) from

the fens of death—most of all are reflected the sweet
countenances which the man has laid in ruins; therefore I
know, bishop, that you also, entering your final dream,
saw Domrémy. That fountain, of which the witnesses
spoke so much, showed itself to your eyes in pure morning
dews: but neither dews, nor the holy dawn, could cleanse
away the bright spots of innocent blood upon its surface.
By the fountain, bishop, you saw a woman seated, that
hid her face. But, as *you* draw near, the woman raises
her wasted features. Would Domrémy know them again
for the features of her child? Ah, but *you* know them,
bishop, well! Oh, mercy! what a groan was *that* which the
servants, waiting outside the bishop's dream at his bedside,
heard from his labouring heart, as at this moment he turned
away from the fountain and the woman, seeking rest in the
forests afar off. Yet not *so* to escape the woman, whom
once again he must behold before he dies. In the forests
to which he prays for pity, will he find a respite? What
a tumult, what a gathering of feet is there! In glades, where
only wild deer should run, armies and nations are assem-
bling; towering in the fluctuating crowd are phantoms that
belong to departed hours. There is the great English Prince,
Regent of France. There is my Lord of Winchester, the
princely cardinal, that died and made no sign. There is
the Bishop of Beauvais, clinging to the shelter of thickets.
What building is that which hands so rapid are raising?
Is it a martyr's scaffold? Will they burn the child of
Domrémy a second time? No: it is a tribunal that rises to
the clouds; and two nations stand around it, waiting for a
trial. Shall my Lord of Beauvais sit again upon the judgment-seat, and again number the hours of the innocent?
Ah no! he is the prisoner at the bar. Already all is waiting:
the mighty audience is gathered, the Court is hurrying to
their seats, the witnesses are arrayed, the trumpets are

sounding, the judge is taking his place. Oh! but this is sudden. My lord, have you no counsel? "Counsel I have none: in heaven above, or on earth beneath, counsellor there is none now that would take a brief from *me:* all are silent." Is it, indeed, come to this? Alas! the time is short, the tumult is wondrous, the crowd stretches away into infinity; but yet I will search in it for somebody to take your brief: I know of somebody that will be your counsel. Who is this that cometh from Domrémy? Who is she in bloody coronation robes from Rheims? Who is she that cometh with blackened flesh from walking the furnaces of Rouen? This is she, the shepherd girl, counsellor that had none for herself, whom I choose, bishop, for yours. She it is, I engage, that shall take my lord's brief. She it is, bishop, that would plead for you: yes, bishop. SHE—when heaven and earth are silent.

THE HERO OF A MAN OF LETTERS: SAMUEL JOHNSON

Thomas Carlyle

I have already written of these three Literary Heroes,[1] expressly or incidentally; what I suppose is known to most of you: what need not be spoken or written a second time. They concern us here as the singular *Prophets* of that singular age; for such they virtually were; and the aspect they and their world exhibit, under this point of view, might lead us into reflections enough! I call them, all three, Genuine Men more or less; faithfully, for most part unconsciously, struggling, to be genuine, and plant themselves on the everlasting truth of things. This to a degree

14   [1] Johnson, Rousseau, and Burns.

that eminently distinguishes them from the poor artificial mass of their contemporaries; and renders them worthy to be considered as Speakers, in some measure, of the ever-lasting truth, as Prophets in that age of theirs. By Nature herself a noble necessity was laid on them to be so. They were men of such magnitude that they could not live on unrealities—clouds, froth, and all inanity gave-way under them: there was no footing for them but on firm earth; no rest or regular motion for them, if they got not footing there. To a certain extent, they were Sons of Nature once more in an age of Artifice; once more, Original Men.

As for Johnson, I have always considered him to be, by nature, one of our great English souls. A strong and noble man; so much left undeveloped in him to the last: in a kindlier element what might he not have been—Poet, Priest, sovereign Ruler! On the whole, a man must not complain of his "element," of his "time," or the like; it is thriftless work doing so. His time is bad: well then, he is there to make it better!—Johnson's youth was poor, isolated, hopeless, very miserable. Indeed, it does not seem possible that, in any the favourablest outward cir-cumstances, Johnson's life could have been other than a painful one. The world might have had more of profitable *work* out of him, or less; but his *effort* against the world's work could never have been a light one. Nature, in return for his nobleness, had said to him, Live in an element of diseased sorrow. Nay, perhaps the sorrow and the noble-ness were intimately and even inseparably connected with each other. At all events, poor Johnson had to go about girded with continual hypochondria, physical and spir-itual pain. Like a Hercules with the burning Nessus'-shirt on him, which shoots in on him dull incurable mis-ery: the Nessus'-shirt not to be stript-off, which is his own natural skin! In this manner *he* had to live. Figure him there, with his scrofulous diseases, with his great greedy heart, and unspeakable chaos of thoughts: stalking mournful as a stranger in this Earth; eagerly devouring what spiritual thing he could come at: school-languages and other merely grammatical stuff, if there were nothing better! The largest soul that was in all England; and provision made for it of "fourpence-halfpenny a day." Yet a giant invincible soul; a true man's. One remembers always that story of the shoes at Oxford: the rough, seamy-faced, rawboned College Servitor stalking about, in winter-season, with his shoes worn-out; how the charitable Gentleman Commoner secretly places a new pair at his door; and the rawboned Servitor, lifting them, looking at them near, with his dim eyes, with what thoughts— pitches them out of window! Wet feet, mud, frost, hunger or what you will; but not beggary: we cannot stand beggary! Rude stubborn self - help here: a whole world of squalor, rudeness, confused misery and want, yet of nobleness and manfulness withal. It is a type of the man's life, this pitching-away of the shoes. An original man;—not a second hand, borrowing or begging man. Let us stand on our own basis, at any rate! On such shoes as we ourselves can get. On frost and mud, if you will, but honestly on that; on the reality and substance which Nature gives *us*, not on the semblance, on the thing she has given another than us!

And yet with all this rugged pride of manhood and self-help, was there ever soul more tenderly affectionate, loyally submissive to what was really higher than he? Great souls are always loyally submissive, reverent to what is over them; only small mean souls are otherwise. I could not find a better proof of what I said the other day, That the sincere man was by nature the obedient man;

that only in a World of Heroes was there loyal Obedience
to the Heroic. The essence of *originality* is not that it be
new: Johnson believed altogether in the old; he found the
old opinions credible for him, fit for him; and in a right
heroic manner lived under them. He is well worth study
in regard to that. For we are to say that Johnson was far
other than a mere man of words and formulas; he was a
man of truths and facts. He stood by the old formulas;
the happier was it for him that *he* could so stand: but in
all formulas that he could stand by, there needed to be a
most genuine substance. Very curious how, in that poor
Paper-age, so barren, artificial, thick-quilted with Pedantries, Hearsays, the great Fact of this Universe glared in,
forever wonderful, indubitable, unspeakable, divine-infernal
upon this man too! How he harmonised his Formulas
with it, how he managed at all under such circumstances:
that is a thing worth seeing. A thing "to be looked at
with reverence, with pity, with awe." That Church of St.
Clement Danes, where Johnson still *worshipped* in the era
of Voltaire, is to me a venerable place.

It was in virtue of his *sincerity*, of his speaking still in
some sort from the heart of Nature, though in the current
artificial dialect, that Johnson was a Prophet. Are not all
dialects "artificial"? Artificial things are not all false;
nay every true Product of Nature will infallibly *shape*
itself; we may say all artificial things are, at the starting
of them, *true*. What we call "Formulas" are not in their
origin bad; they are indispensably good. Formula is
method, habitude; found wherever man is found. Formulas
fashion themselves as Paths do, as beaten Highways,
leading toward some sacred or high object, whither many
men are bent. Consider it. One man, full of heartfelt
earnest impulse, finds-out a way of doing somewhat—were
it of uttering his soul's reverence for the Highest, were it

but of fitly saluting his fellowman.   An inventor was needed to do that, a *poet;* he has articulated the dim-struggling way of doing that; these are his footsteps, the beginning of a "Path."   And now see: the second man travels naturally in the footsteps of his foregoer, it is the *easiest* method. In the footsteps of his foregoer; yet with improvements, with changes where such seem good; at all events with enlargements, the Path ever *widening* itself as more travel it;—till at last there is a broad Highway whereon the whole world may travel and drive.   While there remains a City or Shrine, or any Reality to drive to, at the farther end, the Highway shall be right welcome!   When the City is gone, we will forsake the Highway.   In this manner all Institutions, Practices, Regulated Things in the world have come into existence, and gone out of existence. Formulas all begin by being *full* of substance; you may call them the *skin*, the articulation into shape, into limbs and skin, of a substance that is already there: *they* had not been there otherwise.   Idols, as we said, are not idolatrous till they become doubtful, empty for the worshipper's heart. Much as we talk against Formulas, I hope no one of us is ignorant withal of the high significance of *true* Formulas; that they were, and will ever be, the indispensablest furniture of our habitation in this world.

Mark, too, how little Johnson boasts of his "sincerity." He has no suspicion of his being particularly sincere,—of his being particularly anything!   A hard-struggling, weary-hearted man, or "scholar" as he calls himself, trying hard to get some honest livelihood in the world, not to starve, but to live—without stealing!   A noble unconsciousness is in him.   He does not "engrave *Truth* on his watch-seal"; no, but he stands by truth, speaks by it, works and lives by it.   Thus it ever is.   Think of it once more.   The man whom Nature has appointed to do great things is, first of all, furnished with that openness to Nature which renders him incapable of being *in*sincere! To his large, open, deep-feeling heart Nature is a Fact: all hearsay is hearsay; the unspeakable greatness of this Mystery of Life, let him acknowledge it or not, nay even though he seem to forget it or deny it, is ever present to *him*—fearful and wonderful, on this hand and on that. He has a basis of sincerity; unrecognised, because never questioned or capable of question. Mirabeau, Mahomet, Cromwell, Napoleon: all the Great Men I ever heard-of have this as the primary material of them. Innumerable commonplace men are debating, are talking, everywhere their commonplace doctrines, which they have learned by logic, by rote, at secondhand: to that kind of man all this is still nothing. He must have truth; truth which he feels to be true. How shall he stand otherwise? His whole soul, at all moments, in all ways tells him that there is no standing. He is under the noble necessity of being true. Johnson's way of thinking about this world is not mine, any more than Mahomet's was: but I recognise the everlasting element of heart-*sincerity* in both; and see with pleasure how neither of them remains ineffectual. Neither of them is as *chaff* sown; in both of them is something which the seed-field will *grow*.

Johnson was a Prophet to his people; preached a Gospel to them,—as all like him always do. The highest Gospel he preached we may describe as a kind of Moral Prudence: "in a world where much is to be done, and little is to be known," see how you will *do* it! A thing well worth preaching. "A world where much is to be done, and little is to be known"; do not sink yourselves in boundless bottomless abysses of Doubt, of wretched God-forgetting Unbelief;—you were miserable then, powerless, mad: how could you *do* or work at all? Such Gospel Johnson preached and taught; coupled, theoretically and practically, with this other great Gospel, "Clear your mind of Cant!" Have no trade with Cant: stand on the cold mud in the frosty weather, but let it be in your own *real* torn shoes: "that will be better for you," as Mahomet says! I call this, I call these two things *joined together*, a great Gospel, the greatest perhaps that was possible at that time.

Johnson's Writings, which once had such currency and celebrity, are now, as it were, disowned by the young generation. It is not wonderful; Johnson's opinions are fast becoming obsolete: but his style of thinking and of living, we may hope, will never become obsolete. I find in Johnson's Books the indisputablest traces of a great intellect and great heart;—ever welcome, under what obstructions and perversions soever. They are *sincere* words, those of his; he means things by them. A wondrous buckram style,—the best he could get to then; a measured grandiloquence, stepping or rather stalking along in a very solemn way, grown obsolete now; sometimes a tumid *size* of phraseology not in proportion to the contents of it: all this you will put-up with. For the phraseology, tumid or not, has always *something within it*. So many beautiful styles and books, with *nothing* in them;—a man is a *male*factor to the world who writes such! *They* are the avoidable kind! Had Johnson left nothing but his *Dictionary*, one might have traced there a great intellect, a genuine man. Looking to its clearness of definition, its general solidity, honesty, insight and successful method, it may be called the best of all Dictionaries. There is in it a kind of architectural nobleness; it stands there like a great solid square-built edifice, finished, symmetrically complete; you judge that a true Builder did it.

One word, in spite of our haste, must be granted to poor Bozzy. He passes for a mean, inflated, gluttonous creature; and was so in many senses. Yet the fact of his reverence for Johnson will ever remain noteworthy. The foolish conceited Scotch Laird, the most conceited man of his time, approaching in such awestruck attitude the great dusty Pedagogue in his mean garret there: it is a genuine reverence for Excellence; a *worship* for Heroes, at a time when neither Heroes nor worship were surmised to exist. Heroes, it would seem, exist always, and a certain worship of them! We will also take the liberty to deny altogether that of the witty Frenchman, that no man is a Hero to his valet-de-chambre. Or if so, it is not the Hero's blame, but the Valet's: that his soul, namely, is a mean *valet*-soul! He expects his Hero to advance in royal stage-trappings, with measured step, trains borne behind him, trumpets sounding before him. It should stand rather, No man can be a *Grand-Monarque* to his valet-de-chambre. Strip your Louis Quatorze of his king-gear, and there *is* left nothing but a poor forked radish with a head fantastically carved; admirable to no valet. The Valet does not know a Hero when he sees him! Alas, no: it requires a kind of Hero to do that; and one of the world's wants, in *this* as in other senses, is for most part want of such.

On the whole, shall we not say, that Boswell's admiration was well bestowed; that he could have found no soul in all England so worthy of bending-down before? Shall we not say, of this great mournful Johnson too, that he guided his difficult confused existence wisely; led it *well*, like a right-valiant man? That waste chaos of Authorship by trade; that waste chaos of Scepticism in religion and politics, in life-theory and life-practice; in his poverty, in his dust and dimness, with the sick body and the rusty coat: he made it do for him, like a brave man. Not wholly without a loadstar in the Eternal; he had still a loadstar, as the brave all need to have: with his eye set on that, he would change his course for nothing in these confused vortices of the lower sea of Time. "To the Spirit of Lies, bearing death and hunger, he would in no wise strike his flag." Brave old Samuel: *ultimus Romanorum!*

Dr. Johnson and His Times

Thomas Babington Macaulay

Johnson grown old—Johnson in the fulness of his fame and in the enjoyment of a competent future—is better known to us than any other man in history. Everything about him, his coat, his wig, his figure, his face, his scrofula, his St. Vitus's dance, his rolling walk, his blinking eye, the outward signs which too clearly marked his approbation of his dinner, his insatiable appetite for fish-sauce and veal-pie with plums, his inextinguishable thirst for tea, his trick of touching the posts as he walked, his mysterious practice of treasuring up scraps of orange-peel, his morning slumbers, his midnight disputations, his contortions, his mutterings, his gruntings, his puffings, his vigorous, acute, and ready eloquence, his sarcastic wit, his vehemence, his insolence, his fits of tempestuous rage, his queer inmates, old Mr. Levett and blind Mrs. Williams, the cat Hodge and the negro Frank,—all are as familiar to us as the objects by which we have been surrounded from childhood. But we have no minute information respecting those years of Johnson's life during which his character and his manners became immutably fixed. We know him, not as he was known to the men of his own generation, but as he was known to men whose father he might have been. That celebrated club of which he was the most distinguished member, contained few persons who could remember a time when his fame was not fully established, and his habits completely formed. He had made himself a name in literature while Reynolds and the Wartons were still boys. He was about twenty years older than Burke, Goldsmith, and Gerard Hamilton, about thirty years older than Gibbon, Beauclerk, and Langton, and about forty years older than Lord Stowell, Sir William Jones, and Windham. Boswell and Mrs. Thrale, the two writers from whom we derive most of our knowledge respecting him, never saw him until long after he was fifty years old, till most of his great works had become classical, and till the pension bestowed on him by the Crown had placed him above poverty. Of those eminent men who were his most intimate associates, toward the close of his life, the only one, as far as we remember, who knew him during the first ten or twelve years of his residence in the capital, was David Garrick; and it does not appear that, during those years, David Garrick saw much of his fellow townsman. . . .

At the time when Johnson commenced his literary career, a writer had little to hope from the patronage of powerful individuals. The patronage of the public did not yet furnish the means of comfortable subsistence. The prices paid by booksellers to authors were so low, that a man of considerable talents and unremitting industry could do little more than provide for the day which was passing over him. The lean kine had eaten up the fat kine. The thin and withered ears had devoured the good ears. The season of rich harvests was over, and the period of famine had begun. All that is squalid and miserable might now be summed up in the word Poet. That word denoted a creature dressed like a scare-crow, familiar with compters and spunging-houses, and perfectly qualified to decide on the comparative merits of the Common Side in the King's Bench prison and of Mount Scoundrel in the Fleet. Even the poorest pitied him: and they well might pity him; for, if their condition was equally abject, their aspirings were not equally high, nor their sense of insult equally acute. To lodge in a garret up four pair of stairs, to dine in a cellar among footmen out of place, to translate ten hours a day for the wages of a ditcher, to be hunted by bailiffs from one haunt of beggary and pestilence to another, from Grub Street to St. George's Fields, and from St. George's Fields to the alleys behind St. Martin's Church, to sleep on a bulk in June, and amidst the ashes of a glass-house in December, to die in an hospital and be buried in a parish vault, was the fate of more than one writer who, if he had lived thirty years earlier, would have been admitted to the sittings of the Kit-cat or the Scriblerus club, would have sat in Parliament, and would have been intrusted with embassies to the High Allies—who, if he had lived in our time, would have found encouragement scarcely less munificent in Albemarle Street or in Paternoster Row.

As every climate has its peculiar diseases, so every walk of life has its peculiar temptations. The literary character, assuredly, has always had its share of faults, vanity, jealousy, morbid sensibility. To these faults were now superadded the faults which are commonly found in men whose livelihood is precarious, and whose principles are exposed to the trial of severe distress. All the vices of the gambler and of the beggar were blended with those of the author. The prizes in the wretched lottery of bookmaking were scarcely less ruinous than the blanks. If good fortune came, it came in such a manner that it was almost certain to be abused. After months of starvation and despair, a full third night or a well-received dedication filled the pocket of the lean, ragged, unwashed poet with guineas. He hastened to enjoy those luxuries with the images of which his mind had been haunted while he was sleeping amidst the cinders and eating potatoes at the Irish ordinary in Shoe Lane. A week of taverns soon qualified him for another year of night-cellars. Such was the life of Savage, of Boyce, and of a crowd of others. Sometimes blazing in gold-laced hats and waistcoats; sometimes lying in bed because their coats had gone to pieces, or wearing paper cravats because their linen was in pawn; sometimes drinking champagne and tokay with Betty Careless; sometimes standing at the window of an eating-house in Porridge Island, to snuff up the scent of what they could not afford to taste; they knew luxury; they knew beggary; but they never knew comfort. These men were irreclaimable. They looked on a regular and frugal life with the same aversion which an old gipsy or a Mohawk hunter feels for a stationary abode, and for the restraints and securities of civilized communities. They were as untamable, as much wedded to their desolate freedom, as the wild ass. They could no more be broken into the offices of social man than the unicorn could be trained to serve and abide by the crib. It was well if they did not, like beasts of a still fiercer race, tear the hands which ministered to their necessities. To assist them was impossible; and the most benevolent of mankind at length became weary of giving relief which was dissipated with the wildest profusion as soon as it had been received. If a sum was bestowed on the wretched adventurer, such as, properly husbanded, might have supplied him for six months, it was instantly spent in strange freaks of sensuality, and before forty-eight hours had elapsed the poet was again pestering all his acquaintance for twopence to get a plate of shin of beef at a subterraneous cook-shop. If his friends gave him an asylum in their houses, those houses were forthwith turned into bagnios and taverns. All order was destroyed; all business was suspended. The most good-natured host began to repent of his eagerness to serve a man of genius in distress, when he heard his guest roaring for fresh punch at five o'clock in the morning.

A few eminent writers were more fortunate. Pope had been raised above poverty by the active patronage which, in his youth, both the great political parties had extended to his Homer. Young had received the only pension ever bestowed, to the best of our recollection, by Sir Robert Walpole, as the reward of mere literary merit. One or two of the many poets who attached themselves to the opposition, Thomson in particular and Mallett, obtained, after much severe suffering, the means of subsistence from their political friends. Richardson, like a man of sense, kept his shop; and his shop kept him, which his novels, admirable as they are, would scarcely have done. But nothing could be more deplorable than the state even of the ablest men, who at that time depended for subsistence on their writings. Johnson, Collins, Fielding, and Thomson were certainly four of the most distinguished persons that England produced during the eighteenth century. It is well known that they were all four arrested for debt.

Into calamities and difficulties such as these Johnson plunged in his twenty-eighth year. From that time till he was three or four and fifty, we have little information respecting him—little, we mean, compared with the full and accurate information which we possess respecting his proceedings and habits towards the close of his life. He emerged at length from cock-lofts and sixpenny ordinaries into the society of the polished and the opulent. His fame was established. A pension sufficient for his wants had been conferred on him: and he came forth to astonish a generation with which he had almost as little in common as with Frenchmen or Spaniards.

In his early years he had occasionally seen the great; but he had seen them as a beggar. He now came among them as a companion. The demand for amusement and instruction had, during the course of twenty years, been gradually increasing. The price of literary labour had risen; and those rising men of letters with whom Johnson was henceforth to associate were for the most part persons widely different from those who had walked about with him all night in the streets for want of a lodging. Burke, Robertson, the Wartons, Gray, Mason, Gibbon, Adam Smith, Beattie, Sir William Jones, Goldsmith, and Churchill were the most distinguished writers of what may be called the second generation of the Johnsonian age. Of these men Churchill was the only one in whom we can trace the stronger lineaments of that character which, when Johnson first came up to London, was common among authors. Of the rest, scarcely any had felt the pressure of severe poverty. Almost all had been early admitted into the most respectable society on an equal footing. They were men of quite a different species from the dependents of Curll and Osborne.

Johnson came among them the solitary specimen of a past age, the last survivor of the genuine race of Grub Street hacks; the last of that generation of authors whose abject misery and whose dissolute manners had furnished inexhaustible matter to the satirical genius of Pope. From nature he had received an uncouth figure, a diseased constitution, and an irritable temper. The manner in which the earlier years of his manhood had been passed had given to his demeanor, and even to his moral character, some peculiarities appalling to the civilized beings who were the companions of his old age. The perverse irregularity of his hours, the slovenliness of his person, his fits of strenuous exertion, interrupted by long intervals of sluggishness, his strange abstinence, and his equally strange voracity, his active benevolence, contrasted with the constant rudeness and the occasional ferocity of his manners in society, made him, in the opinion of those with whom he lived during the last twenty years of his life, a complete original. An original he was, undoubtedly, in some respects; but, if we possessed full information concerning those who shared his early hardships, we should probably find that what we call his singularities of manner were, for the most part, failings which he had in common with the class to which he belonged. He ate at Streatham Park as he had been used to eat behind the screen at St. John's Gate, when he was ashamed to show his ragged clothes. He ate as it was natural that a man should eat, who, during a great part of his life, had passed the morning in doubt whether he should have food for the afternoon. The habits of his early life had accustomed him to bear privation with fortitude, but not to taste pleasure with moderation. He could fast; but, when he did not fast, he tore his dinner like a famished wolf, with the veins swelling on his forehead, and the perspiration running down his cheeks. He scarcely ever took wine: but, when he drank it, he drank it greedily and in large tumblers. These were, in fact, mitigated symptoms of that same moral disease which raged with such deadly malignity in his friends Savage and Boyce. The roughness and violence which he showed in society were to be expected from a man whose temper, not naturally gentle, had been long tried by the bitterest calamities, by the want of meat, of fire, and of clothes, by the importunity of creditors, by the insolence of booksellers, by the derision of fools, by the insincerity of patrons, by that bread which is the bitterest of all food, by those stairs which are the most toilsome of all paths, by that deferred hope which makes the heart sick. Through all these things the ill-dressed, coarse, ungainly pedant had struggled manfully up to eminence and command. It was natural that, in the exercise of his power, he should be "eo immitior, quia toleraverat," that, though his heart was undoubtedly generous and humane, his demeanor in society should be harsh and despotic. For severe distress he had sympathy, and not only sympathy, but munificent relief. But for the suffering which a harsh world inflicts upon a delicate mind he had no pity; for it was a kind of suffering which he could scarcely conceive. He would carry home on his shoulders a sick and starving girl from the streets. He turned his house into a place of refuge for a crowd of wretched old creatures who could find no other asylum; nor could all their peevishness and ingratitude weary out his benevolence. But the pangs of wounded vanity seemed to him ridiculous; and he scarcely felt sufficient compassion even for the pangs of wounded affection. He had seen and felt so much of sharp misery, that he was not affected by paltry vexations; and he seemed to think that everybody ought to be as much hardened to those vexations as himself. He was angry with Boswell for complaining of a headache, with Mrs. Thrale for grumbling about the dust on the road or the smell of the kitchen. These were, in his phrase, "foppish lamentations," which people ought to be ashamed to utter in a world so full of sin and sorrow. Goldsmith, crying because the Good-natured Man had failed, inspired him with no pity. Though his own health was not good, he detested and despised valetudinarians. Pecuniary losses, unless they reduced the loser absolutely to beggary, moved him very little. People whose hearts had been softened by prosperity might weep, he said, for such events; but all that could be expected of a plain man was not to laugh. He was not much moved even by the spectacle of Lady Tavistock dying of a broken heart for the loss of her lord. Such grief he considered as a luxury reserved for the idle and the wealthy. A washerwoman, left a widow with nine small children, would not have sobbed herself to death.

A person who troubled himself so little about small or

sentimental grievances was not likely to be very attentive to the feelings of others in the ordinary intercourse of society. He could not understand how a sarcasm or a reprimand could make any man really unhappy. "My dear doctor," said he to Goldsmith, "what harm does it do to a man to call him Holofernes?" "Pooh, ma'am," he exclaimed to Mrs. Carter, "who is the worse for being talked of uncharitably?" Politeness has been well defined as benevolence in small things. Johnson was impolite, not because he wanted benevolence, but because small things appeared smaller to him than to people who had never known what it was to live for fourpence-halfpenny a day.

A Visit to Wordsworth[1]

Ralph Waldo Emerson

On the 28th August, I went to Rydal Mount, to pay my respects to Mr. Wordsworth. His daughters called in their father, a plain, elderly, white-haired man, not prepossessing, and disfigured by green goggles. He sat down, and talked with great simplicity. He had just returned from a journey. His health was good, but he had broken a tooth by a fall, when walking with two lawyers, and had said, that he was glad it did not happen forty years ago; whereupon they had praised his philosophy.

He had much to say of America, the more that it gave occasion for his favourite topic,—that society is being enlightened by a superficial tuition, out of all proportion to its being restrained by moral culture. Schools do no good. Tuition is not education. He thinks more of the education of circumstances than of tuition. 'Tis no question whether there are offences of which the law takes cognizance, but whether there are offences of which the law does not take cognizance. Sin is what he fears, and how society is to escape without gravest mischiefs from this source—? He has even said, what seemed a paradox, that they needed a civil war in America, to teach the necessity of knitting the social ties stronger. "There may be," he said, "in America some vulgarity in manner, but that's not important. That comes of the pioneer state of things. But I fear they are too much given to the making of money; and secondly, to politics; that they make political distinction the end, and not the means. And I fear they lack a class of men of leisure,—in short, of gentlemen,—to give a tone of honour to the community. I am told that things are boasted of in the second class of society there, which, in England,—God knows, are done in England every day,— but would never be spoken of. In America I wish to know not how many churches or schools, but what newspapers? My friend, Colonel Hamilton, at the foot of the hill, who was a year in America, assures me that the newspapers are atrocious, and accuse members of Congress of stealing spoons!" He was against taking off the tax on newspapers in England, which the reformers represent as a tax upon knowledge, for this reason, that they would be inundated with base prints. He said, he talked on political aspects, for he wished to impress on me and all good Americans to cultivate the moral, the conservative, &c., &c., and never to call into action the physical strength of the people, as had just now been done in England in the Reform Bill,— a thing prophesied by Delolme. He alluded once or twice to his conversation with Doctor Channing, who had recently visited him (laying his hand on a particular chair in which the Doctor had sat).

The conversation turned on books. Lucretius he esteems a far higher poet than Virgil: not in his system, which is nothing, but in his power of illustration. Faith is necessary to explain anything, and to reconcile the foreknowledge of God with human evil. Of Cousin (whose lectures we had all been reading in Boston), he knew only the name.

I inquired if he had read Carlyle's critical articles and translations. He said, he thought him sometimes insane. He proceeded to abuse Goethe's Wilhelm Meister heartily. It was full of all manner of fornication. It was like the crossing of flies in the air. He had never gone further than the first part; so disgusted was he that he threw the book across the room. I deprecated this wrath, and said what I could for the better parts of the book; and he courteously promised to look at it again. Carlyle, he said, wrote most obscurely. He was clever and deep, but he defied the sympathies of everybody. Even Mr. Coleridge wrote more clearly, though he had always wished Coleridge would write more to be understood. He led me out into his garden, and showed me the gravel walk in which thousands of his lines were composed. His eyes are much inflamed. This is no loss, except for reading, because he never writes prose, and of poetry he carries even hundreds of lines in his head before writing them. He had just returned from a visit to Staffa, and within three days had made three sonnets on Fingal's Cave, and was composing a fourth, when he was called in to see me. He said, "If you are interested in my verses, perhaps you will like to hear these lines." I gladly assented; and he recollected himself for a few moments, and then stood forth and repeated, one after the other, the three entire sonnets with great animation. I fancied the second and third more beautiful than his poems are wont to be. The third is addressed to the flowers, which, he said, especially the oxeye daisy, are very abundant on the top of the rock. The second alludes to the name of the cave, which is "Cave of Music"; the first to the circumstance of its being visited by the promiscuous company of the steamboat.

This recitation was so unlooked for and surprising,—he, the old Wordsworth, standing apart, and reciting to me in a garden-walk, like a schoolboy declaiming,—that I at first was near to laugh; but recollecting myself, that I had come thus far to see a poet, and he was chanting poems to me, I saw that he was right and I was wrong, and gladly gave myself up to hear. I told him how much the few printed extracts had quickened the desire to possess his unpublished poems. He replied, he never was in haste to publish; partly, because he corrected a good deal, and every alteration is ungraciously received after printing; but what he had written would be printed, whether he lived or died. I said, "Tintern Abbey" appeared to be the favourite poem with the public, but more contemplative readers preferred the first books of the "Excursion," and the sonnets. He said, "Yes, they are better." He preferred such of his poems as touched the affections, to any others; for whatever is didactic,—what theories of society, and so on,—might perish quickly; but whatever combined a truth with an affection was πτῆμα ἐραει, good to-day and good forever. He cited the sonnet "On the feelings of a high-minded Spaniard," which he preferred to any other (I so understood him), and the "Two Voices"; and quoted, with evident pleasure, the verses addressed "To the Skylark." In this connection, he said of the Newtonian theory, that it might yet be superseded and forgotten; and Dalton's atomic theory.

When I prepared to depart, he said he wished to show me what a common person in England could do, and he led me into the enclosure of his clerk, a young man, to whom he had given this slip of ground, which was laid out, as its natural capabilities showed, with much taste. He then said he would show me a better way toward the inn; and he walked a good part of a mile, talking, and ever and anon stopping short to impress the word or the verse, and finally parted from me with great kindness, and returned across the fields.

Wordsworth honoured himself by his simple adherence to truth, and was very willing not to shine; but he surprised by the hard limits of his thought. To judge from a single conversation, he made the impression of a narrow and very English mind; of one who paid for his rare elevation by general tameness and conformity. Off his own beat, his opinions were of no value. It is not very rare to find persons loving sympathy and ease, who expiate their departure from the common, in one direction, by their conformity in every other.

THE LOVES OF STELLA AND THE DEAN [1]

William Makepeace Thackeray

We view the world with our own eyes, each of us; and we make from within us the world we see. A weary heart gets no gladness out of sunshine; a selfish man is sceptical about friendship, as a man with no ear doesn't care for music. A frightful self-consciousness it must have been, which looked on mankind so darkly through those keen eyes of Swift.

A remarkable story is told by Scott, of Delany, who interrupted Archbishop King and Swift in a conversation which left the prelate in tears, and from which Swift rushed

---

[1] From *The English Humourists of the Eighteenth Century.*

away with marks of strong terror and agitation in his countenance, upon which the Archbishop said to Delany, "You have just met the most unhappy man on earth; but on the subject of his wretchedness you must never ask a question."

The most unhappy man on earth—*Miserrimus*—what a character of him! And at this time all the great wits of England had been at his feet. All Ireland had shouted after him, and worshipped him as a liberator, a saviour, the greatest Irish patriot and citizen. Dean Drapier Bicker-staff Gulliver—the most famous statesmen and the great poets of his day had applauded him and done him homage; and at this time, writing over to Bolingbroke from Ireland, he says, "It is time for me to have done with the world, and so I would if I could get into a better before I was called into the best, *and not die here in a rage, like a poisoned rat in a hole.*"

We have spoken about the men, and Swift's behaviour to them; and now it behooves us not to forget that there are certain other persons in the creation who had rather intimate relations with the great Dean. Two women whom he loved and injured are known by every reader of books so familiarly that if we had seen them, or if they had been relatives of our own, we scarcely could have known them better. Who hasn't in his mind an image of Stella? Who does not love her? Fair and tender creature: pure and affectionate heart! Boots it to you, now that you have been at rest for a hundred and twenty years, not divided in death from the cold heart which caused yours, whilst it beat, such faithful pangs of love and grief—boots it to you now, that the whole world loves and deplores you? Scarce any man, I believe, ever thought of that grave, that did not cast a flower of pity on it, and write over it a sweet epitaph. Gentle lady, so loving, so unhappy! you have had countless champions; millions of manly hearts mourning for you. From generation to generation we take up the fond tradition of your beauty, we watch and follow your tragedy, your bright morning love and purity, your constancy, your grief, your sweet martyrdom. We know your legend by heart. You are one of the saints of English story.

And if Stella's love and innocence are charming to contemplate, I will say that, in spite of ill-usage, in spite of drawbacks, in spite of mysterious separation and union, of hope delayed and sickened heart—in the teeth of Vanessa, and that little episodical aberration which plunged Swift into such woful pitfalls and quagmires of amorous perplexity—in spite of the verdicts of most women, I believe, who, as far as my experience and conversation go, generally take Vanessa's part in the controversy—in spite of the tears which Swift caused Stella to shed, and the rocks and barriers which fate and temper interposed, and which prevented the pure course of that true love from running smoothly—the brightest part of Swift's story, the pure star in that dark and tempestuous life of Swift's, is his love for Hester Johnson. It has been my business, professionally of course, to go through a deal of sentimental reading in my time, and to acquaint myself with love-making, as it has been described in various languages, and at various ages of the world, and I know of nothing more manly, more tender, more exquisitely touching, than some of those brief notes, written in what Swift calls "his little language" in his journal to Stella. He writes to her night and morning often. He never sends away a letter to her but he begins a new one on the same day. He can't bear to let go her kind little hand, as it were. He knows that she is thinking of him, and longing for him far away in Dublin yonder. He takes her letters from under his pillow and

talks to them, familiarly, paternally, with fond epithets
and pretty caresses—as he would to the sweet and artless
creature who loved him.   "Stay," he writes one morning—
it is the 14th of December, 1710—"Stay, I will answer some
of your letters this morning in bed.   Let me see.   Come
and appear, little letter!   Here I am, says he, and what
say you to Stella this morning fresh and fasting?   And can
Stella read this writing without hurting her dear eyes?" he
goes on, after more kind prattle and fond whispering.
The dear eyes shine clearly upon him then—the good angel
of his life is with him and blessing him.   Ah, it was a sad
fate that wrung from them so many tears, and stabbed
pitilessly that pure and tender bosom.   A hard fate: but
would she have changed it?   I have heard a woman say
that she would have taken Swift's cruelty to have had his
tenderness.   He had a sort of worship for her whilst he
wounded her.   He speaks of her after she is gone; of her
wit, of her kindness, of her grace, of her beauty, with a
simple love and reverence that are indescribably touching;
in contemplation of her goodness his hard heart melts into
pathos; his cold rhyme kindles and glows into poetry, and
he falls down on his knees, so to speak, before the angel
whose life he had embittered, confesses his own wretchedness and unworthiness, and adores her with cries of remorse
and love:

> "When on my sickly couch I lay,
>   Impatient both of night and day,
>   And groaning in unmanly strains,
>   Called every power to ease my pains,
>   Then Stella ran to my relief,
>   With cheerful face and inward grief,
>   And though by Heaven's severe decree
>   She suffers hourly more than me,
>   No cruel master could require
>   From slaves employed for daily hire,

What Stella, by her friendship warmed,
With vigour and delight performed.
Now, with a soft and silent tread,
Unheard she moves about my bed:
My sinking spirits now supplies
With cordials in her hands and eyes.
Best pattern of true friends! beware
You pay too dearly for your care
If, while your tenderness secures
My life, it must endanger yours:
For such a fool was never found
Who pulled a palace to the ground,
Only to have the ruins made
Materials for a house decayed."

One little triumph Stella had in her life—one dear little piece of injustice was performed in her favour, for which I confess, for my part, I can't help thanking fate and the Dean. *That other person* was sacrificed to her—that—that young woman, who lived five doors from Doctor Swift's lodgings in Bury Street, and who flattered him, and made love to him in such an outrageous manner—Vanessa was thrown over.

Swift did not keep Stella's letters to him in reply to those he wrote her. He kept Bolingbroke's, and Pope's, and Harley's, and Peterborough's: but Stella "very carefully," the *Lives* say, kept Swift's. Of course; that is the way of the world: and so we cannot tell what her style was, or of what sort were the little letters which the Doctor placed there at night, and bade to appear from under his pillow of a morning. But in Letter IV. of that famous collection he describes his lodging in Bury Street, where he has the first floor, a dining-room and bed-chamber, at eight shillings a week; and in Letter VI. he says "he has visited a lady just come to town," whose name somehow is not mentioned; and in Letter VIII. he enters a query of Stella's—"What do you mean 'that boards near me, that I dine with now and then?' What the deuce! You know whom I have dined with every day since I left you, better than I do." Of course she does. Of course Swift has not the slightest idea of what she means. But in a few letters more it turns out that the Doctor had been to dine "gravely" with a Mrs. Vanhomrigh: then that he has been to "his neighbour": then that he has been unwell, and means to dine for the whole week with his neighbour! Stella was quite right in her previsions. She saw from the very first hint what was going to happen; and scented Vanessa in the air. The rival is at the Dean's feet. The pupil and teacher are reading together, and drinking tea together, and going to prayers together, and learning Latin together, and conjugating *amo, amas, amavi* together. The "little language" is over for poor Stella. By the rule of grammar and the course of conjugation, doesn't *amavi* come after *amo* and *amas?*

The loves of Cadenus and Vanessa you may peruse in Cadenus's own poem on the subject, and in poor Vanessa's vehement expostulatory verses and letters to him; she adores him, implores him, admires him, thinks him something godlike, and only prays to be admitted to lie at his feet. As they are bringing him home from church, those divine feet of Doctor Swift's are found pretty often in Vanessa's parlour. He likes to be admired and adored. He finds Miss Vanhomrigh to be a woman of great taste and spirit, and beauty and wit, and a fortune too. He sees her every day; he does not tell Stella about the business; until the impetuous Vanessa becomes too fond of him, until the Doctor is quite frightened by the young woman's ardour, and confounded by her warmth. He wanted to marry neither of them—that I believe was the truth; but if he had not married Stella, Vanessa would have had him in spite of himself. When he went back to Ireland, his Ariadne, not content to remain in her isle, pursued the fugitive Dean. In vain he protested, he vowed, he soothed, and bullied, the news of the Dean's marriage with Stella at last came to her, and it killed her—she died of that passion.

And when she died, and Stella heard that Swift had written beautifully regarding her, "That doesn't surprise me," said Mrs. Stella, "for we all know the Dean could write beautifully about a broomstick." A woman—a true woman! Would you have had one of them forgive the other?

In a note in his biography, Scott says that her friend Doctor Tuke, of Dublin, has a lock of Stella's hair, enclosed in a paper by Swift, on which are written, in the Dean's hand, the words: *"Only a woman's hair."* An instance, says Scott, of the Dean's desire to veil his feelings under the mask of cynical indifference.

See the various notions of critics! Do these words indicate indifference or an attempt to hide feeling? Did you ever hear or read four words more pathetic? Only a woman's hair; only love, only fidelity, only purity, innocence, beauty; only the tenderest heart in the world stricken and wounded, and passed away now out of reach of pangs of hope deferred, love insulted, and pitiless desertion:—only that lock of hair left; and memory and remorse, for the guilty lonely wretch, shuddering over the grave of his victim.

And yet to have had so much love, he must have given some. Treasures of wit and wisdom, and tenderness, too, must that man have had locked up in the caverns of his gloomy heart, and shown fitfully to one or two whom he took in there. But it was not good to visit that place. People did not remain there long, and suffered for having been there. He shrank away from all affections sooner or later. Stella and Vanessa both died near him, and away from him. He had not heart enough to see them die. He broke from his fastest friend, Sheridan; he slunk away from his fondest admirer, Pope. His laugh jars on one's ear after seven score years. He was always alone—alone and gnashing in the darkness, except when Stella's sweet smile came and shone upon him. When that went, silence and utter night closed over him. An immense genius: an awful downfall and ruin. So great a man he seems to me, that thinking of him is like thinking of an empire falling. We have other great names to mention—none, I think, however, so great or so gloomy.

THE GREAT ARMADA'S HOME-COMING[1]

James Anthony Froude

They had done all that men could do. On the miserable day when their commander[2] decided to turn his back and fly they would have forced him upon a more honourable course, and given the forlorn adventure an issue less utterly ignominious. But their advice had been rejected. They had sailed away from an enemy whose strength at most was not greater than theirs. They had escaped from a battle with a human foe to a more fatal war with the elements, and they had seen their comrades perish round them, victims of folly and weakness. The tremendous catastrophe broke their hearts, and they lay down and died. Oquendo's *Capitana* had been blown up after the

---

[1] From *The Spanish Story of The Armada and Other Essays.* Copyright, 1892, by Messrs. Charles Scribner's Sons and here printed by the courtesy of their permission.

[2] Medina Sidonia.

fight at Plymouth. By a strange fatality the ship which brought him home blew up also in the harbour of St. Sebastian. The explosion may have been the last sound that reached his failing sense. The stragglers came in one by one; sixty-five ships only of the hundred and thirty who, in July, had sailed out of Corunna full of hope and enthusiasm. In those hundred and thirty had been twenty-nine thousand human creatures, freshly dedicated to what they called the service of their Lord. Nine or ten thousand only returned; a ragged remnant, shadows of themselves, sinking under famine and fever and scurvy which carried them off like sheep with the rot. When they had again touched Spanish soil, a wail of grief rose over the whole peninsula, as of Rachel weeping for her children; yet above it all rose the cry, Where was Alonzo de Leyva? Where was the flower of Spanish chivalry? Cuellar knew his fate; but Cuellar was with his Irish chief far away. Weeks, even months, passed before certain news arrived, and rumour invented imaginary glories for him. He had rallied the missing galleons, he had fallen in with Drake, had beaten and captured him, and had sunk half the English fleet. Vain delusion! De Leyva, like Oquendo and Recalde, had done all which could be done by man, and God had not interposed to help him. He had fought his *Rata Coronado* till her spars were shot away and her timbers pierced like a sieve. She became water-logged in the gales on the Irish coast. A second galleon and a surviving galeass were in his company. The *Rata* and the galleon drove ashore. De Leyva, in the galeass, made Killybegs harbour, and landed there with fourteen hundred men. It was the country of the O'Neil. They were treated with the generous warmth which became the greatest of the Irish chieftains. But their presence was known in Dublin. O'Neil was threatened, and De Leyva honourably refused to be an occasion of danger to him. He repaired the galeass at Killybegs. The October weather appeared to have settled at last, and he started again with as many of his people as the galeass would carry to make the coast of Scotland. She had passed round the north of Donegal, she had kept along the land and had almost reached the Giant's Causeway, when she struck a rock and went to pieces, and De Leyva and his companions went the way of the rest.

The men who came back seemed as if they had been smitten by a stroke from which they could not rally. One of them describes pathetically the delight with which, after those desperate storms, and hunger and cold and thirst, they felt the warmth of the Spanish sun again; saw Spanish grapes in the gardens at Santander, and the fruit hanging on the trees; had pure bread to eat and pure water to drink. But the change brought no return of health. For the first weeks they were left on board their ships, no preparation on shore having been made to receive them. When the mortality was found rather to increase than diminish, they were moved to hospitals, but they died still by hundreds daily, as if destiny or Providence was determined to sweep off the earth every innocent remnant of the shattered expedition, while those who were really to blame escaped unpunished.

Medina Sidonia had been charged by Philip to report his progress to him as often as messengers could be sent off. He had written when off the Lizard before his first contact with the enemy. He had written again on August 21, among the Atlantic rollers, when he believed that he was bringing home his charge at least safe if not victorious. On September 22 he arrived at Santander, and on the 23d reported briefly the close of the tragedy so far as it was then known to him. The weather, he said, had been

terrible since he last wrote. Sixty-one vessels were then
with him. They had held tolerably well together till
September 18, when they were caught in another gale,
and fifty of them had gone he knew not where. Eleven
only had remained with himself. They had made the coast
near Corunna, and had signalled for help, but none had
come off. They had then struggled on to Santander and
were lying there at anchor. He had himself gone on
shore, being broken down by suffering. The miseries
which they had experienced had exceeded the worst that
had ever before been heard of. In some ships there had not
been a drop of water for fourteen days. A hundred and
eighty of the crew of the *San Martin* had died, the rest
were down with putrid fever. Of his personal attendants
all were dead but two. There was not food enough left
on board for those who were alive to last two days. The
Duke "blessed the Lord for all that He had ordained";
but prayed the King to see instantly to their condition,
and to send them money, for they had not a maravedi in
the fleet. He was himself too ill to do anything. There
was no person whose duty it was to help them, neither
inspector, purveyor, nor paymaster. They could obtain
nothing that they wanted. He had written to the Archbishop of Burgos for assistance in establishing a hospital.

The opinion in Spain was savagely hostile to the Duke.
It was thought that if he had possessed the feelings of a
gentleman, he would have died of the disgrace like Oquendo
and Recalde. The Duke, so far from feeling that he was
himself to blame, considered that he above the rest had
most reason to complain of having been forced into a position which he had not sought and for which he had protested his unfitness. Being Lord High Admiral, his business was to remain with the fleet, however ill he might be,
till some other responsible officer could be sent to relieve

him. His one desire was to escape from the sight of the ships and everything belonging to them, and hide himself and recover his spirits in his palace at San Lucar. Not Sancho, when he left his island, could be in greater haste to rid himself of his office and all belonging to it.

On September 27, before an answer could arrive from Philip, he wrote again to Secretary Idiaquez. Almost all the sailors were dead, he said. Many of the ships were dismasted; no one could believe the state in which they were. Idiaquez must look to it. For himself, his health was broken; he was unfit for further duty, and even if he was perfectly well he would never go on shipboard again. He was absolutely without any knowledge either of navigation or of war, and the King could have no object in forcing him to continue in a service from which the State could derive no possible advantage. He begged that he might be thought of no more in connection with the navy, and that, since the Lord had not been pleased to call him to that vocation, he might not be compelled to return in a situation of which he could not, as he had many times explained, conscientiously discharge the duties. His Majesty, he said, could not surely wish the destruction of a faithful subject. With sea affairs he neither could nor would meddle any further, though it should cost him his head. Better so than fail in an office of the duties of which he was ignorant, and where he had to be guided by the advice of others, in whose honesty of intention he could feel no confidence.

The last allusion was of course to Diego Florez, on whom, since it was necessary to punish some one, the blame was allowed to fall. In justice, if justice was to have a voice in the matter, the person really guilty was Don Philip. Of the subordinates, Diego Florez was probably the most in fault, and he was imprisoned in the Castle of Burgos.

For the rest, Philip was singularly patient, his conscience perhaps telling him that if he was to demand a strict account he would have to begin with himself. The popular story of the composure with which he heard of the fate of the Armada is substantially true, though rather too dramatically pointed. The awful extent of the catastrophe became known to him only by degrees, and the end of Alonzo de Leyva, which distressed him most of all, he only heard of at Christmas.

To the Duke's letter he replied quietly and affectionately, without a syllable of reproach. Unlike Elizabeth, who left the gallant seamen who had saved her throne to die of want and disease in the streets of Margate, and had to be reminded that the pay of those who had been killed in her service was still due to their relations, Philip ordered clothes, food, medicine, everything that was needed, to be sent down in hottest haste to Corunna and Santander. The widows and orphans of the dead sailors and soldiers were sought out and pensioned at the cost of the State. To Medina Sidonia he sent the permission which the Duke had asked for, to leave the fleet and go home. He could not in fairness have blamed the commander-in-chief for having failed in a situation for which he had protested his incompetence. The fault of Philip as a king and statesman was a belief in his own ability to manage things. In sending out the Armada he had set in motion a mighty force, not intending it to be used mightily, but that he might accomplish with it what he regarded as a master-stroke of tame policy. He had selected Medina Sidonia as an instrument who would do what he was told and would make no rash experiments. And the effect was to light a powder-magazine which blew to pieces the naval power of Spain. It is to his credit, however, that he did not wreak his disappointment upon his instruments, and endured patiently what had be-

16

fallen him as the Will of God. The Will of God, indeed, created a difficulty. The world had been informed so loudly that the Armada was going on the Lord's work, the prayers of the Church had been so long and so enthusiastic, and a confidence in what the Lord was to do had been generated so universally that when the Lord had not done it, there was at once a necessity for acknowledging the judgment, and embarrassment in deciding the terms in which the truth was to be acknowledged. Philip's formal piety provided a solution which might have been missed by a more powerful intellect, and on October 13th the following curious letter was addressed by him to the bishops and archbishops throughout his dominions:

MOST REVEREND,—The uncertainties of naval enterprise are well known, and the fate which had befallen the Armada is an instance in point. You will have already heard that the Duke of Medina Sidonia has returned to Santander, bringing with him part of the fleet. Others of the ships have reached various ports, some of them having suffered severely from their long and arduous voyage. We are bound to give praise to God for all things which He is pleased to do. I on the present occasion have given thanks to Him for the mercy which He has shown. In the foul weather and violent storms to which the Armada has been exposed, it might have experienced a worse fate; and that the misfortune has not been heavier is no doubt due to the prayers which have been offered in its behalf so devoutly and continuously.

These prayers must have entailed serious expense and trouble on those who have conducted them. I wish you, therefore, all to understand that while I am, so far, well pleased with your exertions, they may now cease. You may wind up in the cathedrals and churches of your dioceses with a solemn Thanksgiving Mass on any day which you may appoint, and for the future I desire all ecclesiastics and other devout persons to continue to commend my actions to the Lord in their secret devotions, that He may so direct them as shall be for His own service, the exaltation of His Church, the welfare and safety of Christendom, which are the objects always before me.—*From the Escurial: October* 13, 1588.

Medina Sidonia reconsidered his resolution to have no more to do with ships and fighting. He was continued in his office of Lord High Admiral; he was again appointed Governor of Cadiz, and he had a second opportunity of measuring himself against English seamen, with the same result as before. Essex went into Cadiz in 1596, as Drake had gone in 1587. The Duke acted in the same manner, and withdrew to Seville to seek for reinforcements. He ventured back only after the English had gone, and was again thanked by his master for his zeal and courage. As if this was not enough, Philip, in 1598, raised him to the rank of Consejero altisimo de Estado y Guerra, Supreme Councillor in Politics and War. Who can wonder that under such a King the Spanish Empire went to wreck?

The people were less enduring. Clamours were raised that he had deserted the fleet at Santander, that he had shown cowardice in action, that he had neglected the counsels of his wisest admirals, that he was as heartless as he was incapable, and that, leaving the seamen and soldiers to die, he had hastened home to his luxuries at San Lucar. In reality he had gone with the King's permission, because he was useless and was better out of the way. He was accused of having carried off with him a train of mules loaded with ducats. He had told Philip that he had not brought home a maravedi, and if he had really taken money he would have done it less ostentatiously and with precautions for secrecy.

But nothing could excuse him to Spain. Every calumny found credit. He had shown "cobardia y continual pavor y miedo de morir, avaricia, dureza y crueldad"—cowardice, constant terror, and fear of death, avarice, harshness and cruelty. His real faults were enough without piling others on him of which he was probably innocent. With or without his will, he had been in the thickest and hottest parts of the hardest engagements, and the *San Martin* had suffered as severely as any ship in the fleet. He knew nothing of the work which he was sent to do; that is probably the worst which can be justly said of him; and he had not sought an appointment for which he knew that he was unfit. But an officer who tried to defend him was obliged to admit that it would have been happy for his country if the Duke had never been born; that he threw away every chance which was offered him, and that he talked and consulted when acts and not words were wanted.

His journey home across Castile was a procession of ignominy. The street boys in Salamanca and Medina del Campo pelted him with stones; crowds shouted after him "A las gallinas, à las almadradas" (To the hens and the tunnies)—the tunnies being the fattest and the most timid of fish, and the tunny fishing being a monopoly of his dukedom. He was told that he had disgraced his illustrious ancestors, and that had he the spirit of a man he would not have outlived his shame.

History does not record the reception which he met with from his wife when he reached his palace.

Emerson, the Lecturer [1]

James Russell Lowell

The bother with Mr. Emerson is that, though he writes in prose, he is essentially a poet. If you undertake to paraphrase what he says, and to reduce it to words of one syllable for infant minds, you will make as sad work of it as the good monk with his analysis of Homer in the "Epistolæ Obscurorum Virorum." We look upon him as one of the few men of genius whom our age has produced, and there needs no better proof of it than his masculine faculty of fecundating other minds. Search for his eloquence in his books and you will perchance miss it, but meanwhile you will find that it has kindled all your thoughts. For choice and pith of language he belongs to a better age than ours, and might rub shoulders with Fuller and Browne—though he does use that abominable word *reliable*. His eye for a fine, telling phrase that will carry true is like that of a backwoodsman for a rifle; and he will dredge you up a choice word from the mud of Cotton Mather himself. A diction at once so rich and so homely as his I know not where to match in these days of writing by the page; it is like homespun cloth-of-gold. The many cannot miss his meaning, and only the few can find it. It is the open secret of all true genius. It is wholesome to angle in those profound pools, though one be rewarded with nothing more than the leap of a fish that flashes his freckled side in the sun and as suddenly absconds in the dark and dreamy waters again. There is keen excitement, though there be no ponderable acquisition. If we carry nothing home in our baskets, there is ample gain in dilated lungs

[1] From *My Study Windows*, by James Russell Lowell, by permission of Messrs. Houghton, Mifflin & Co.

and stimulated blood. What does he mean, quotha? He means inspiring hints, a diving-rod to your deeper nature. No doubt, Emerson, like all original men, has his peculiar audience, and yet I know none that can hold a promiscuous crowd in pleased attention so long as he. As in all original men, there is something for every palate. "Would you know," says Goethe, "the ripest cherries? Ask the boys and the blackbirds."

The announcement that such a pleasure as a new course of lectures by him is coming, to people as old as I am, is something like those forebodings of spring that prepare us every year for a familiar novelty, none the less novel, when it arrives, because it is familiar. We know perfectly well what we are to expect from Mr. Emerson, and yet what he says always penetrates and stirs us, as is apt to be the case with genius, in a very unlooked-for fashion. Perhaps genius is one of the few things which we gladly allow to repeat itself—one of the few that multiply rather than weaken the force of their impression by iteration! Perhaps some of us hear more than the mere words, are moved by something deeper than the thoughts? If it be so, we are quite right, for it is thirty years and more of "plain living and high thinking" that speak to us in this altogether unique lay-preacher. We have shared in the beneficence of this varied culture, this fearless impartiality in criticism and specula-tion, this masculine sincerity, this sweetness of nature which rather stimulates than cloys, for a generation long. If ever there was a standing testimonial to the cumulative power and value of Character (and we need it sadly in these days), we have it in this gracious and dignified presence. What an antiseptic is a pure life! At sixty-five (or two years beyond his grand climacteric, as he would prefer to call it) he has that privilege of soul which abolishes the calendar, and presents him to us always the unwasted contemporary of his own prime. I do not know if he seems old to his younger hearers, but we who have known him so long wonder at the tenacity with which he maintains himself even in the outposts of youth. I suppose it is not the Emerson of 1868 to whom we listen. For us the whole life of the man is distilled in the clear drop of every sentence, and behind each word we divine the force of a noble character, the weight of a large capital of thinking and being. We do not go to hear what Emerson says so much as to hear Emerson. Not that we perceive any falling-off in anything that ever was essential to the charm of Mr. Emerson's peculiar style of thought or phrase. The first lecture, to be sure, was more disjointed even than common. It was as if, after vainly trying to get his paragraphs into sequence and order, he had at last tried the desperate expedient of *shuffling* them. It was chaos come again, but it was a chaos full of shooting-stars, a jumble of creative forces. The second lecture, on "Criticism and Poetry," was quite up to the level of old times, full of that power of strangely subtle association whose indirect approaches startle the mind into almost painful attention, of those flashes of mutual understanding between speaker and hearer that are gone ere one can say it lightens. The vice of Emerson's criticism seems to be, that while no man is so sensitive to what is poetical, few men are less sensible than he of what makes a poem. He values the solid meaning of thought above the subtler meaning of style. He would prefer Donne, I suspect, to Spenser, and sometimes mistakes the queer for the original.

To be young is surely the best, if the most precarious, gift of life; yet there are some of us who would hardly consent to be young again, if it were at the cost of our recollection of Mr. Emerson's first lectures during the consulate of Van Buren. We used to walk in from the country to the Masonic Temple (I think it was), through the crisp winter night, and listen to that thrilling voice of his, so charged with subtle meaning and subtle music, as shipwrecked men on a raft to the hail of a ship that came with unhoped-for food and rescue. Cynics might say what they liked. Did our own imaginations transfigure dry remainder-biscuit into ambrosia? At any rate, he brought us *life*, which, on the whole, is no bad thing. Was it all transcendentalism? magic-lantern pictures on mist? As you will. Those, then, were just what we wanted. But it was not so. The delight and the benefit were that he put us in communication with a larger style of thought, sharpened our wits with a more pungent phrase, gave us ravishing glimpses of an ideal under the dry husk of our New England; made us conscious of the supreme and everlasting originality of whatever bit of soul might be in any of us; freed us, in short, from the stocks of prose in which we had sat so long that we had grown well-nigh contented in our cramps. And who that saw the audience will ever forget it, where every one still capable of fire, or longing to renew in them the half-forgotten sense of it, was gathered? Those faces, young and old, agleam with pale intellectual light, eager with pleased attention, flash upon me once more from the deep recesses of the years with an exquisite pathos. Ah, beautiful young eyes, brimming with love and hope, wholly vanished now in that other world we call the Past, or peering doubtfully through the pensive gloaming of memory, your light impoverishes these cheaper days! I hear again that rustle of sensation, as they turned to exchange glances over some pithier thought, some keener flash of that humour which always played about the horizon of his mind like heat-lightning, and it seems now like the sad whisper of the autumn leaves that are whirling around me. But would my picture be complete if I forgot that

ample and vegete countenance of Mr. R—— of W——
—how, from its regular post at the corner of the front
bench, it turned in ruddy triumph to the profaner audience,
as if he were the inexplicably appointed fugleman of ap-
preciation? I was reminded of him by those hearty
cherubs in Titian's Assumption, that look at you as who
should say, "Did you ever see a Madonna like *that?* Did
you ever behold one hundred and fifty pounds of womanhood mount heavenward before like a rocket?"

To some of us that long-past experience remains as the
most marvellous and fruitful we have ever had. Emerson
awakened us, saved us from the body of this death. It
is the sound of the trumpet that the young soul longs
for, careless what breath may fill it. Sidney heard it in
the ballad of "Chevy Chase," and we in Emerson. Nor
did it blow retreat, but called to us with assurance of
victory. Did they say he was disconnected? So were
the stars, that seemed larger to our eyes, still keen with
that excitement, as we walked homeward with prouder
stride over the creaking snow. And were *they* not knit
together by a higher logic than our mere sense could
master? Were we enthusiasts? I hope and believe we
were, and am thankful to the man who made us worth
something for once in our lives. If asked what was left?
what we carried home? we should not have been careful
for an answer. It would have been enough if we had
said that something beautiful had passed that way. Or
we might have asked in return what one brought away
from a symphony of Beethoven? Enough that he had set
that ferment of wholesome discontent at work in us. There
is one, at least, of those old hearers, so many of whom are
now in the fruition of that intellectual beauty of which
Emerson gave them both the desire and the foretaste, who
will always love to repeat:

"Che in la mente m' è fitta, ed or m' accuora
La cara e buona immagine paterna
Di voi, quando nel mondo ad ora ad ora
M' insegnavaste come l' uom s' eterna."

THE DEATH OF THOMAS CARLYLE[1]

Walt Whitman

February 10, '81.—And so the flame of the lamp, after long wasting and flickering, has gone out entirely.

As a representative author, a literary figure, no man else will bequeath to the future more significant hints of our stormy era, its fierce paradoxes, its din, and its struggling parturition periods, than Carlyle. He belongs to our own branch of the stock too; neither Latin nor Greek, but altogether Gothic. Rugged, mountainous, volcanic, he was himself more a French revolution than any of his volumes. In some respects, so far in the nineteenth century, the best equipt, keenest mind, even from the college point of view, of all Britain; only he had an ailing body. Dyspepsia is to be traced in every page, and now and then fills the page. One may include among the lessons of his life—even though that life stretch'd to amazing length—how behind the tally of genius and morals stands the stomach, and gives a sort of casting vote.

Two conflicting agonistic elements seem to have contended in the man, sometimes pulling him different ways like wild horses. He was a cautious, conservative Scotchman, fully aware what a fœtid gas-bag much of modern radicalism is; but then his great heart demanded reform, demand-

---

[1] From *Specimen Days in America*. Here printed by the permission and courtesy of Mr. Thomas B. Harned, and of the publishers, Messrs. G. P. Putnam's Sons.

ed change—often terribly at odds with his scornful brain. No author ever put so much wailing and despair into his books, sometimes palpable, oftener latent. He reminds me of that passage in Young's poems where as death presses closer and closer for his prey, the soul rushes hither and thither, appealing, shrieking, berating, to escape the general doom.

Of short-comings, even positive blur-spots, from an American point of view, he had serious share.

Not for his merely literary merit (though that was great), not as "maker of books," but as launching into the self-complacent atmosphere of our days a rasping, questioning, dislocating agitation and shock, is Carlyle's final value. It is time the English-speaking peoples had some true idea about the vertebra of genius, namely power. As if they must always have it cut and bias'd to the fashion, like a lady's cloak! What a needed service he performs! How he shakes our comfortable reading circles with a touch of the old Hebraic anger and prophecy—and indeed it is just the same. Not Isaiah himself, more scornful, more threatening: "The crown of pride, the drunkards of Ephraim, shall be trodden under feet: And the glorious beauty which is on the head of the fat valley shall be a fading flower." (The word prophecy is much misused; it seems narrow'd to prediction merely. That is not the main sense of the Hebrew word translated "prophet"; it means one whose mind bubbles up and pours forth as a fountain, from inner, divine spontaneities revealing God. Prediction is a very minor part of prophecy. The great matter is to reveal and outpour the God-like suggestions pressing for birth in the soul. This is briefly the doctrine of the Friends or Quakers.)

Then the simplicity and amid ostensible frailty the towering strength of this man—a hardy oak knot, you could never wear out—an old farmer dress'd in brown clothes, and not handsome — his very foibles fascinating. Who cares that he wrote about Doctor Francia, and "Shooting Niagara"—and "The Nigger Question"—and didn't at all admire our United States? (I doubt if he ever thought or said half as bad words about us as we deserve.) How he splashes like leviathan in the seas of modern literature and politics! Doubtless, respecting the latter, one needs first to realize, from actual observation, the squalor, vice, and doggedness ingrain'd in the bulk-population of the British Islands, with the red tape, the fatuity, the flunkey-ism everywhere, to understand the last meaning of his pages. Accordingly, though he was no chartist or radical, I consider Carlyle's by far the most indignant comment or protest anent the fruits of feudalism to-day in Great Britain—the increasing poverty and degradation of the homeless, landless twenty millions, while a few thousands, or rather a few hundreds, possess the entire soil, the money, and the fat berths. Trade and shipping, and clubs and culture, and prestige, and guns, and a fine select class of gentry and aristocracy, with every modern improve-ment, cannot begin to salve or defend such stupendous hoggishness.

The way to test how much he had left his country were to consider, or try to consider, for a moment, the array of British thought, the resultant *ensemble* of the last fifty years, as existing to-day, *but with Carlyle left out*. It would be like an army with no artillery. The show were still a gay and rich one—Byron, Scott, Tennyson, and many more—horsemen and rapid infantry, and banners flying—but the last heavy roar so dear to the ear of the train'd soldier, and that settles fate and victory, would be lacking.

For the last three years we in America have had trans-mitted glimpses of a thin-bodied, lonesome, wifeless, child-

less, very old man, lying on a sofa, kept out of bed by in-
domitable will, but, of late, never well enough to take the
open air.   I have noted this news from time to time in brief
descriptions in the papers.   A week ago I read such an
item just before I started out for my customary evening
stroll between eight and nine.   In the fine cold night, un-
usually clear (February 5, '81), as I walk'd some open
grounds adjacent, the condition of Carlyle, and his approaching—perhaps even then actual—death, filled me
with thoughts eluding statement, and curiously blending
with the scene.   The planet Venus, an hour high in the
west, with all her volume and lustre recover'd (she has been
shorn and languid for nearly a year,) including an additional
sentiment I never noticed before—not merely voluptuous,
Paphian, steeping, fascinating—now with calm command-
ing seriousness and hauteur—the Milo Venus now.   Upward to the zenith, Jupiter, Saturn, and the moon past her
quarter, trailing in procession, with the Pleiades following
and the constellation Taurus, and red Aldebaran.   Not a
cloud in heaven.   Orion strode through the southeast, with
his glittering belt—and a trifle below hung the sun of the
night, Sirius.   Every star dilated, more vitreous, nearer
than usual.   Not as in some clear nights when the larger
stars entirely outshine the rest.   Every little star or cluster
just as distinctly visible, and just as high.   Berenice's
Hair showing every gem, and new ones.   To the northeast
and north the Sickle, the Goat and Kids, Cassiopea, Castor
and Pollux, and the two Dippers.   While through the
whole of this silent indescribable show, inclosing and bath-
ing my whole receptivity, ran the thought of Carlyle dying.
(To soothe and spiritualize, and, as far as may be, solve
the mysteries of death and genius, consider them under
the stars at midnight.)

And now that he has gone hence, can it be that Thomas

Carlyle, soon to chemically dissolve in ashes and by winds, remains an identity still? In ways perhaps eluding all the statements, lore, and speculations of ten thousand years— eluding all possible statements to mortal sense—does he yet exist, a definite, vital being, a spirit, an individual— perhaps now wafted in space among those stellar systems, which, suggestive and limitless as they are, merely edge more limitless, far more suggestive systems? I have no doubt of it. In silence, of a fine night, such questions are answer'd to the soul, the best answers that can be given. With me, too, when depress'd by some specially sad event, or tearing problem, I wait till I go out under the stars for the last voiceless satisfaction.

THOMAS GRAY

Matthew Arnold

James Brown, Master of Pembroke Hall at Cambridge, Gray's friend and executor, in a letter written a fortnight after Gray's death to another of his friends, Dr. Wharton of Old Park, Durham, has the following passage:

"Everything is now dark and melancholy in Mr. Gray's room, not a trace of him remains there; it looks as if it had been for some time uninhabited, and the room be- spoke for another inhabitant. The thoughts I have of him will last, and will be useful to me the few years I can ex- pect to live. He never spoke out, but I believe from some little expressions I now remember to have dropped from him, that for some time past he thought himself nearer his end than those about him apprehended."

He never spoke out. In these four words is contained the whole history of Gray, both as a man and as a poet. The words fell naturally, and as it were by chance, from their writer's pen; but let us dwell upon them, and press into their meaning, for in following it we shall come to understand Gray.

He was in his fifty-fifth year when he died, and he lived in ease and leisure, yet a few pages hold all his poetry; *he never spoke out* in poetry. Still, the reputation which he had achieved by his few pages is extremely high. . . .

Beattie, at the end of the eighteenth century, writing to Sir William Forbes, says: "Of all the English poets of this age Mr. Gray is most admired, and I think with justice." Cowper writes: "I have been reading Gray's works, and think him the only poet since Shakespeare entitled to the character of sublime. Perhaps you will remember that I once had a different opinion of him. I was prejudiced." Adam Smith says: "Gray joins to the sublimity of Milton the elegance and harmony of Pope; and nothing is wanting to render him, perhaps, the first poet in the English language, but to have written a little more." And, to come nearer to our own times, Sir James Mackintosh speaks of Gray thus: "Of all English poets he was the most finished artist. He attained the highest degree of splendour of which poetical style seemed to be capable."

In a poet of such magnitude, how shall we explain his scantiness of production? Shall we explain it by saying that to make of Gray a poet of this magnitude is absurd; that his genius and resources were small, and that his production, therefore, was small also, but that the popularity of a single piece, the *Elegy*,—a popularity due in great measure to the subject,—created for Gray a reputation to which he has really no right? He himself was not deceived by the favour shown to the *Elegy*. "Gray told me with a good deal of acrimony," writes Doctor Gregory, "that the *Elegy* owed its popularity entirely to the subject, and that the public would have received it as well if it had

been written in prose." This is too much to say; the
Elegy is a beautiful poem, and in admiring it the public
showed a true feeling for poetry. But it is true that the
Elegy owed much of its success to its subject, and that it
has received a too unmeasured and unbounded praise.

Gray himself, however, maintained that the *Elegy* was
not his best work in poetry, and he was right. High as
is the praise due to the *Elegy*, it is yet true that in other
productions of Gray he exhibits poetical qualities even
higher than those exhibited in the *Elegy*. He deserves,
therefore, his extremely high reputation as a poet, although
his critics and the public may not always have praised him
with perfect judgment. We are brought back, then, to
the question: How, in a poet so really considerable, are
we to explain his scantiness of production? . . .

Gray's letters and the records of him by his friends have
happily made it possible for us thus to know him, and to
appreciate his high qualities of mind and soul. Let us see
these in the man first, and then observe how they appear
in his poetry; and why they cannot enter into it more
freely and inspire it with more strength, render it more
abundant.

We will begin with his acquirements. "Mr. Gray was,"
writes his friend Temple, "perhaps the most learned man
in Europe. He knew every branch of history both natural
and civil; had read all the original historians of England,
France, and Italy; and was a great antiquarian. Criticism, metaphysics, morals, politics, made a principal part
of his study. Voyages and travels of all sorts were his
favourite amusements; and he had a fine taste in painting,
prints, architecture, and gardening." The notes in his
interleaved copy of Linnæus remained to show the extent
and accuracy of his knowledge in the natural sciences,
particularly in botany, zoology, and entomology. Ento-

mologists testified that his account of English insects was more perfect than any that had then appeared. His notes and papers, of which some have been published, others remain still in manuscript, give evidence, besides, of his knowledge of literature ancient and modern, geography and topography, painting, architecture and antiquities, and of his curious researches in heraldry. He was an excellent musician. Sir James Mackintosh reminds us, moreover, that to all the other accomplishments and merits of Gray we are to add this: "That he was the first discoverer of the beauties of nature in England, and has marked out the course of every picturesque journey that can be made in it." . . .

Gray's quality of mind, then, we see; his quality of soul will no less bear inspection. His reserve, his delicacy, his distaste for many of the persons and things surrounding him in the Cambridge of that day,—"this silly, dirty place," as he calls it,—have produced an impression of Gray as being a man falsely fastidious, finical, effeminate. But we have already had that grave testimony to him from the Master of Pembroke Hall: "The thoughts I have of him will last, and will be useful to me the few years I can expect to live." And here is another to the same effect from a younger man, from Gray's friend Nicholls:—

"You know," he writes to his mother, from abroad, when he heard of Gray's death, "that I considered Mr. Gray as a second parent, that I thought only of him, built all my happiness on him, talked of him forever, wished him with me whenever I partook of any pleasure, and flew to him for revenge whenever I felt any uneasiness. To whom now shall I talk of all I have seen here? Who will teach me to read, to think, to feel? I protest to you, that whatever I did or thought had a reference to him. If I met with any chagrins, I comforted myself that I had a treasure at home; if all the world had despised and hated

17

me, I should have thought myself perfectly recompensed in his
friendship.   There remains only one loss more; if I lose you, I
am left alone in the world.   At present I feel that I have lost
half of myself."

Testimonies such as these are not called forth by a fastidious effeminate weakling; they are not called forth,
even, by mere qualities of mind; they are called forth by
qualities of soul.   And of Gray's high qualities of soul, of
his σπουδαιότης, his excellent seriousness, we may gather
abundant proof from his letters. . . .

Seriousness, character, was the foundation of things
with him; where this was lacking he was always severe,
whatever might be offered to him in its stead.   Voltaire's
literary genius charmed him, but the faults of Voltaire's
nature he felt so strongly that when his young friend
Nicholls was going abroad in 1771, just before Gray's
death, he said to him: "I have one thing to beg of you
which you must not refuse."   Nicholls answered: "You
know you have only to command; what is it?"—"Do
not go to see Voltaire," said Gray; and then added: "No
one knows the mischief that man will do."   Nicholls
promised compliance with Gray's injunction; "But what,"
he asked, "could a visit from me signify?"—"Every tribute to such a man signifies," Gray answered. . . .

And with all this strenuous seriousness, a pathetic sentiment, and an element, likewise, of sportive and charming
humour.   At Keswick, by the lakeside on an autumn evening, he has the accent of the *Rêveries*, or of Obermann, or
Wordsworth:—

"In the evening walked down alone to the lake by the side of
Crow Park after sunset and saw the solemn colouring of night
draw on, the last gleam of sunshine fading away on the hill-tops,
the deep serene of the waters, and the long shadows of the mountains thrown across them, till they nearly touched the hither-

most shore. At a distance heard the murmur of many water-falls, not audible in the daytime. Wished for the Moon, but she was *dark to me and silent, hid in her vacant interlunar cave.*"

Of his humour and sportiveness his delightful letters are full; his humour appears in his poetry too, and is by no means to be passed over there. Horace Walpole said that "Gray never wrote anything easily but things of humour; humour was his natural and original turn."

Knowledge, penetration, seriousness, sentiment, humour, Gray had them all; he had the equipment and endowment for the office of poet. But very soon in his life appear traces of something obstructing, something disabling; of spirits failing, and health not sound; and the evil increases with years. He writes to West in 1737:—

"Low spirits are my true and faithful companions; they get up with me, go to bed with me, make journeys and returns as I do; nay, pay visits and will even affect to be jocose and force a feeble laugh with me; but most commonly we sit alone together, and are the prettiest insipid company in the world."

The tone is playful, Gray was not yet twenty-one. "Mine," he tells West four or five years later, "mine, you are to know, is a white Melancholy, or rather *Leuco-choly*, for the most part; which, though it seldom laughs or dances, nor ever amounts to what one calls joy or pleasure, yet is a good easy sort of a state." But, he adds in the same letter:—

"But there is another sort, black indeed, which I have now and then felt, that has something in it like Tertullian's rule of faith, *Credo quia impossibile est;* for it believes, nay, is sure of everything that is unlikely, so it be but frightful; and on the other hand excludes and shuts its eyes to the most possible hopes, and everything that is pleasurable; from this the Lord deliver us! for none but he and sunshiny weather can do it." . . .

And in 1757 he writes to Hurd:—

"To be employed is to be happy. This principle of mine (and I am convinced of its truth) has, as usual, no influence on my practice. I am alone, and *ennuyé* to the last degree, yet do nothing. Indeed I have no excuse; my health (which you have so kindly inquired after) is not extraordinary. It is no great malady, but several little ones, that seem brewing no good to me."

From thence to the end his languor and depression, though still often relieved by occupation and travel, keep fatally gaining on him. At last the depression became constant, became mechanical. "Travel I must," he writes to Doctor Wharton, "or cease to exist. Till this year I hardly knew what *mechanical* low spirits were; but now I even tremble at an east wind." Two months afterward he died.

What wonder, that with this troublous cloud, throughout the whole term of his manhood, brooding over him and weighing him down, Gray, finely endowed though he was, richly stored with knowledge though he was, yet produced so little, found no full and sufficient utterance, " *never*," as the Master of Pembroke Hall said, " *spoke out.*" . . .

Bonstetten, that mercurial Swiss who died in 1832 at the age of eighty-seven, having been younger and livelier from his sixtieth year to his eightieth than at any other time in his life, paid a visit in his early days to Cambridge, and saw much of Gray, to whom he attached himself with devotion. Gray, on his part, was charmed with his young friend; "I never saw such a boy," he writes; "our breed is not made on this model." Long afterward Bonstetten published his reminiscences of Gray. "I used to tell Gray," he says, "about my life and my native country, but *his* life was a sealed book to me; he never would talk of himself, never would allow me to speak to him of his poetry. If I quoted lines of his to him, he kept silence like an obstinate child. I said to him sometimes: 'Will you have the goodness to give me an answer?' But not a word issued from his lips." *He never spoke out.* Bonstetten thinks that Gray's life was poisoned by an unsatisfied sensibility, was withered by his having never loved; by his days being passed in the dismal cloisters of Cambridge, in the company of a set of monastic bookworms, "whose existence no honest woman ever came to cheer." Sainte-Beuve, who was much attracted and interested by Gray, doubts whether Bonstetten's explanation of him is admissible; the secret of Gray's melancholy he finds rather in the sterility of his poetic talent, "so distinguished, so rare, but so stinted"; in the poet's despair at his own unproductiveness.

But to explain Gray, we must do more than allege his sterility, as we must look further than to his reclusion at Cambridge. What caused his sterility? Was it his ill-health, his hereditary gout? Certainly we will pay all respect to the powers of hereditary gout for afflicting us poor mortals. But Goethe, after pointing out that Schiller, who was so productive, was "almost constantly ill," adds the true remark that it is incredible how much the spirit can do, in these cases, to keep up the body. Pope's animation and activity through all the course of what he pathetically calls "that long disease, my life," is an example presenting itself signally, in Gray's own country and time, to confirm what Goethe here says. What gave the power to Gray's reclusion and ill-health to induce his sterility?

The reason, the indubitable reason as I cannot but think it, I have already given elsewhere. Gray, a born poet, fell upon an age of prose. He fell upon an age whose task was such as to call forth in general men's powers of under-

standing, wit and cleverness, rather than their deepest
powers of mind and soul. As regards literary production,
the task of the eighteenth century in England was not the
poetic interpretation of the world, its task was to create
a plain, clear, straightforward, efficient prose. Poetry
obeyed the bent of mind requisite for the due fulfilment
of this task of the century. It was intellectual, argu-
mentative, ingenious; not seeing things in their truth and
beauty, not interpretative. Gray, with the qualities of
mind and soul of a genuine poet, was isolated in his century. Maintaining and fortifying them by lofty studies,
he yet could not fully educe and enjoy them; the want of
a genial atmosphere, the failure of sympathy in his contemporaries, were too great. Born in the same year with
Milton, Gray would have been another man; born in the
same year with Burns, he would have been another man.
A man born in 1608 could profit by the larger and more
poetic scope of the English spirit in the Elizabethan age;
a man born in 1759 could profit by that European renew-
ing of men's minds of which the great historical manifes-
tation is the French Revolution. Gray's alert and bril-
liant young friend, Bonstetten, who would explain the
void in the life of Gray by his having never loved, Bonstetten himself loved, married, and had children. Yet at
the age of fifty he was bidding fair to grow old, dismal and
torpid like the rest of us, when he was roused and made
young again for some thirty years, says M. Sainte-Beuve,
by the events of 1789. If Gray, like Burns, had been just
thirty years old when the French Revolution broke out,
he would have shown, probably, productiveness and animation in plenty. Coming when he did, and endowed as
he was, he was a man born out of date, a man whose full
spiritual flowering was impossible. The same thing is to
be said of his great contemporary, Butler, the author of

the *Analogy*. In the sphere of religion, which touches that of poetry, Butler was impelled by the endowment of his nature to strive for a profound and adequate conception of religious things, which was not pursued by his contemporaries, and which at that time, and in that atmosphere of mind, was not fully attainable. Hence, in Butler too, a dissatisfaction, a weariness, as in Gray; "great labour and weariness, great disappointment, pain and even vexation of mind." A sort of spiritual east wind was at that time blowing; neither Butler nor Gray could flower. They *never spoke out*.

THE FIRST EXPEDITION OF JEAN RIBAUT[1]

Francis Parkman

In the year 1562 a cloud of black and deadly portent was thickening over France. Surely and swiftly she glided towards the abyss of the religious wars. None could pierce the future, perhaps none dared to contemplate it: the wild rage of fanaticism and hate, friend grappling with friend, brother with brother, father with son; altars profaned, hearthstones made desolate; the robes of Justice herself bedrenched with murder. In the gloom without lay Spain, imminent and terrible. As on the hill by the field of Dreux, her veteran bands of pikemen, dark masses of organized ferocity, stood biding their time while the battle surged below, then swept downward to the slaughter,— so did Spain watch and wait to trample and crush the hope of humanity.

In these days of fear, a second Huguenot colony sailed for the New World. . . . An excellent seaman and stanch

[1] From *Pioneers of France in the New World*.

Protestant, Jean Ribaut of Dieppe, commanded the expedition. Under him, besides sailors, were a band of veteran soldiers, and a few young nobles. Embarked in two of those antiquated craft, whose high poops and tublike proportions are preserved in the old engravings of De Bry, they sailed from Havre on the eighteenth of February 1562. They crossed the Atlantic, and on the thirtieth of April, in the latitude of twenty-nine and a half degrees saw the long, low line where the wilderness of waves met the wilderness of woods. It was the coast of Florida. Soon they descried a jutting point, which they called French Cape, perhaps one of the headlands of Matanzas Inlet. They turned their prows northward, skirting the fringes of that waste of verdure which rolled in shadowy undulation far to the unknown West.

On the next morning, the first of May, they found themselves off the mouth of a great river. Riding at anchor on a sunny sea, they lowered their boats, crossed the bar that obstructed the entrance, and floated on a basin of deep and sheltered water, alive with leaping fish. Indians were running along the beach, and out upon the sand-bars beckoning them to land. They pushed their boats ashore and disembarked,—sailors, soldiers, and eager young nobles. Corselet and morion, arquebuse and halberd, flashed in the sun that flickered through innumerable leaves, as, kneeling on the ground, they gave thanks to God who had guided their voyage to an issue full of promise. The Indians seated gravely under the neighbouring trees, looked on in silent respect, thinking that they worshipped the sun. They were in full paint, in honour of the occasion, and in a most friendly mood. With their squaws and children, they presently drew near, and, strewing the earth with laurel-boughs, sat down among the Frenchmen. The latter were much pleased with them, and Ribaut gave the chief, whom he calls the king, a robe of cloth, worked in yellow with the regal fleur-de-lis.

But Ribaut and his followers, just escaped from the dull prison of their ships, were intent on admiring the wild scenes around them. Never had they known a fairer May-Day. The quaint old narrative is exuberant with delight. The tranquil air, the warm sun, woods fresh with young verdure, meadows bright with flowers; the palm, the cypress, the pine, the magnolia; the grazing deer; herons, curlews, bitterns, woodcock, and unknown water-fowl that waded in the ripple of the beach; cedars bearded from crown to root with long, gray moss; huge oaks smothering in the serpent folds of enormous grape-vines: such were the objects that greeted them in their roamings, till their new-discovered land seemed "the fairest, fruitfullest, and pleasantest of all the world."

They found a tree covered with caterpillars, and here-upon the ancient black-letter says—"Also there be Silke wormes in meruielous number, a great deale fairer and better then be our silk wormes. To bee short, it is a thing vnspeakable to consider the thinges that bee seene there, and shalbe founde more and more in this incomperable lande."

Above all, it was plain to their excited fancy, that the country was rich in gold and silver, turquoises and pearls. One of the latter, "as great as an Acorne at ye least," hung from the neck of an Indian who stood near their boats as they reëmbarked. They gathered, too, from the signs of their savage visitors, that the wonderful land of Cibola, with its seven cities and its untold riches, was distant but twenty days' journey by water. In truth, it was on the Gila, two thousand miles off, and its wealth a fable.

They named the river the River of May,—it is now the St. John's,—and on its southern shore, near its mouth, they planted a stone pillar engraved with the arms of France. Then, once more embarked, they held their course northward, happy in the benign decree which locks from mortal eyes the secrets of the future.

Next they anchored near Fernandina, and to a neighbouring river, probably the St. Mary's, gave the name of the Seine. Here, as morning broke on the fresh, moist meadows hung with mists, and on broad reaches of inland waters which seemed like lakes, they were tempted to land again, and soon "espied an innumerable number of foote steps of great Hartes and Hindes of a wonderfull greatnesse, the steppes being all fresh and new, and it seemeth that the people doe nourish them like tame Catell." By two or three weeks of exploration they seemed to have gained a clear idea of this rich semi-aquatic region. Ribaut describes it as "a countrie full of hauens riuers and Ilands of such fruitfulnes, as cannot with tongue be expressed." Slowly moving northward, they named each river, or inlet supposed to be a river, after the streams of France,—the Loire, the Charente, the Garonne, the Gironde. At length, they reached a scene made glorious in after-years. Opening betwixt flat and sandy shores, they saw a commodious haven and named it Port Royal.

On the twenty-seventh of May they crossed the bar, where the war-ships of Dupont crossed three hundred years later. They passed Hilton Head, where in an after-generation Rebel batteries belched their vain thunder, and, dreaming nothing of what the rolling centuries should bring forth, held their course along the peaceful bosom of Broad River. On the left they saw a stream which they named Libourne, probably Skull Creek; on the right, a wide river, probably the Beaufort. When they landed, all was solitude. The frightened Indians had fled, but they lured them back with knives, beads, and looking-glasses, and enticed two of them on board their ships. Here, by feeding, clothing, and caressing them, they tried to wean them from their fears; but the captive warriors moaned and lamented day and night, till Ribaut, with the prudence and humanity, which seem always to have characterised him, gave over his purpose of carrying them to France, and set them ashore again.

Ranging the woods, they found them full of game, wild turkeys and partridges, bears and lynxes. Two deer, of unusual size, leaped up from the underbrush. Cross-bow and arquebuse were brought to the level; but the Huguenot captain, "moved with the singular fairness and bigness of them," forbade his men to shoot.

Preliminary exploration, not immediate settlement, had been the object of the voyage; but all was still rose-color in the eyes of the voyagers, and many of their number would fain linger in the New Canaan. Ribaut was more than willing to humour them. He mustered his company on deck, and made them a stirring harangue. He appealed to their courage and their patriotism, told them how, from a mean origin, men rise by enterprise and daring to fame and fortune, and demanded who among them would stay behind and hold Port Royal for the King. The greater part came forward, and "with such a good will and joly corage," writes the commander, "as we had much to do to stay their importunitie." Thirty were chosen, and Albert de Pierria was named to command them.

A fort was forthwith begun, on a small stream called the Chenonceau, probably Archer's Creek, about six miles from the site of Beaufort. They named it Charlesfort, in honor of the unhappy son of Catherine de Medici, Charles the Ninth, the future hero of St. Bartholomew. Ammunition and stores were sent on shore, and, on the eleventh of June, with his diminished company, Ribaut, again embarking, spread his sails for France.

From the beach at Hilton Head, Albert and his companions might watch the receding ships, growing less and less on the vast expanse of blue, dwindling to faint specks, then vanishing on the pale verge of the waters. They were alone in these fearful solitudes. From the North Pole to Mexico there was no Christian denizen but they.

But how were they to subsist? Their thought was not of subsistence, but of gold. Of the thirty, the greater number were soldiers and sailors, with a few gentlemen, that is to say, men of the sword, born within the pale of nobility, who at home could neither labour nor trade without derogation from their rank. For a time they busied themselves with finishing their fort, and, this done, set forth in quest of adventures.

The Indians had lost fear of them. Ribaut had enjoined upon them to use all kindness and gentleness in their dealing with the men of the woods; and they more than obeyed him. They were soon hand in glove with chiefs, warriors, and squaws; and as with Indians the adage, that familiarity breeds contempt, holds with peculiar force, they quickly divested themselves of the prestige which had attached at the outset to their supposed character of children of the Sun. Good-will, however, remained, and this the colonists abused to the utmost.

Roaming by river, swamp, and forest, they visited in turn the villages of five petty chiefs, whom they called kings, feasting everywhere on hominy, beans, and game, and loaded with gifts. One of these chiefs, named Audusta, invited them to the grand religious festival of his tribe. Thither, accordingly, they went. The village was alive with preparation, and troops of women were busied in sweeping the great circular area, where the ceremonies were to take place. But as the noisy and impertinent guests showed a disposition to undue merriment, the chief shut them all in his wigwam, lest their Gentile eyes should profane the mysteries. Here, immured in darkness, they listened to the howls, yelpings, and lugubrious songs that resounded from without. One of them, however, by some artifice, contrived to escape, hid behind a bush, and saw the whole solemnity; the procession of the medicine-men and the bedaubed and befeathered warriors; the drumming, the dancing, the stamping; the wild lamentation of the women, as they gashed the arms of the young girls with sharp mussel-shells and flung the blood into the air with dismal outcries. A scene of ravenous feasting followed, in which the French, released from durance, were summoned to share.

Their carousal over, they returned to Charlesfort, where they were soon pinched with hunger. The Indians, never niggardly of food, brought them supplies as long as their own lasted; but the harvest was not yet ripe, and their means did not match their good-will. They told the French of two other kings, Ouadé and Couexis, who dwelt towards the South, and were rich beyond belief in maize, beans, and squashes. Embarking without delay, the mendicant colonists, steered for the wigwams of these potentates, not by the open sea, but by a perplexing inland navigation, including, as it seems, Calibogue Sound and neighbouring waters. Arrived at the friendly villages, on or near the Savannah, they were feasted to repletion, and their boat was laden with vegetables and corn. They returned rejoicing; but their joy was short. Their storehouse at Charlesfort, taking fire in the night, burned to the ground, and with it their newly acquired stock. Once more they set forth for the realms of King Ouadé, and once more returned laden with supplies. Nay, the generous savage assured them, that, so long as his cornfields yielded their harvests, his friends should not want.

How long this friendship would have lasted may well be matter of doubt. With the perception that the dependants on their bounty were no demigods, but a crew of idle and helpless beggars, respect would soon have changed to contempt and contempt to ill-will. But it was not to Indian war-clubs that the embryo colony was to owe its ruin. Within itself it carried its own destruction. The ill-assorted band of landsmen and sailors, surrounded by that influence of the wilderness which wakens the dormant savage in the breasts of men, soon fell into quarrels. Albert, a rude soldier, with a thousand leagues of ocean betwixt him and responsibility, grew harsh, domineering, and violent beyond endurance. None could question or oppose him without peril of death. He hanged a drummer who had fallen under his displeasure, and banished La Chère, a soldier, to a solitary island, three leagues from the fort, where he left him to starve. For a time his comrades chafed in smothered fury. The crisis came at length. A few of the fiercer spirits leagued together, assailed their tyrant, and murdered him. The deed done, and the famished soldier delivered, they called to the command one Nicholas Barré, a man of merit. Barré took the command, and thenceforth there was peace.

Peace, such as it was, with famine, homesickness, disgust. The rough ramparts and rude buildings of Charlesfort, hatefully familiar to their weary eyes, the sweltering forest, the glassy river, the eternal silence of the lifeless wilds around them, oppressed the senses and the spirits. Did they feel themselves the pioneers of religious freedom, the advance-guard of civilisation? Not at all. They dreamed of ease, of home, of pleasures across the sea—of the evening cup on the bench before the cabaret, of dances with kind damsels of Dieppe. But how to escape? A continent was their solitary prison, and the pitiless Atlantic closed the egress. Not one of them knew how to build a ship; but Ribaut had left them a forge, with tools and iron, and strong desire supplied the place of skill. Trees were hewn down and the work begun. Had they put forth, to maintain themselves at Port Royal, the energy and resource which they exerted to escape from it, they might have laid the corner-stone of a solid colony.

All, gentle and simple, laboured with equal zeal. They calked the seams with the long moss which hung in profusion from the neighbouring trees; the pines supplied them with pitch; the Indians made for them a kind of cordage; and for sails they sewed together their shirts and bedding. At length a brigantine worthy of Robinson Crusoe floated on the waters of the Chenonceau. They laid in what provision they might, gave all that remained of their goods to the delighted Indians, embarked, descended the river, and put to sea. A fair wind filled their patchwork sails and bore them from the hated coast. Day after day they held their course, till at length the favoring breeze died away and a breathless calm fell on the face of the waters. Florida was far behind; France farther yet before. Floating idly on the glassy waste, the craft lay motionless. Their supplies gave out. Twelve kernels of maize a day were each man's portion; then the maize failed, and they ate their shoes and leather jerkins. The water-barrels were drained, and they tried to slake their thirst with brine. Several died, and the rest, giddy with exhaustion and crazed with thirst, were forced to ceaseless labour, baling out the water that gushed through every seam. Head-winds set in, increasing to a gale, and the wretched brigantine, her sails close-reefed, tossed among the savage billows at the mercy of the storm. A heavy sea rolled

down upon her, and threw her on her side.   The surges
broke over her, and, clinging with desperate gripe to spars
and cordage, the drenched voyagers gave up all for lost.
At length she righted.   The gale subsided, the wind changed
and the crazy, water-logged vessel again bore slowly
towards France.

Gnawed with deadly famine, they counted the leagues of
barren ocean that still stretched before.   With haggard,
wolfish eyes they gazed on each other, till a whisper passed
from man to man, that one, by his death, might ransom
all the rest.   The choice was made.   It fell on La Chère,
the same wretched man whom Albert had doomed to
starvation on a lonely island, and whose mind was burdened with the fresh memories of his anguish and despair.
They killed him, and with ravenous avidity portioned out
his flesh.   The hideous repast sustained them till the
French coast rose in sight, when, it is said, in a delirium of
joy, they could no longer steer their vessel, but let her drift
at the will of the tide.   A small English bark bore down
upon them, took them all on board, and after landing the
feeblest, carried the rest prisoners to Queen Elizabeth.

Thus closed another of those scenes of woe whose lurid
clouds were thickly piled around the stormy dawn of
American history.

THE MARQUIS OF MONTROSE[1]

Sir John Skelton

To do what Montrose did, to win successive victories over
seven or eight trained armies, each of them superior in

[1] From *Essays in History and Biography, including the Defence of
Mary Stuart*.   Published by William Blackwood & Sons, Edinburgh,
1883.

numbers, discipline, and organisation to that which he led, must be counted no small achievement; but the peculiar difficulty which he had to meet, and which none but a really great man could have met with success, resulted from the peculiar constitution of his army. The Highlander was brave, and he liked fighting. But he liked plunder better, and he liked to secure his plunder. So that the general was placed in a singular dilemma. Whenever he gained a battle, he lost his army. The victor, in the hour of victory, was left at the mercy of the vanquished. It is assuredly not the least remarkable fact in his career, that he contrived to secure permanent and enduring results; in effect, to subdue and pacify the whole of Scotland; with an army that continually melted away, and to which victory was, in truth, more fatal than defeat. Any energetic Celtic robber could issue from the passes, harry the plain, reive the black cattle of his Lowland neighbours, and then retire swiftly with the spoil into his mountain lair. He could do this; it was all that he could do. Montrose, through the felicity and daring of his genius, contrived to make these fickle and inconstant instruments work out a great scheme of national liberation. For though the body dissolved like the snow, the spirit, the *man*, remained—a man who acted as a magnet, who drew soldiers out of every valley through which he passed, at whose war-cry the red-shanks gathered together from their remotest hills. Such a man was a nucleus, a centre, a rallying-point; and so long as their dreaded enemy lived, the rebel government felt that its supremacy in Scotland was not secure.

When, on his way to England, he is at last worsted, forced to quit his own country, and take refuge at a foreign court, he is not cast down nor depressed. He is still fertile in expedients; still prompt, resolute, and hopeful; still gentle, true, and of a good conscience. The elastic vigour of his

18

mind is as noticeable in adversity as in victory. Charles's death indeed stung him very sorely; he felt it keenly; perhaps he was never quite the old man after it; probably it prompted that wild descent from the Orkneys, when he came back with the king's standard in black, and *nil medium* upon his own.

One sometimes wishes that Montrose had died in battle —in victory—wrapt, it may be, in the flag he had kept so bravely. But it was better not. A stormy death on the battle-field was fitter for Dundee. We have said that Montrose's was a well-balanced character; his life also was well-balanced. But it needed the last scene to perfect it. The death gives it a beautiful lyric completeness which most lives, however distinguished in their incidents, want. It is a noble poem from beginning to end; breaking into a solemn dirge and wail of funeral music at the close.

That which enables the martyr to endure is the consciousness that each indignity of his martyrdom represents a great principle. And so widely has this been felt by men and women, so nobly in consequence have they been able to bear, that the degrading instruments of torture and death have escaped from the executioner's hand. They have ceased to be the instruments of infamy; and have become the symbols of heroic constancy and deathless honour. Christendom bows humbly before the Cross. The crown of thorns has become a crown of light. No martyr ever met a meaner death more nobly than Montrose. He saw with wonderful clearness the dignity of the indignities that were heaped upon him. The halter, the scaffold, the dismembered limb, had each its noble side, on which it represented honour, loyalty, and unspotted faith. It is easy to write thus now; but it was thus, undoubtedly, that Montrose saw them—spontaneously, not by resolute effort of the will. The neat reflections, the epigrammatic sayings, which seem to critical men and artists (who pause over the scene fastidiously and at their leisure), best to befit the solemnity, remain on well-authenticated testimony as those which, in these forlorn hours, naturally occurred to his mind. "I think it," he exclaims, "a greater honour to have my head standing on the post of this town for this cause, than to have my picture in the king's bedchamber. I am beholden to you," he adds, referring to the terms of his sentence, "that lest my loyalty should be forgotten, ye have appointed five of your most eminent towns to bear witness of it to posterity." Again, as they are tying his hands, "I felt not more honoured," he says, with perfect simplicity, "when his Majesty sent me the Garter." Montrose was a true poet; the poetic form being used instinctively by him in moments of strong emotion; and these his last verses were dictated by the same spontaneous feeling:

> "Let them bestow on every airth a limb,
>   Then open all my veins, that I may swim
>   To Thee, my Maker, in that crimson lake,—
>   Then place my parboil'd head upon a stake,
>   Scatter my ashes—strew them in the air;—
> Lord! since thou know'st where all these atoms are,
>   I'm hopeful Thou'lt recover once my dust,
>   And confident Thou'lt raise me with the just!"

But in his demeanour there is no rudeness or bravado, only grave courtesy and polished irony—the sole weapons his enemies have left him. The greatest of saints, he blandly assures them, have their own peculiar weaknesses. When they apologise for the extremities to which their brethren have proceeded in England, he answers only, "Error is infinite," a reply involving endless philosophies as well as subtlest sarcasm. Nay, he can even afford to jest with them, courtly and stately jesting as becomes the

Marquis. For whatever happens, this at least is evident, that he will not allow these men to *close* with him; they are to be held at arm's length; they are to be kept away from the inner chambers of his soul. So he continues to converse with them, seasoning his discourse with quaint allusion and Latin apophthegm, "very handsomely," as they admit; yet somewhat "too airy and volage," grave-visaged Patrick Simson thinks, for the occasion.

When at length his doom was read to him in the crowded house, "he lifted up his face without any word speaking." *He lifted up his face*. A grand speech—eloquent in its solemn simplicity. A silent protest: a silent appeal. Was it with him as with an older martyr?

> "And *looking upward*, full of grace,
>   He prayed, and from a happy place,
>   God's glory smote him on the face."

So died James Graeme, sometime Marquis of Montrose. He went through "the trying scene," his biographer assures us, "with the grace and gallantry of a perfect gentleman," as if he had engaged to dance a minuet with one of her Majesty's maids of honour, and did it, though he felt his duty rather irksome. Fancy a man entering the next world "with the grace and gallantry of a perfect gentleman." And yet, though the expression is somewhat unhappy when applied to the grave serenity of Montrose, it does not inaptly describe the way in which men died in those times. They prided themselves on doing it with perfect correctness and good breeding. Their lace ruffles stiff with starch; their long locks elaborately curled; and the neat little speech, with its not over-hackneyed quotation from Horace or Catullus, to wind up with. Sir Thomas More set the fashion; it was kept up by all his successors during the reigns of Mary and Elizabeth; one of the last

and most perfect specimens of an art that has died out is
the speech of the Lord Grey of Wilton, who was tried with
Raleigh in 1603.   When asked if he had anything to say
why death should not be pronounced, these only were his
words: "I have nothing to say"; there he paused long;
"and yet a word of Tacitus comes in my mind—'non
eadem omnibus decora'; the house of the Wiltons have
spent many lives in their prince's service, and Grey cannot
beg his.   God send the king a long and prosperous reign,
and to your Lordships all honour."   Neat and curt as an
epigram, and surviving as such to the present day, while
more words have been spent vainly—a warning to Parliamentary orators.

But Graeme's is unique.   "He lifted up his face without
any word speaking."

V

Impassioned Prose

Impassioned Prose

A VERY brief note is sufficient to indicate what is meant by impassioned prose. It may be described as prose so impregnated with emotion that it is elevated to an equality with poetry. It must not be confused, however, with what is sometimes called the "prose-poem," a bastard form of writing, which usually fails of being either good prose or good poetry. When, for example, Dickens becomes dithyrambic over his frequent death-beds, it is not impassioned prose he writes, but hysteric prose, and its effect upon a critical taste is to produce a sense of nausea and absurdity. When, however, the Hebrew prophets, aflame with a hatred of injustice, rise to the height of their great argument, they write truly impassioned prose, which increases in dignity in the degree of its emotional vehemence. We find the same quality in Wycliff and Latimer for the same reason; each is a prophet pleading for the rights of the poor. Across their pages there sweeps the gust of the Spirit, as it does at times over the page of Milton; a wind that blows through the members, a flame that burns upon the heights of logic; something that fuses and transfuses the form of thought, until the whole is indistinguishable from poetic or prophetic utterance.

Such a form of writing is necessarily rare. In Baxter, from whose *Saints' Everlasting Rest* we quote, it is manifestly the fruit of spiritual emotion. From the great religious and devotional writers many similar passages might be selected, but Baxter's may stand as the example of all. It should be noted how closely related this passage of Baxter's is to oratory, and indeed it is very probable that it was actually preached—another illustration of the relation of the essay to the spoken word. In De Quincey the spirit and method are wholly different, and are not altogether free from the suspicion of artifice; yet there is no mistaking the seer-like quality of the writing. And this is always the most marked outward characteristic of impassioned prose, *it is vision*. It is of imagination all compact; imagination paints the picture, emotion pours into each reticulation of the picture a pulse of life, which makes it less a picture than a vision. We *see* things; with Baxter that far-off land, where "every day is a noon, every month is harvest, every year a jubilee, every age is a full manhood, and all this is one eternity"; with De Quincey, "Death, the crowned Phantom, with all the equippage of his terrors . . . suddenly as from the chambers of the air opening in revelation . . . with the flashing of cataracts"—rushing on his victim. Here we have the true apocalyptic quality, which asking larger freedom for itself than the forms of metre admit, finds its adequate expression in impassioned prose.

Ruskin is much less simple than Baxter, much more ornate than De Quincey, but in his highest moments is equally the *seer*, the man who sees. His pictures of Venice are a continuous pageant, so essentially pictures in their objective quality and their appeal to the imagination, that had he possessed the equipment of the painter, he would have found in color a better vehicle for their interpretation than in words. The passage chosen from Ruskin illustrates this pictorial power, but it must not be forgotten that his prophetic power was equally great. Word-painting is but a part of his gift; behind it lies the rarer gift of passion, and his greatest prose passages are the product of his moral passion. In no English writer is the influence of the Bible so manifest. He himself has told us that one of the chief intellectual exercises of his childhood was the systematic absorption of the English Bible. Mr. Frederick Harrison has noted no fewer than sixty references to the Bible in one of his famous passages. With a soul saturated with the spirit of the Hebrew prophets, a mind exquisitely sensitive to their sonorous eloquence, a nature easily wrought into ecstasies of indignation over wrong, ecstasies of rapture over loveliness of form or action, Ruskin needed for his message to the world something that lay between poetry which he could not write, and mere pedestrian prose which he scorned to write, and he found his medium in impassioned prose. Matthew Arnold's famous apostrophe to Oxford is well known. In his essays, as in his poetry, he has something of the defect which he noted in Gray—he does not speak out. No one can be franker than he in the expression of opinion, few men have been more reticent in the expression of emotion. But in his apostrophe to Oxford he allows his emotion to speak as it rarely spoke even in his poetry. And it has the singular charm of entire spontaneity; here he speaks from the heart, and the speech is the more affecting because it is the brief and habitually denied emotion of a man naturally reticent. In Walter Pater the source of passion is the love of beauty. With a style definitely intricate, subtle, and full of artifice, Pater also has his passionate moments, when his page grows lyric, and his exquisite modulations affect us like the passing of a strain of music. Stevenson has done more for the essay than any writer since Lamb. He has endued it with new qualities, carried it to a completer perfection. Always by genius and deliberate aim a great stylist, a lover of phrases, a master of form, in his essays the genuine man speaks; a man not only genuine but deep-hearted, with a message for his age which he himself has won out of the long discipline of suf-

fering.   It is the urging of this message which enables him
to rise from time to time into impassioned prose.   He can
write as an artist only, gemming his page with curious
felicities that surprise and delight us; sometimes he is the
acute critic, sometimes the ironic observer, the familiar
philosopher, or the gentle humourist, but from time to time
a deeper chord is struck, the gravity and splendour of human
life seizes on him, the doubtfulness and solemnity of human
destiny, and then he also is among the prophets, and
speaks a prophet's language.   The passage selected from
Stevenson is an admirable specimen of this grave and
lofty mood, and it certainly does not suffer in contrast
with the great writers who preceded him.

THE   SAINTS'   REST [1]

Richard Baxter

Rest! how sweet the sound!   It is melody to my ears!
It lies as a reviving cordial at my heart, and from thence
sends forth lively spirits which beat through all the pulses
of my soul!   Rest, not as the stone that rests on the earth,
nor as this flesh shall rest in the grave, nor such a rest as
the carnal world desires.   O blessed rest! when we rest not
day and night saying, "Holy, holy, holy, Lord God Almighty": when we shall rest from sin, but not from worship; from suffering and sorrow, but not from joy!   O
blessed day! when I shall rest with God! when I shall rest
in the bosom of my Lord! when my perfect soul and body
shall together perfectly enjoy the most perfect God! when
God, who is love itself, shall perfectly love me, and rest in
this love to me, as I shall rest in my love to Him; and

----

[1] From *The Saints' Everlasting Rest.*

rejoice over me with joy, and joy over me with singing, as I shall rejoice in Him!

This is that joy which was procured by sorrow, that crown which was procured by the Cross. My Lord wept that now my tears might be wiped away; He bled that I might now rejoice; He was forsaken that I might not now be forsook; He then died that I might now live. O free mercy, that can exalt so vile a wretch! Free to me, though dear to Christ: free grace that hath chosen me, when thousands were forsaken. This is not like our cottages of clay, our prisons, our earthly dwellings. This voice of joy is not like our old complaints, our impatient groans and sighs; nor this melodious praise like the scoffs and revilings, or the oaths and curses, which we heard on earth. This body is not like that we had, nor this soul like the soul we had, nor this life like the life we lived. We have changed our place and state, our clothes and thoughts, our looks, language, and company. Before, a saint was weak and despised; but now, how happy and glorious a thing is a saint! Where is now their body of sin, which wearied themselves and those about them? Where are now our different judgments, reproachful names, divided spirits, exasperated passions, strange looks, uncharitable censures? Now are all of one judgment, of one name, of one heart, house, and glory. O sweet reconciliation! happy union! Now the Gospel shall no more be dishonoured through our folly. No more, my soul, shalt thou lament the sufferings of the saints, or the church's ruins, or mourn thy suffering friends, nor weep over their dying beds or their graves. Thou shalt never suffer thy old temptations from Satan, the world, or thy own flesh. Thy pains and sickness are all cured; thy body shall no more burden thee with weakness and weariness; thy aching head and heart, thy hunger and thirst, thy sleep and labour, are all gone. O what a mighty change is this. From the dunghill to the throne! From persecuting sinners to praising saints! From a vile body to this which shines as the brightness of the firmament! From a sense of God's displeasure to the perfect enjoyment of Him in love! From all my fearful thoughts of death to this joyful life! Blessed change! Farewell sin and sorrow for ever; farewell my rocky, proud, unbelieving heart; my worldly, sensual, carnal heart; and welcome my most holy, heavenly nature. Farewell repentance, faith, and hope; and welcome love, and joy, and praise. I shall now have my harvest without ploughing or sowing: my joy without a preacher or a promise: even all from the face of God Himself. Whatever mixture is in the streams, there is nothing but pure joy in the fountain. Here shall I be encircled with eternity, and ever live, and ever, ever praise the Lord. My face will not wrinkle nor my hair be gray: for this corruptible shall have put on incorruption; and this mortal, immortality; and death shall be swallowed up in victory. O death where is now thy sting? O grave where is thy victory? The date of my lease will no more expire, nor shall I trouble myself with thoughts of death, nor lose my joys through fear of losing them. When millions of ages are past, my glory is but beginning; and when millions more are past, it is no nearer ending. Every day is all noon, every month is harvest, every year is a jubilee, every age is a full manhood, and all this is one eternity. O blessed eternity! the glory of my glory, the perfection of my perfection.

THE VISION OF SUDDEN DEATH

Thomas De Quincey

What is to be taken as the predominant opinion of man, reflective and philosophic, upon SUDDEN DEATH? It is remarkable that, in different conditions of society, sudden death has been variously regarded as the consummation of an earthly career most fervently to be desired, or, again, as that consummation which is with most horror to be deprecated. Cæsar the Dictator, at his last dinner-party (*cœna*), on the very evening before his assassination, when the minutes of his earthly career were numbered, being asked what death, in *his* judgment, might be pronounced the most eligible, replied "That which should be most sudden." On the other hand, the divine Litany of our English Church, when breathing forth supplications, as if in some representative character, for the whole human race prostrate before God, places such a death in the very van of horrors: "From lightning and tempest; from plague, pestilence, and famine; from battle and murder, and from SUDDEN DEATH—*Good Lord, deliver us.*" Sudden death is here made to crown the climax in a grand ascent of calamities; it is ranked among the last of curses; and yet by the noblest of Romans it was ranked as the first of blessings.

* * * * * * *

The incident, so memorable in itself by its features of horror, and so scenical by its grouping for the eye, which furnished the text for this reverie upon *Sudden Death*, occurred to myself in the dead of night, as a solitary spectator, when seated on the box of the Manchester and Glasgow mail, in the second or third summer after Waterloo. . . .

Having mounted the box, I took a small quantity of laudanum, having already travelled two hundred and fifty miles—viz. from a point seventy miles beyond London. In the taking of laudanum there was nothing extraordinary. But by accident it drew upon me the special attention of my assessor on the box, the coachman. And in *that* also there was nothing extraordinary. But by accident, and with great delight, it drew my own attention to the fact that this coachman was a monster in point of bulk, and that he had but one eye. In fact, he had been foretold by Virgil as

"Monstrum horrendum, informe, ingens, cui lumen ademptum."

He answered to the conditions in every one of the items:— 1, a monster he was; 2, dreadful; 3, shapeless; 4, huge; 5, who had lost an eye. But why should *that* delight me? Had he been one of the Calendars in the "Arabian Nights," and had paid down his eye as the price of his criminal curiosity, what right had *I* to exult in his misfortune? I did *not* exult; I delighted in no man's punishment, though it were even merited. But these personal distinctions (Nos. 1, 2, 3, 4, 5) identified in an instant an old friend of mine whom I had known in the south for some years as the most masterly of mail-coachmen. He was the man in all Europe that could (if *any* could) have driven six-in-hand full gallop over *Al Sirat*—that dreadful bridge of Mahomet, with no side battlements, and of *extra* room not enough for a razor's edge—leading right across the bottomless gulf. Under this eminent man, whom in Greek I cognominated Cyclops *Diphrélates* (Cyclops the Charioteer), I, and others known to me, studied the diphrelatic art. . . .

During the first stage, I found out that Cyclops was mortal: he was liable to the shocking affection of sleep— a thing which previously I had never suspected. If a man indulges in the vicious habit of sleeping, all the skill in aurigation of Apollo himself, with the horses of Aurora to execute his notions, avails him nothing. "Oh, Cyclops!" I exclaimed, "thou art mortal. My friend, thou snorest." Through the first eleven miles, however, this infirmity— which I grieve to say that he shared with the whole Pagan

Pantheon—betrayed itself only by brief snatches. On waking up, he made an apology for himself which, instead of mending matters, laid open a gloomy vista of coming disasters. The summer assizes, he reminded me, were now going on at Lancaster: in consequence of which for three nights and three days he had not lain down in a bed. During the day he was waiting for his own summons as a witness on the trial in which he was interested, or else, lest he should be missing at the critical moment, was drinking with the other witnesses under the pastoral surveillance of the attorneys. During the night, or that part of it which at sea would form the middle watch, he was driving. This explanation certainly accounted for his drowsiness, but in a way which made it much more alarming; since now, after several days' resistance to this infirmity, at length he was steadily giving way. Throughout the second stage he grew more and more drowsy. In the second mile of the third stage he surrendered himself finally and without a struggle to his perilous temptation. All his past resistance had but deepened the weight of this final oppression. Seven atmospheres of sleep rested upon him; and, to consummate the case, our worthy guard, after singing "Love amongst the Roses" for perhaps thirty times, without invitation and without applause, had in revenge moodily resigned himself to slumber—not so deep, doubtless, as the coachman's, but deep enough for mischief. And thus at last, about ten miles from Preston, it came about that I found myself left in charge of his Majesty's London and Glasgow mail, then running at the least twelve miles an hour. . . .

The usual silence and solitude prevailed along the road. Not a hoof nor a wheel was to be heard. And, to strengthen this false luxurious confidence in the noiseless roads, it happened also that the night was one of peculiar solemnity and peace. For my own part, though slightly alive to the possibilities of peril, I had so far yielded to the influence of the mighty calm as to sink into a profound reverie. . . .

Suddenly I was awakened to a sullen sound, as of some motion on the distant road. It stole upon the air for a moment; I listened in awe; but then it died away. Once roused, however, I could not but observe with alarm the quickened motion of our horses. Ten years' experience had made my eye learned in the valuing of motion; and I saw that we were now running thirteen miles an hour. I pretend to no presence of mind. On the contrary, my fear is that I am miserably and shamefully deficient in that quality as regards action. The palsy of doubt and distraction hangs like some guilty weight of dark unfathomed remembrances upon my energies when the signal is flying for *action*. But, on the other hand, this accursed gift I have, as regards *thought*, that in the first step towards the possibility of a misfortune I see its total evolution; in the radix of the series I see too certainly and too instantly its entire expansion; in the first syllable of the dreadful sentence I read already the last. It was not that I feared for ourselves. *Us* our bulk and impetus charmed against peril in any collision. And I had ridden through too many hundreds of perils that were frightful to approach, that were matter of laughter to look back upon, the first face of which was horror, the parting face a jest—for any anxiety to rest upon *our* interests. The mail was not built, I felt assured, nor bespoke, that could betray *me* who trusted to its protection. But any carriage that we could meet would be frail and light in comparison of ourselves. And I remarked this ominous accident of our situation,—we were on the wrong side of the road. But then, it may be said, the other party, if other there was, might also be on the wrong side; and two wrongs might make a right. *That* was not likely. The same motive which had drawn *us* to the right-hand side of the road—viz. the luxury of the soft beaten sand as contrasted with the paved centre—would prove attractive to others. The two adverse carriages would therefore, to a certainty, be travelling on the same side; and from this side, as not being ours in law, the crossing over to the other would, of course, be looked for from *us*. Our lamps, still lighted, would give the impression of vigilance on our part. And every creature that met us would rely upon *us* for quartering. All this, and if the separate links of the anticipation had been a thousand times more, I saw, not discursively, or by effort, or by succession, but by one flash of horrid simultaneous intuition.

Under this steady though rapid anticipation of the evil which *might* be gathering ahead, ah! what a sullen mystery of fear, what a sigh of woe, was that which stole upon the air, as again the far-off sound of a wheel was heard! A whisper it was—a whisper from, perhaps, four miles off— secretly announcing a ruin that, being foreseen, was not the less inevitable; that, being known, was not therefore healed. What could be done—who was it that could do it—to check the storm-flight of these maniacal horses? Could I not seize the reins from the grasp of the slumbering coachman? You, reader, think that it would have been in *your* power to do so. And I quarrel not with your estimate of yourself. But, from the way in which the coachman's hand was viced between his upper and lower thigh, this was impossible. Easy was it? See, then, that bronze equestrian statue. The cruel rider has kept the bit in his horse's mouth for two centuries. Unbridle him for a minute, if you please, and wash his mouth with water. Easy was it? Unhorse me, then, that imperial rider; knock me those marble feet from those marble stirrups of Charlemagne.

The sounds ahead strengthened, and were now too clearly the sounds of wheels. Who and what could it be? Was it industry in a taxed cart? Was it youthful gaiety in a gig? Was it sorrow that loitered, or joy that raced? For as yet the snatches of sound were too intermitting, from distance, to decipher the character of the motion. Whoever were the travellers, something must be done to warn them. Upon the other party rests the active responsibility, but upon *us*—and, woe is me! that *us* was reduced to my frail opium-shattered self—rests the responsibility of warning. Yet, how should this be accomplished? Might I not sound the guard's horn? Already, on the first thought, I was making my way over the roof to the guard's seat. But this, from the accident which I have mentioned, of the foreign mails being piled upon the roof, was a difficult and even dangerous attempt to one cramped by nearly three hundred miles of outside travelling. And, fortunately, before I had lost much time in the attempt, our frantic horses swept round an angle of the road which opened upon us that final stage where the collision must be accomplished and the catastrophe sealed. All was apparently finished. The court was sitting; the case was heard; the judge had finished; and only the verdict was yet in arrear.

Before us lay an avenue straight as an arrow, six hundred yards, perhaps, in length; and the umbrageous trees, which rose in a regular line from either side, meeting high overhead, gave to it the character of a cathedral aisle. These trees lent a deeper solemnity to the early light; but there was still light enough to perceive, at the further end of this Gothic aisle, a frail reedy gig, in which were seated a young man, and by his side a young lady. Ah, young sir! what are you about? If it is requisite that you should whisper your communications to this young lady—though really I see nobody, at an hour and on a road so solitary, likely to overhear you—is it therefore requisite that you should carry your lips forward to hers? The little carriage is creeping on at one mile an hour; and the parties within it, being thus tenderly engaged, are naturally bending down their heads. Between them and eternity, to all human calculation, there is but a minute and a half. Oh, heavens! what is it that I shall do? Speaking or acting, what help can I offer? Strange it is, and to a mere auditor of the tale might seem laughable, that I should need a suggestion from the "Iliad" to prompt the sole resource that remained. Yet so it was. Suddenly I remembered the shout of Achilles, and its effect. But could I pretend to shout like the son of Peleus, aided by Pallas? No: but then I needed not the shout that should alarm all Asia militant; such a shout would suffice as might carry terror into the hearts of two thoughtless young people and one gig-horse. I shouted—and the young man heard me not. A second time I shouted—and now he heard me, for now he raised his head.

Here, then, all had been done that, by me, *could* be done; more on *my* part was not possible. Mine had been the first step; the second was for the young man; the third was for God. If, said I, this stranger is a brave man, and if indeed he loves the young girl at his side—or, loving her not, if he feels the obligation, pressing upon every man worthy to be called a man, of doing his utmost for a woman confided to his protection—he will at least make some effort to save her. If *that* fails, he will not perish the more, or by a death more cruel, for having made it; and he will die as a brave man should, with his face to the danger, and with his arm about the woman that he sought in vain to save. But, if he makes no effort,—shrinking without a struggle from his duty,—he himself will not the less certainly perish for this baseness of poltroonery. He will die

no less: and why not? Wherefore should we grieve that
there is one craven less in the world? No; *let* him perish,
without a pitying thought of ours wasted upon him; and,
in that case, all our grief will be reserved for the fate of the
helpless girl who now, upon the least shadow of failure in
him, must by the fiercest of translations—must without
time for a prayer—must within seventy seconds—stand
before the judgment-seat of God.

But craven he was not: sudden had been the call upon
him, and sudden was his answer to the call. He saw, he
heard, he comprehended, the ruin that was coming down;
already its gloomy shadow darkened above him; and already he was measuring his strength to deal with it. Ah!
what a vulgar thing does courage seem when we see nations
buying it and selling it for a shilling a-day: ah! what a
sublime thing does courage seem when some fearful summons on the great deeps of life carries a man, as if running
before a hurricane, up to the giddy crest of some tumultuous
crisis from which lie two courses, and a voice says to him
audibly, "One way lies hope; take the other, and mourn
for ever!" How grand a triumph if, even then, amidst the
raving of all around him, and the frenzy of the danger,
the man is able to confront his situation—is able to retire
for a moment into solitude with God, and to seek his counsel
from *Him!*

For seven seconds, it might be, of his seventy, the stranger
settled his countenance steadfastly upon us, as if to search
and value every element in the conflict before him. For
five seconds more of his seventy he sat immovably, like one
that mused on some great purpose. For five more, perhaps, he sat with eyes upraised, like one that prayed in
sorrow, under some extremity of doubt, for light that should
guide him to the better choice. Then suddenly he rose;
stood upright; and, by a powerful strain upon the reins,

raising his horse's fore-feet from the ground, he slewed him
round on the pivot of his hind-legs, so as to plant the little
equipage in a position nearly at right angles to ours. Thus
far his condition was not improved; except as a first step
had been taken towards the possibility of a second. If no
more were done, nothing was done; for the little carriage
still occupied the very centre of our path, though in an
altered direction. Yet even now it may not be too late:
fifteen of the seventy seconds may still be unexhausted;
and one almighty bound may avail to clear the ground.
Hurry, then, hurry! for the flying moments—*they* hurry.
Oh, hurry, hurry, my brave young man! for the cruel hoofs
of our horses—*they* also hurry! Fast are the flying moments, faster are the hoofs of our horses. But fear not for
him, if human energy can suffice; faithful was he that drove
to his terrific duty; faithful was the horse to *his* command.
One blow, one impulse given with voice and hand, by the
stranger, one rush from the horse, one bound as if in the
act of rising to a fence, landed the docile creature's fore-
feet upon the crown or arching centre of the road. The
larger half of the little equipage had then cleared our over-
towering shadow: *that* was evident even to my own agitated
sight. But it mattered little that one wreck should float
off in safety if upon the wreck that perished were embarked the human freightage. The rear part of the carriage
—was *that* certainly beyond the line of absolute ruin?
What power could answer the question? Glance of eye,
thought of man, wing of angel, which of these had speed
enough to sweep between the question and the answer,
and divide the one from the other? Light does not tread
upon the steps of light more indivisibly than did our all-
conquering arrival upon the escaping efforts of the gig.
That must the young man have felt too plainly. His back
was now turned to us; not by sight could he any longer

communicate with the peril; but, by the dreadful rattle of our harness, too truly had his ear been instructed that all was finished as regarded any effort of *his*. Already in resignation he had rested from his struggle; and perhaps in his heart he was whispering, "Father, which art in heaven, do Thou finish above what I on earth have attempted." Faster than ever mill-race we ran past them in our inexorable flight. Oh, raving of hurricanes that must have sounded in their young ears at the moment of our transit! Even in that moment the thunder of collision spoke aloud. Either with the swingle-bar, or with the haunch of our near leader, we had struck the off-wheel of the little gig; which stood rather obliquely, and not quite so far advanced as to be accurately parallel with the near-wheel. The blow, from the fury of our passage, resounded terrifically. I rose in horror, to gaze upon the ruins we might have caused. From my elevated station I looked down, and looked back upon the scene; which in a moment told its own tale, and wrote all its records on my heart for ever.

Here was the map of the passion that now had finished. The horse was planted immovably, with his fore-feet upon the paved crest of the central road. He of the whole party might be supposed untouched by the passion of death. The little cany carriage—partly, perhaps, from the violent torsion of the wheels in its recent movement, partly from the thundering blow we had given to it—as if it sympathized with human horror, was all alive with tremblings and shiverings. The young man trembled not, nor shivered. He sat like a rock. But *his* was the steadiness of agitation frozen into rest by horror. As yet he dared not to look round; for he knew that, if anything remained to do, by him it could no longer be done. And as yet he knew not for certain if their safety were accomplished. But the lady—

But the lady—! Oh, heavens! will that spectacle ever depart from my dreams, as she rose and sank upon her seat, sank and rose, threw up her arms wildly to heaven, clutched at some visionary object in the air, fainting, praying, raving, despairing? Figure to yourself, reader, the elements of the case; suffer me to recall before your mind the circumstances of that unparalleled situation. From the silence and deep peace of this saintly summer night—from the pathetic blending of this sweet moonlight, dawnlight, dreamlight—from the manly tenderness of this flattering, whispering, murmuring love—suddenly as from the woods and fields—suddenly as from the chambers of the air opening in revelation—suddenly as from the ground yawning at her feet, leaped upon her, with the flashing of cataracts, Death the crowned phantom, with all the equipage of his terrors, and the tiger roar of his voice.

The moments were numbered; the strife was finished; the vision was closed. In the twinkling of an eye, our flying horses had carried us to the termination of the umbrageous aisle; at the right angles we wheeled into our former direction; the turn of the road carried the scene out of my eyes in an instant, and swept it into my dreams for ever.

The Entry into Venice[1]

John Ruskin

In the olden days of travelling, now to return no more, in which distance could not be vanquished without toil, but in which that toil was rewarded, partly by the power of deliberate survey of the countries through which the journey lay, and partly by the happiness of the evening

[1] From *The Stones of Venice*, vol. ii, chap. i, sections 1 and 2.

hours, when, from the top of the last hill he had surmounted, the traveller beheld the quiet village where he was to rest, scattered among the meadows beside its valley stream; or, from the long-hoped-for turn in the dusty perspective of the causeway, saw, for the first time, the towers of some famed city, faint in the rays of sunset—hours of peaceful and thoughtful pleasure, for which the rush of the arrival in the railway station is perhaps not always, or to all men, an equivalent—in those days, I say, when there was something more to be anticipated and remembered in the first aspect of each successive halting-place, than a new arrangement of glass roofing and iron girder, there were few moments of which the recollection was more fondly cherished by the traveller than that which brought him within sight of Venice, as his gondola shot into the open lagoon from the canal of Mestre. Not but that the aspect of the city itself was generally the source of some slight disappointment, for, seen in this direction, its buildings are far less characteristic than those of the other great towns of Italy; but this inferiority was partly disguised by distance, and more than atoned for by the strange rising of its walls and towers out of the midst, as it seemed, of the deep sea, for it was impossible that the mind of the eye could at once comprehend the shallowness of the vast sheet of water which stretched away in leagues of rippling lustre to the north and south, or trace the narrow line of islets bounding it to the east. The salt breeze, the white moaning sea-birds, the masses of black weed separating and disappearing gradually, in knots of heaving shoal, under the advance of the steady tide, all proclaimed it to be indeed the ocean on whose bosom the great city rested so calmly; not such blue, soft, lake-like ocean as bathes the Neapolitan promontories, or sleeps beneath the marble rocks of Genoa, but a sea with the bleak power of our own northern waves, yet subdued

into a strange spacious rest, and changed from its angry
pallor into a field of burnished gold, as the sun declined
behind the belfry tower of the lonely island church, fitly
named "St. George of the Seaweed." As the boat drew
nearer to the city, the coast which the traveller had just
left sank behind him into one long, low, sad-coloured line,
tufted irregularly with brushwood and willows: but, at
what seemed its northern extremity, the hills of Arqua rose
in a dark cluster of purple pyramids, balanced on the bright
mirage of the lagoon; two or three smooth surges of inferior
hill extended themselves about their roots, and beyond
these, beginning with the craggy peaks above Vicenza,
the chain of the Alps girded the whole horizon to the north
—a wall of jagged blue, here and there showing through its
clefts a wilderness of misty precipices, fading far back into
the recesses of Cadore, and itself rising and breaking away
eastward, where the sun struck opposite upon its snow,
into mighty fragments of peaked light, standing up behind
the barred clouds of evening, one after another, countless,
the crown of the Adriatic Sea, until the eye turned back
from pursuing them, to rest upon the nearer burning of the
campaniles of Murano, and on the great city, where it
magnified itself along the waves, as the quick silent pacing
of the gondola drew nearer and nearer. And at last, when
its walls were reached, and the outmost of its untrodden
streets were entered, not through towered gate or guarded
rampart, but as a deep inlet between two rocks of coral in
the Indian sea; when first upon the traveller's sight opened
the long ranges of columned palaces—each with its black
boat moored at the portal—each with its image cast down,
beneath its feet, upon that green pavement which every
breeze broke into new fantasies of rich tessellation; when
first at the extremity of the bright vista, the shadowy
Rialto threw its colossal curve slowly forth from behind the

palace of the Camerlenghi; that strange curve, so delicate, so adamantine, strong as a mountain cavern, graceful as a bow just bent; when first, before its moon-like circumference was all risen, the gondolier's cry, "Ah! Stalì," struck sharp upon the ear, and the prow turned aside under the mighty cornices that half met over the narrow canal, where the plash of the water followed close and loud, ringing along the marble by the boat's side; and when at last that boat darted forth upon the breadth of silver sea, across which the front of the Ducal palace, flushed with its sanguine veins, looks to the snowy dome of Our Lady of Salvation, it was no marvel that the mind should be so deeply entranced by the visionary charm of a scene so beautiful and so strange, as to forget the darker truths of its history and its being. Well might it seem that such a city had owed her existence rather to the rod of the enchanter, than the fear of the fugitive; that the waters which encircled her had been chosen for the mirror of her state, rather than the shelter of her nakedness; and that all which in nature was wild or merciless—Time and Decay, as well as the waves and tempests—had been won to adorn her instead of to destroy, and might still spare, for ages to come, that beauty which seemed to have fixed for its throne the sands of the hour-glass as well as of the sea.

And although the last few eventful years, fraught with change to the face of the whole earth, have been more fatal in their influence on Venice than the five hundred that preceded them; though the noble landscape of approach to her can now be seen no more, or seen only by a glance, as the engine slackens its rushing on the iron line; and though many of her palaces are for ever defaced, and many in desecrated ruins, there is still so much of magic in her aspect, that the hurried traveller, who must leave her before the wonder of that first aspect has been worn away, may still be led to forget the humility of her origin, and to shut his eyes to the depth of her desolation. They, at least, are little to be envied, in whose hearts the great charities of the imagination lie dead, and for whom the fancy has no power to repress the importunity of painful impressions, or to raise what is ignoble, and disguise what is discordant, in a scene so rich in its remembrances, so surpassing in its beauty. But for this work of the imagination there must be no permission during the task which is before us. The impotent feelings of romance, so singularly characteristic of this century, may indeed gild, but never save the remains of those mightier ages to which they are attached like climbing flowers; and they must be torn away from the magnificent fragments, if we would see them as they stood in their own strength. Those feelings, always as fruitless as they are fond, are in Venice not only incapable of protecting but even of discerning, the objects to which they ought to have been attached. The Venice of modern fiction and drama is a thing of yesterday, a mere efflorescence of decay, a stage dream which the first ray of daylight must dissipate into dust. No prisoner, whose name is worth remembering, or whose sorrow deserved sympathy, ever crossed that "Bridge of Sighs," which is the centre of the Byronic ideal of Venice; no great merchant of Venice ever saw that Rialto under which the traveller now passes with breathless interest; the statue which Byron makes Faliero address as of one of his great ancestors was erected to a soldier of fortune a hundred and fifty years after Faliero's death; and the most conspicuous parts of the city have been so entirely altered in the course of the last three centuries, that if Henry Dandolo or Francis Foscari could be summoned from their tombs, and stood each on the deck of his galley at the entrance of the Grand Canal, that renowned entrance, the painter's favourite subject, the novelist's

favorite scene, where the water first narrows by the steps
of the Church of La Salute,—the mighty Doges would not
know in what spot of the world they stood, would literally
not recognise one stone of the great city, for whose sake,
and by whose ingratitude, their grey hairs had been brought
down with bitterness to the grave.   The remains of *their*
Venice lie hidden behind the cumbrous masses which
were the delight of the nation in its dotage; hidden in many
a grass-grown court, and silent pathway, and lightless
canal, where the slow waves have sapped their foundations
for five hundred years, and must soon prevail over them
for ever.   It must be our task to glean and gather them
forth, and restore out of them some faint image of the lost
city, more gorgeous a thousand-fold than that which now
exists, yet not created in the day-dream of the prince, nor
by the ostentation of the noble, but built by iron hands
and patient hearts, contending against the adversity of
nature and the fury of man, so that its wonderfulness cannot be grasped by the indolence of imagination, but only
after frank inquiry into the true nature of that wild and
solitary scene, whose restless tides and trembling sands
did indeed shelter the birth of the city, but long denied her
dominion.

OXFORD[1]

Matthew Arnold

Oxford, the Oxford of the past, has many faults: and she
has heavily paid for them in defeat, in isolation, in want of
hold upon the modern world.   Yet we in Oxford, brought
up amidst the beauty and sweetness of that beautiful place,
have not failed to seize one truth: the truth that beauty

[1] From the essay on " Sweetness and Light," in *Culture and Anarchy.*

and sweetness are essential characters of a complete human perfection. When I insist on this, I am all in the faith and tradition of Oxford. I say boldly that this our sentiment for beauty and sweetness, our sentiment against hideousness and rawness, has been at the bottom of our attachment to so many beaten causes, of our opposition to so many triumphant movements. And the sentiment is true, and has never been wholly defeated, and has shown its power even in its defeat. We have not won our political battles, we have not carried our main points, we have not stopped our adversaries' advance, we have not marched victoriously with the modern world; but we have told silently upon the mind of the country, we have prepared currents of feeling which sap our adversaries' position when it seems gained, we have kept up our own communications with the future. Look at the course of the great movement which shook Oxford to its centre some thirty years ago! It was directed, as any one who reads Doctor Newman's "Apology" may see, against what in one word may be called "Liberalism." Liberalism prevailed; it was the appointed force to do the work of the hour; it was necessary, it was inevitable that it should prevail. The Oxford movement was broken, it failed; our wrecks are scattered on every shore:—

Quæ regio in terris nostri non plena laboris?

*   *   *   *   *   *   *

[1] We are all seekers still! seekers often make mistakes, and I wish mine to redound to my own discredit only, and not to touch Oxford. Beautiful city! so venerable, so lovely, so unravaged by the fierce intellectual life of our century, so serene!

"There are our young barbarians, all at play!"

[1] From the Preface to *Essays in Criticism* (1865).

And yet, steeped in sentiment as she lies, spreading her gardens to the moonlight, and whispering from her towers the last enchantments of the Middle Age, who will deny that Oxford, by her ineffable charm, keeps ever calling us nearer to the true goal of all of us, to the ideal, to perfection,—to beauty, in a word, which is only truth seen from another side?—nearer, perhaps, than all the science of Tübingen. Adorable dreamer, whose heart has been so romantic! who hast given thyself so prodigally, given thyself to sides and to heroes not mine, only never to the Philistines! home of lost causes, and forsaken beliefs, and unpopular names, and impossible loyalties! what example could ever so inspire us to keep down the Philistine in ourselves, what teacher could ever so save us from that bondage to which we are all prone, that bondage which Goethe, in his incomparable lines on the death of Schiller, makes it his friend's highest praise (and nobly did Schiller deserve the praise) to have left miles out of sight behind him;—the bondage of *"was uns alle bändigt,* DAS GEMEINE!" She will forgive me, even if I have unwittingly drawn upon her a shot or two aimed at her unworthy son; for she is generous, and the cause in which I fight is, after all, hers. Apparitions of a day, what is our puny warfare against the Philistines, compared with the warfare which this queen of romance has been waging against them for centuries, and will wage after we are gone?

PHILOSOPHY OF LIFE[1]

Walter Pater

The service of philosophy, of speculative culture, towards the human spirit is to rouse, to startle it into sharp and

[1] From the " Conclusion " to *The Renaissance: Studies in Art and Poetry.*

eager observation. Every moment some form grows perfect in hand or face; some tone on the hills or the sea is choicer than the rest; some mood of passion or insight or intellectual excitement is irresistibly real and attractive for us—for that moment only. Not the fruit of experience, but experience itself, is the end. A counted number of pulses only is given to us of a variegated, dramatic life. How may we see in them all that is to be seen in them by the finest senses? How shall we pass most swiftly from point to point, and be present always at the focus where the greatest number of vital forces unite in their purest energy?

To burn always with this hard, gem-like flame, to maintain this ecstasy, is success in life. In a sense it might even be said that our failure is to form habits; for, after all, habit is relative to a stereotyped world, and meantime it is only the roughness of the eye that makes any two persons, things, situations, seem alike. While all melts under our feet, we may well catch at any exquisite passion, or any contribution to knowledge that seems by a lifted horizon to set the spirit free for a moment, or any stirring of the senses, strange dyes, strange colours, and curious odours, or work of the artist's hands, or the face of one's friend. Not to discriminate every moment some passionate attitude in those about us, and in the brilliancy of their gifts some tragic dividing of forces on their ways, is, on this short day of frost and sun, to sleep before evening. With this sense of the splendour of our experience and of its effort to see and touch, we shall hardly have time to make theories about the things we see and touch. What we have to do is to be for ever curiously testing new opinions and courting new impressions, never acquiescing in a facile orthodoxy of Comte, or of Hegel, or of our own. Philosophical theories or ideas, as points of view, instruments of

20

criticism, may help us to gather up what might otherwise pass unregarded by us. "Philosophy is the microscope of thought." The theory or idea or system which requires of us the sacrifice of any part of this experience, in consideration of some interest into which we cannot enter, or some abstract theory we have not identified with ourselves, or what is only conventional, has no real claim upon us.

One of the most beautiful passages in the writings of Rousseau is that in the sixth book of the *Confessions*, where he describes the awakening in him of the literary sense. An undefinable taint of death had always clung about him, and now in early manhood he believed himself smitten by mortal disease. He asked himself how he might make as much as possible of the interval that remained; and he was not biassed by anything in his previous life when he decided that it must be by intellectual excitement, which he found just then in the clear, fresh writings of Voltaire. Well! we are all *condamnés*, as Victor Hugo says: we are all under sentence of death, but with a sort of indefinite reprieve—*les hommes sont tous condamnés à mort avec des sursis indéfinis:* we have an interval, and then our place knows us no more. Some spend this interval in listlessness, some in high passions, the wisest, at least among "the children of this world," in art and song. For our one chance lies in expanding that interval, in getting as many pulsations as possible into the given time. Great passions may give us this quickened sense of life, ecstasy and sorrow of love, the various forms of enthusiastic activity, disinterested or otherwise, which come naturally to many of us. Only be sure it is passion—that it does yield you this fruit of a quickened, multiplied consciousness. Of this wisdom, the poetic passion, the desire of beauty, the love of art for art's sake, has most; for art comes to you professing frankly

to give nothing but the highest quality to your moments
as they pass, and simply for those moments' sake.

1868.

PAN'S PIPES

Robert Louis Stevenson

The world in which we live has been variously said and
sung by the most ingenious poets and philosophers: these
reducing it to formulæ and chemical ingredients, those
striking the lyre in high-sounding measures for the handi-
work of God. What experience supplies is of a mingled
tissue, and the choosing mind has much to reject before it
can get together the materials of a theory. Dew and
thunder, destroying Atilla and the Spring lambkins, belong
to an order of contrasts which no repetition can assimilate.
There is an uncouth, outlandish strain throughout the
web of the world, as from a vexatious planet in the house
of life. Things are not congruous and wear strange disguises: the consummate flower is fostered out of dung,
and after nourishing itself awhile with heaven's delicate
distillations, decays again into indistinguishable soil; and
with Cæsar's ashes, Hamlet tells us, the urchins make dirt
pies and filthily besmear their countenances. Nay, the
kindly shine of summer, when tracked home with the
scientific spy-glass, is found to issue from the most portentous nightmare of the universe—the great, conflagrant
sun: a world of hell's squibs, tumultuary, roaring aloud,
inimical to life. The sun itself is enough to disgust a
human being of the scene which he inhabits; and you
would not fancy there was a green or habitable spot in a
universe thus awfully lighted up. And yet it is by the
blaze of such a conflagration, to which the fire of Rome

was but a spark, that we do all our fiddling, and hold domestic tea-parties at the arbour door.

The Greeks figured Pan, the god of Nature, now terribly stamping his foot, so that armies were dispersed; now by the woodside on a summer noon trolling on his pipe till he charmed the hearts of upland ploughmen. And the Greeks, in so figuring, uttered the last word of human experience. To certain smoke-dried spirits matter and motion and elastic æthers, and the hypothesis of this or that other spectacled professor, tell a speaking story; but for youth and all ductile and congenial minds, Pan is not dead, but of all the classic hierarchy alone survives in triumph; goat-footed, with a gleeful and an angry look, the type of the shaggy world: and in every wood, if you go with a spirit properly prepared, you shall hear the note of his pipe.

For it is a shaggy world, and yet studded with gardens; where the salt and tumbling sea receives clear rivers running from among reeds and lilies; fruitful and austere; a rustic world; sunshiny, lewd, and cruel. What is it the birds sing among the trees in pairing time? What means the sound of the rain falling far and wide upon the leafy forest? To what tune does the fisherman whistle, as he hauls in his net at morning, and the bright fish are heaped inside the boat? These are all airs upon Pan's pipe; he it was who gave them breath in the exultation of his heart, and gleefully modulated their outflow with his lips and fingers. The coarse mirth of herdsmen, shaking the dells with laughter and striking out high echoes from the rock; the tune of moving feet in the lamplit city, or on the smooth ballroom floor; the hooves of many horses, beating the wide pastures in alarm; the song of hurrying rivers; the colour of clear skies; and smiles and the live touch of hands; and the voice of things, and their significant look, and the renovating influence they breathe forth—these are his joyful measures, to which the whole earth treads in choral harmony. To this music the young lambs bound as to a tabor, and the London shop-girl skips rudely in the dance. For it puts a spirit of gladness in all hearts; and to look on the happy side of nature is common, in their hours, to all created things. Some are vocal under a good influence, are pleasing whenever they are pleased, and hand on their happiness to others, as a child, who, looking upon lovely things, looks lovely. Some leap to the strains with unapt foot, and make a halting figure in the universal dance. And some, like sour spectators at the play, receive the music into their hearts with an unmoved countenance, and walk like strangers through the general rejoicing. But let him feign never so carefully, there is not a man but has his pulses shaken when Pan trolls out a stave of ecstasy and sets the world a-singing.

Alas if that were all! But oftentimes the air is changed; and in the screech of the night wind, chasing navies, subverting the tall ships and the rooted cedar of the hills; in the random deadly levin or the fury of headlong floods, we recognise the "dread foundation" of life and the anger in Pan's heart. Earth wages open war against her children, and under her softest touch hides treacherous claws. The cool hearth burns up in the hour of sleep, and makes an end of all. Everything is good or bad, helpful or deadly, not in itself, but by its circumstances. For a few bright days in England the hurricane must break forth and the North Sea pay a toll of populous ships. And when the universal music has led lovers into the path of dalliance, confident of Nature's sympathy, suddenly the air shifts into a minor, and death makes a clutch from his ambuscade below the bed of marriage. For death is given a kiss; the dearest kindnesses are fatal; and into this life, where one thing preys upon another, the child too often makes its

entrance from the mother's corpse. It is no wonder,
with so traitorous a scheme of things, if the wise people
who created for us the idea of Pan thought that of all fears
the fear of him was the most terrible, since it embraces all.
And still we preserve the phrase: a panic terror. To reckon
dangers too curiously, to hearken too intently for the
threat that runs through all the winning music of the
world, to hold back the hand from the rose because of the
thorn, and from life because of death: this it is to be afraid
of Pan. Highly respectable citizens who flee life's pleasures and responsibilities and keep, with upright hat, upon
the midway of custom, avoiding the right hand and the
left, the ecstasies and the agonies, how surprised they would
be if they could hear their attitude mythologically expressed, and knew themselves as tooth-chattering ones,
who flee from Nature because they fear the hand of Nature's
God! Shrilly sound Pan's pipes; and behold the banker
instantly concealed in the bank parlour! For to distrust
one's impulses is to be recreant to Pan.

There are moments when the mind refuses to be satisfied
with evolution, and demands a ruddier presentation of the
sum of man's experience. Sometimes the mood is brought
about by laughter at the humorous side of life, as when,
abstracting ourselves from earth, we imagine people plod-
ding on foot, or seated in ships and speedy trains, with
the planet all the while whirling in the opposite direction,
so that, for all their hurry, they travel back-foremost
through the universe of space. Sometimes it comes by the
spirit of delight, and sometimes by the spirit of terror.
At least, there will always be hours when we refuse to be
put off by the feint of explanation, nicknamed science;
and demand instead some palpitating image of our estate,
that shall represent the troubled and uncertain element
in which we dwell, and satisfy reason by the means of art.

Science writes of the world as if with the cold finger of a starfish; it is all true; but what is it when compared to the reality of which it discourses! where hearts beat high in April, and death strikes, and hills totter in the earthquake, and there is a glamour over all the objects of sight, and a thrill in all noises among men? So we come back to the old myth, and hear the goat-footed piper making the music which is itself the charm and terror of things; and when a glen invites our visiting footsteps, fancy that Pan leads us thither with a gracious tremolo; or when our hearts quail at the thunder or the cataract, tell ourselves that he has stamped his foot in the nigh thicket.

VI

The Familiar Essay

THE FAMILIAR ESSAY

THE familiar essay marks the final development of the essay. In Addison's day the essay was subject to many trammels, especially that of politics. It was also oppressed by a deadly weight of classicism. Addison and Steele certainly enfranchised and lightened it, but they never made it genuinely sprightly. It was still burdened and in part ruined by quotations from the classics, which to the modern man appear absurdly pedantic and out of place. A notable example of Addison's use of his learning to restrain emotion is found in the essay called *A Death-bed Scene*. Steele wrote the first half of this essay, in a straightforward and unaffected style, drawing his inspiration from his own experience and observation of life. Addison writes the second half, and immediately falls back upon what other men have said and done, quoting endlessly, as is the habit of the merely bookish man. First it is Seneca to whom he refers, and what the Roman philosopher had to say upon the virtues and death of the wife of Macrinus. Then it is Milton on the additional satisfaction which men derive from pleasures shared in the company of those they love. Here follow eighteen lines from the soliloquy of Eve, when, though in Paradise, she finds herself no longer pleased with the beautiful objects that surround her, unless she sees them in comradeship with Adam. Out of this quotation arises a little criticism of Dryden, because he "has said, in his preface to Juvenal, that he could meet with no turn of words in Milton." Lastly, as a conclusion to a death-bed scene, he remarks, "I might here, since I am accidentally led into the subject, show several passages in Milton that have as excellent turns of this nature as any of our English poets whatsoever, but shall only mention that which follows." He forthwith describes one of the passages, quoting it to the extent of five lines, thus concluding an essay which was begun with an exquisitely human account of the conduct of a good woman and the behaviour of her broken-hearted husband and children in the solemn trial of death, with the different ways in which persons of various ages have expressed their grief under similar circumstances.

It was not for lack of better models that Addison thus misjudged the nature of the essay. Addison, if he had willed, might have learned much from Cowley, of whom Johnson said, "His thoughts are natural, and his style has a smooth and placid equability, which has never yet obtained its due commendation. Nothing is far-sought or hard-laboured, but is easy without feebleness, and *familiar* without grossness." The final clause of this verdict is significant of what literary familiarity was wont to mean in Johnson's day. The truth is that Addison has been greatly over-rated. He had singular good fortune as a writer; he achieved immediate fame, and was rewarded with a munificence out of all proportion to his merit; for when we examine his work it is with a sense of strong disappointment we discover how little there is in it of original force. What has often been called stateliness in Addison is really stiffness and pedantry. He was much too cold and self-centred a man to be capable of the familiar essay, and he had not the humility to learn the lesson that Cowley had already taught, and Steele was even then teaching him.

In Johnson's day the essay had become much more

free, but it was still over-weighted by the habit of ponderous phraseology. For this Johnson himself was largely responsible. "Johnsonese" has come to be a synonym for a style based on artificial antithesis, for a laboured and scholastic method of writing, which mistakes turgidity for eloquence and ponderousness for majesty. Yet, in close association with Johnson, there was one man who was destined to simplify the entire literary style of his age, Oliver Goldsmith. Goldsmith began his prose writing by the imitation of Johnson. It was the convention of the day, and one which no hack-writer, as Goldsmith then was, could afford to disregard. It is very likely that Goldsmith knew perfectly well that his contributions to periodic literature would have had a precarious chance of acceptance unless they had obeyed the Johnsonian tradition. Goldsmith's first essays were sent to *The Bee*, and it is amusing to remember that Boswell, always jealous for the sole rule of his deity, somewhat angrily accused Goldsmith of having patterned himself on Johnson. This imitative phase of Goldsmith's writing did not last long. It was absolutely foreign to the nature of his genius, and was shaken off as a mere disguise, the moment he had attained a sufficient reputation to write as he pleased. The real Goldsmith, wise, simple, foolish, friendly, then appeared; the Goldsmith who wrote of real things, and always with a captivating lucidity of style.

One of the most memorable things to be remarked in Goldsmith is the note of world-wideness which he introduced into literature. There is a total absence in him of local prejudice, which is in strong contrast with the vigorous and almost barbaric insularity of Johnson. He had once thought of emigrating to America, and would have done so but for one of those humorous accidents so common in his haphazard life. He knew France and Italy with a thoroughness never attained by those who made the grand tour under circumstances of pomp and luxury. The most such travellers learned of the countries they traversed was superficial; their attitude was supercilious, and what they observed did little more than strengthen that unamiable patriotism which thrives upon the depreciation of other nations. This habit is so common that it has been accepted as characteristic of the travelling Englishman, who, to quote Ian Maclaren, "sniffs" his way across a continent. But Goldsmith went afoot, mixing with the common people, quick to recognise in them lovable and sterling qualities. "He was perhaps the only writer of his day," it has been said, "who thoroughly understood the social condition of the Continent. Nor was he less observant of English society; the *Deserted Village* has often been quoted by economists in illustration of the change which has gradually substituted large estates for the small holdings of a numerous yeomanry." In this quality of world-wideness he stands alone among his contemporaries. And this quality is reflected in his essays. He is large-hearted, because he has had a large acquaintance with mankind. He is among the first of humanitarians, using that word to indicate an interest in mankind as a whole. He is in reality what he described his mythical philosopher to be, a *Citizen of the World*.

The only point in which Goldsmith fails of the true familiar essay is that he does not explicitly relate his own experiences. He writes under a pseudonym as Lamb did; but the disguise is so transparent that it conceals nothing. No one needs to be informed that it is no Chinese observer who conceived the following passage: "The clock has just struck two; what a gloom hangs all around! No sound is heard but the chiming of the clock, or the distant watchdog. How few appear in these streets, which but some few hours ago were crowded! But who are these that make the street their couch, and find a short repose from wretchedness at the doors of the opulent? They are strangers, wanderers, and orphans, whose circumstances are too humble to expect redress, and whose distresses are too great even for pity. Some are without the covering even of rags, and others emaciated with disease; the world has disclaimed them; society turns its back upon their distress, and has given them up to nakedness and hunger. . . . Why, why was I born a man, and yet see the suffering of wretches I cannot relieve! Poor houseless creatures! The world will give you reproaches, but will not give you relief!" No pseudonym can conceal for a moment the vital autobiographic truth of this picture. It has the poignant pathos of personal confession, it is the houseless Goldsmith himself we see, the ill-paid drudge, drifting helpless through the populous Infernos of London misery, and finding his only shelter among the outcasts and beggars of Axe Lane.

Charles Lamb inherits the tradition of Goldsmith and extends it. He also writes under a pseudonym which is the most transparent of disguises. It will be observed, however, that he has none of Goldsmith's world-wideness, nor has he Goldsmith's delicate sense of natural beauty. He is a city-dweller, essentially local in spirit, who boldly confesses, in a day when a new movement toward Nature was attracting men like Wordsworth and Coleridge, and in a more limited degree Byron and Shelley, that he prefers Fleet Street to Skiddaw. It is hard to place Lamb, for he was an exotic. His style, in its suggestive quaintness, is a harking back to Fuller and Sir Thomas Browne. His method, however, and the nature of his themes, relate him vitally to the familiar essay. He uses the essay with the utmost freedom; indulges his sentiment, whim, and fancy without restraint; can be grotesque, eloquent, pathetic in turn; is very much of a conscious humourist, whose humour expresses itself in a kind of genial irresponsibility, which is best described by the word "fun." He sees everything at so odd an angle that all he writes is intimately personal, and his charm lies in this constant intimate revelation of himself. He can be wise and tender; but he is delightfully boyish in his good spirits, his love of laughter, his quick sense of the ridiculous. Perhaps the word "delightful" best expresses his charm; he is "the gentle Elia," who is either our friend or makes no appeal whatever to us.

Thoreau is a writer who has never received from his countrymen the praise to which he is entitled, probably because the man himself has not been truly understood. In the year 1845 he built for himself a hut on the shore of Walden Pond, and commenced the life of the solitary, which lasted for two years. Here he read assiduously, studied Nature intimately, and arrived at certain truths about the simplification of life which were to constitute his message to the world. On his return to society, after great difficulty and long search he found a publisher for his first book—*A Week on the Concord and Merrimac Rivers*. The book was not appreciated, and found few readers. A few years later he gathered together the greater part of his first editions, stored them in a garret, and wrote in his journal, "I have now a library of 900 volumes, over 700 *of which I wrote myself*." In 1854 he published his second book, *Walden*, and it is on this book his fame is based. Mr. Lowell, in a passage of truly monumental misapprehension, has said "Thoreau had no humour, and this implies that he was a sorry logician." It is not easy to see what Lowell meant by this implication, or what is the connection between humour and logic; but it is certain that no statement could be more manifestly false. Thoreau is a singularly acute logician, and his power of humour is sufficiently proved by the selection in this volume. He is not humourous in Lamb's way, it is true; his more frequent mood is dry irony; but when he apologises for not doing good by saying that he has tried it fairly, and is satisfied that it does not agree with his constitution, he achieves a kind of quaintness in which Lamb would have delighted. Thoreau, like all familiar essayists, writes of himself. He is not lovable, not genial, but he is so original in his attitude to life and society that he never fails to excite our interest. And it must also be added that no modern writer has ever loved Nature with a more real passion, or has written of natural objects with surer accuracy.

Of the two remaining writers quoted in this volume little need be said. Stevenson has passed away so recently, and his work is so well known, that the general characteristics of his work are familiar to all cultured readers. As an essayist he had many modes, and was successful in each. He has written the sermonic essay, although he writes rather as a friendly adviser than a preacher; he has written excellent critical and biographical essays, as for example the essay on Burns; but his chief merit is that he imparts to all he writes the intimate and familiar note. He is the familiar of all things. The roadside beggar, children at play, the priest, the mule-driver, the tavern companion of a night, interest him as deeply as Burns or Villon. In this broad humanitarianism and worldwideness he resembles Goldsmith. As a stylist he is supreme. He loves words for their own sake, perceives their colour and value with the exigent eye of the artist, and yet always uses them as a means to accurate and sometimes subtle thought. It may be said finally of Stevenson's familiar essays that, more than any other modern, he has brought the essay back to Montaigne; with him also "My subject is my-selfe."

One other essayist, Richard Dowling, is included in this series, because he affords an admirable example of the perfection to which the essay has come among modern writers who are comparatively unknown. Dowling lived and died unappreciated by his contemporaries. The literary journals which recorded his death could find nothing to comment on but his personal qualities; upon his work they were silent, or scornfully condescending. Yet Dowling wrote at least one essay which is worthy to rank with the best in English Literature—viz., the essay which is included in this volume. The fact that such a piece of work is totally unknown illustrates something more than the blindness of contemporary criticism; it is significant of the amount of excellent essay-work which was before the world that this should be unnoticed. And in this reflection we reach the last word upon the English essay. What has been said in a previous volume of this series on the art of letter-writing is equally true of the essay; it is one of the forms of literature that is marked by a steady progression toward a more generally diffused excellence. In the great literary journals, and often in the popular press, there appear to-day many essays of which neither Defoe nor Addison, Goldsmith nor Johnson, had they lived to-day, would have had cause to be ashamed. But while the model has been surpassed, the value of the model can never be ignored; all can grow the flower, but only a few can supply the seed; and the chief object of this work is to furnish a compact account of the evolution of the essay from seed to flower, from its first diffident attempt at separate expression to its final triumph as a recognised form of literary art.

A City Night-Piece

Oliver Goldsmith

The clock has just struck two, the expiring taper rises and sinks in the socket, the watchman forgets the hour in slumber, the laborious and the happy are at rest, and nothing wakes but meditation, guilt, revelry, and despair. The drunkard once more fills the destroying bowl, the robber walks his midnight round, and the suicide lifts his guilty arm against his own sacred person.

Let me no longer waste the night over the page of antiquity or the sallies of contemporary genius, but pursue the solitary walk, where Vanity, ever changing, but a few hours past walked before me, where she kept up the pageant, and now, like a froward child, seems hushed with her own importunities.

What a gloom hangs all around! The dying lamp feebly emits a yellow gleam; no sound is heard but of the chiming clock, or the distant watch-dog. All the bustle of human pride is forgotten; an hour like this may well display the emptiness of human vanity.

There will come a time when this temporary solitude may be made continual, and the city itself, like its inhabitants, fade away, and leave a desert in its room.

What cities, as great as this, have once triumphed in existence! had their victories as great, joy as just and as unbounded, and, with short-sighted presumption, promised themselves immortality! Posterity can hardly trace the situation of some; the sorrowful traveller wanders over the awful ruins of others; and, as he beholds, he learns wisdom, and feels the transience of every sublunary possession.

"Here," he cries, "stood their citadel, now grown over with weeds; there, their senate house, but now the haunt of every noxious reptile; temples and theatres stood here, now only an undistinguished heap of ruin. They are fallen: for luxury and avarice first made them feeble. The rewards of the state were conferred on amusing and not on useful members of society. Their riches and opulence invited the invaders, who, though at first repulsed, returned again, conquered by perseverance, and at last swept the defendants into undistinguished destruction."

How few appear in those streets which, but some few hours ago, were crowded! and those who appear now no longer wear their daily mask, nor attempt to hide their lewdness or their misery.

But who are those who make the streets their couch, and find a short repose from wretchedness at the doors of the opulent? These are strangers, wanderers, and orphans, whose circumstances are too humble to expect redress, and whose distresses are too great even for pity. Their wretchedness rather excites horror than pity. Some are without the covering even of rags, and others emaciated with disease: the world has disclaimed them; society turns its back upon their distress, and has given them up to nakedness and hunger. These poor shivering females have once seen happier days and been flattered into beauty. They have been prostituted to the gay, luxurious villain, and are now turned out to meet the severity of winter. Perhaps, now lying at the doors of their betrayers, they sue to wretches whose hearts are insensible, to debauchees who may curse but will not relieve them.

Why, why was I born a man, and yet see the sufferings of wretches I cannot relieve! Poor houseless creatures! the world will give you reproaches, but will not give you relief. The slightest misfortunes of the great, the most imaginary uneasinesses of the rich, are aggravated with all the power of eloquence, and held up to engage our attention and sympathetic sorrow. The poor weep unheeded, persecuted by every subordinate species of tyranny; and every law, which gives others security, becomes an enemy to them.

Why was this heart of mine formed with so much sensibility! or why was not my fortune adapted to its impulse! Tenderness, without a capacity of relieving, only makes the man who feels it more wretched than the object which sues for assistance. Adieu.

CHRIST'S HOSPITAL FIVE AND THIRTY YEARS AGO

Charles Lamb

In Mr. Lamb's "Works," published a year or two since, I find a magnificent eulogy on my old school, such as it was, or now appears to him to have been, between the years 1782 and 1789. It happens, very oddly, that my own standing at Christ's was nearly corresponding with his; and, with all gratitude to him for his enthusiasm for the cloisters, I think he has contrived to bring together whatever can be said in praise of them, dropping all the other side of the argument most ingeniously. . . .

I was a hypochondriac lad; and the sight of a boy in fetters, upon the day of my first putting on the blue clothes, was not exactly fitted to assuage the natural terrors of initiation. I was of tender years, barely turned of seven; and had only read of such things in books, or seen them but in dreams. I was told he had *run away*. This was the punishment for the first offence.—As a novice I was soon after taken to see the dungeons. These were little, square, Bedlam cells, where a boy could just lie at his length upon straw and a blanket—a mattress, I think, was afterwards substituted—with a peep of light, let in askance, from a prison-orifice at top, barely enough to read by. Here the poor boy was locked in by himself all day, without sight of any but the porter who brought him his bread and water —who *might not speak to him;*—or of the beadle, who came twice a week to call him out to receive his periodical chastisement, which was almost welcome, because it separated him for a brief interval from solitude: and here he was shut up by himself *of nights*, out of the reach of any sound, to suffer whatever horrors the weak nerves, and superstition incident to his time of life, might subject him to. This was the penalty for the second offence.—Wouldst thou like, reader, to see what became of him in the next degree?

The culprit, who had been a third time an offender, and whose expulsion was at this time deemed irreversible, was brought forth, as at some solemn *auto da fé*, arrayed in uncouth and most appalling attire—all trace of his late "watchet weeds" carefully effaced, he was exposed in a jacket, resembling those which London lamplighters formerly delighted in, with a cap of the same. The effect of this divestiture was such as the ingenious devisers of it could have anticipated. With his pale and frighted features, it was as if some of those disfigurements in Dante had seized upon him. In this disguisement he was brought into the hall (*L.'s favourite state-room*), where awaited him the whole number of his schoolfellows, whose joint lessons and sports he was thenceforth to share no more; the awful presence of the steward, to be seen for the last time; of the executioner beadle, clad in his state robe for the occasion; and of two faces more, of direr import, because never but in these extremities visible. These were governors; two of whom, by choice, or charter, were always accustomed to officiate at these *Ultima Supplicia;* not to mitigate (so at least we understood it), but to enforce the uttermost stripe. Old Bamber Gascoigne, and Peter Aubert, I remember, were colleagues on one occasion, when the beadle turning rather pale, a glass of brandy was ordered to prepare him for the mysteries. The scourging was, after the old Roman fashion, long and stately. The lictor accompanied the criminal quite round the hall. We were generally too faint with attending to the previous disgusting circumstances, to make accurate report with our eyes of the degree of corporal suffering inflicted. Report, of course, gave out the back knotty and livid. After scourging, he was made over, in his *San Benito*, to his friends, if he had any (but commonly such poor runagates were friendless), or to his parish officer, who, to enhance the effect of the scene, had his station allotted to him on the outside of the hall gate.

These solemn pageantries were not played off so often as to spoil the general mirth of the community. We had plenty of exercise and recreation *after* school hours; and, for myself, I must confess that I was never happier than *in* them. The Upper and Lower Grammar Schools were held in the same room, and an imaginary line only divided their bounds. Their character was as different as that of the inhabitants on the two sides of the Pyrenees. The Rev. James Boyer was the Upper Master: but the Rev. Matthew Field presided over that portion of the apartment, of which I had the good fortune to be a member. We lived a life as careless as birds. We talked and did just what we pleased, and nobody molested us. We carried an accidence, or a grammar, for form; but, for any trouble it gave us, we might take two years in getting through the verbs deponent, and another two in forgetting all that we had learned about them. There was now and then the formality of saying a lesson, but if you had not learned it, a brush across the shoulders (just enough to disturb a fly) was the sole re-

monstrance. Field never used the rod; and in truth he
wielded the cane with no great good will—holding it "like
a dancer." It looked in his hands rather like an emblem
than an instrument of authority; and an emblem, too, he
was ashamed of. He was a good easy man, that did not
care to ruffle his own peace, nor perhaps set any great consideration upon the value of juvenile time. He came
among us, now and then, but often staid away whole days
from us; and when he came, it made no difference to us—
he had his private room to retire to, the short time he staid,
to be out of the sound of our noise. Our mirth and uproar
went on. We had classics of our own, without being beholden to "insolent Greece or haughty Rome," that passed
current among us—Peter Wilkins—the Adventures of the
Hon. Capt. Robert Boyle—the Fortunate Blue Coat Boy
—and the like. Or we cultivated a turn for mechanic or
scientific operations; making little sun-dials of paper; or
weaving those ingenious parentheses, called *cat-cradles;*
or making dry peas to dance upon the end of a tin-pipe; or
studying the art military over that laudable game "French
and English," and a hundred other such devices to pass
away the time—mixing the useful with the agreeable—as
would have made the souls of Rousseau and John Locke
chuckle to have seen us.

Matthew Field belonged to that class of modest divines
who affect to mix in equal proportion the *gentleman,* the
scholar, and the *Christian;* but, I know not how, the first
ingredient is generally found to be the predominating dose
in the composition. He was engaged in gay parties, or with
his courtly bow at some episcopal levée, when he should have
been attending upon us. He had for many years the classical charge of a hundred children, during the four or five
first years of their education; and his very highest form
seldom proceeded further than two or three of the intro-

ductory fables of Phædrus. How things were suffered to
go on thus, I cannot guess. Boyer, who was the proper
person to have remedied these abuses, always affected,
perhaps felt, a delicacy in interfering in a province not
strictly his own. I have not been without my suspicions
that he was not altogether displeased at the contrast we
presented to his end of the school. We were a sort of
Helots to his young Spartans. He would sometimes, with
ironic deference, send to borrow a rod of the Under Master,
and then, with Sardonic grin, observe to one of his upper
boys, "how neat and fresh the twigs looked." While his
pale students were battering their brains over Xenophon and
Plato, with a silence as deep as that enjoined by the Samite,
we were enjoying ourselves at our ease in our little Goshen.
We saw a little into the secrets of his discipline, and the
prospect did but the more reconcile us to our lot. His
thunders rolled innocuous for us; his storms came near, but
never touched us; contrary to Gideon's miracle, while all
around were drenched, our fleece was dry. His boys turned
out the better scholars? we, I suspect, have the advantage
in temper. His pupils cannot speak of him without something of terror allaying their gratitude; the remembrance
of Field comes back with all the soothing images of indolence
and summer slumbers, and work like play, and innocent
idleness, and Elysian exemptions, and life itself a "playing
holiday."

Though sufficiently removed from the jurisdiction of
Boyer, we were near enough (as I have said) to understand
a little of his system. We occasionally heard sounds of
the *Ululantes* and caught glances of Tartarus. B. was a
rabid pedant. His English style was crampt to barbarism.
His Easter anthems (for his duty obliged him to those
periodical flights) were grating as scrannel pipes.—He would
laugh, ay, and heartily, but then it must be at Flaccus's

quibble about *Rex*—— or at the *tristis severitas in vultu*, or *inspicere in patinas*, of Terence—thin jests, which at their first broaching could hardly have had *vis* enough to move a Roman muscle.—He had two wigs, both pedantic, but of different omen. The one serene, smiling, fresh powdered, betokening a mild day. The other, an old discoloured, unkempt, angry caxon, denoting frequent and bloody execution. Woe to the school, when he made his morning appearance in his *passy*, or *passionate wig*. No comet expounded surer.—J. B. had a heavy hand. I have known him double his knotty fist at a poor trembling child (the maternal milk hardly dry upon its lips) with a "Sirrah, do you presume to set your wits at me?"—Nothing was more common than to see him make a headlong entry into the schoolroom, from his inner recess, or library, and, with turbulent eye, singling out a lad, roar out, "Od's my life, sirrah," (his favourite adjuration) "I have a great mind to whip you,"—then, with as sudden a retracting impulse, fling back into his lair—and, after a cooling lapse of some minutes (during which all but the culprit had totally forgotten the context), drive headlong out again, piecing out his imperfect sense, as if it had been some Devil's Litany, with the expletory yell—"*and I* WILL *too*."—In his gentler moods, when the *rabidus furor* was assuaged, he had resort to an ingenious method, peculiar, for what I have heard, to himself, of whipping the boy, and reading the Debates, at the same time; a paragraph, and a lash between; which in those times, when parliamentary oratory was most at a height and flourishing in these realms, was not calculated to impress the patient with a veneration for the diffuser graces of rhetoric.

Once, and but once, the uplifted rod was known to fall ineffectual from his hand—when droll squinting W—— having been caught putting the inside of the master's desk to a use for which the architect had clearly not designed it, to justify himself, with great simplicity averred, that *he did not know that the thing had been forewarned*. This exquisite irrecognition of any law antecedent to the *oral* or *declaratory*, struck so irresistibly upon the fancy of all who heard it (the pedagogue himself not excepted) that remission was unavoidable.

L. has given credit to B.'s great merits as an instructor. Coleridge, in his literary life, has pronounced a more intelligible and ample encomium on them. The author of the Country Spectator doubts not to compare him with the ablest teachers of antiquity. Perhaps we cannot dismiss him better than with the pious ejaculation of C.—when he heard that his old master was on his death-bed—"Poor J. B.!—may all his faults be forgiven; and may he be wafted to bliss by little cherub-boys, all head and wings, with no *bottoms* to reproach his sublunary infirmities."

Under him were many good and sound scholars bred.— First Grecian of my time was Lancelot Pepys Stevens, kindest of boys and men, since Co-grammar-master (and inseparable companion) with Dr. T——e. What an edifying spectacle did this brace of friends present to those who remembered the anti-socialities of their predecessors!— You never met the one by chance in the street without a wonder, which was quickly dissipated by the almost immediate subappearance of the other. Generally arm in arm, these kindly coadjutors lightened for each other the toilsome duties of their profession, and when, in advanced age, one found it convenient to retire, the other was not long in discovering that it suited him to lay down the fasces also. Oh, it is pleasant, as it is rare, to find the same arm linked in yours at forty, which at thirteen helped it to turn over the *Cicero De Amicitia*, or some tale of Antique Friendship, which the young heart even then was burning to

anticipate!—Co-Grecian with S. was Th——, who has since
executed with ability various diplomatic functions at the
Northern courts.   Th—— was a tall, dark, saturnine youth,
sparing of speech, with raven locks.—Thomas Fanshaw
Middleton followed him (now Bishop of Calcutta), a scholar
and a gentleman in his teens.   He has the reputation of an
excellent critic; and is author (besides the Country Spectator) of a Treatise on the Greek Article, against Sharpe.—
M. is said to bear his mitre high in India, where the *regni
novitas* (I dare say) sufficiently justifies the bearing.   A
humility quite as primitive as that of Jewel or Hooker might
not be exactly fitted to impress the minds of those Anglo-
Asiatic diocesans with a reverence for home institutions,
and the church which those fathers watered.   The manners
of M. at school, though firm, were mild, and unassuming·
—Next to M. (if not senior to him) was Richards, author of
the Aboriginal Britons, the most spirited of the Oxford
Prize Poems; a pale, studious Grecian.—Then followed poor
S——, ill-fated M——! of those the Muse is silent.

> Finding some of Edward's race
> Unhappy, pass their annals by.

Come back into memory, like as thou wert in the day-
spring of thy fancies, with hope like a fiery column before
thee—the dark pillar not yet turned—Samuel Taylor
Coleridge—Logician, Metaphysician, Bard!—How have
I seen the casual passer through the Cloisters stand still,
entranced with admiration (while he weighed the dis-
proportion between the *speech* and the *garb* of the young
Mirandula), to hear thee unfold, in thy deep and sweet
intonations, the mysteries of Jamblichus, or Plotinus (for
even in those years thou waxedst not pale at such philosophic draughts), or reciting Homer in his Greek, or
Pindar—while the walls of the old Grey Friars re-echoed to

the accents of the *inspired charity-boy!* Many were the
"witcombats" (to dally awhile with the words of old
Fuller), between him and C. V. Le G——, "which two I behold like a Spanish great galleon,and an English man-of-war;
Master Coleridge, like the former, was built far higher in
learning, solid, but slow in his performances. C. V. L.,
with the English man-of-war, lesser in bulk, but lighter in
sailing, could turn with all tides, tack about and take
advantage of all winds, by the quickness of his wit and
invention."

Nor shalt thou, their compeer, be quickly forgotten,
Allen, with the cordial smile, and still more cordial laugh,
with which thou wert wont to make the old Cloisters shake,
in thy cognition of some poignant jest of theirs; or the anticipation of some more material, and peradventure, practical one, of thine own. Extinct are those smiles, with that
beautiful countenance, with which (for thou wert the
Nireus formosus of the school), in the days of thy maturer
waggery, thou didst disarm the wrath of infuriated town-
damsel, who, incensed by provoking pinch, turning tigress-
like round, suddenly converted by thy angel-look, exchanged the half-formed terrible *"bl——,"* for a gentler
greeting—*"bless thy handsome face!"*

Next follow two, who ought to be now alive, and the
friends of Elia—the junior Le G—— and F——; who impelled, the former by a roving temper, the latter by too
quick a sense of neglect—ill capable of enduring the slights
poor Sizars are sometimes subject to in our seats of learning—exchanged their Alma Mater for the camp; perishing,
one by climate, and one on the plains of Salamanca:—Le
G——, sanguine, volatile, sweet-natured; F——, dogged,
faithful, anticipative of insult, warm-hearted, with something of the old Roman height about him.

Fine, frank-hearted Fr——, the present master of Hertford, with Marmaduke T——, mildest of Missionaries—and both my good friends still—close the catalogue of Grecians in my time.

PHILANTHROPY FROM A PERSONAL POINT OF VIEW

Henry David Thoreau

I confess that I have hitherto indulged very little in philanthropic enterprises. I have made some sacrifices to a sense of duty, and among others have sacificed this pleasure also. There are those who have used all their arts to persuade me to undertake the support of some poor family in the town; and if I had nothing to do,—for the devil finds employment for the idle,—I might try my hand at some such pastime as that. However, when I have thought to indulge myself in this respect, and lay their Heaven under an obligation by maintaining certain poor persons in all respects as comfortably as I maintain myself, and have even ventured so far as to make them the offer, they have one and all unhesitatingly preferred to remain poor. While my townsmen and women are devoted in so many ways to the good of their fellows, I trust that one at least may be spared to other and less humane pursuits. You must have a genius for charity as well as for anything else. As for doing good, that is one of the professions which are full. Moreover, I have tried it fairly, and, strange as it may seem, am satisfied that it does not agree with my constitution. Probably I should not consciously and deliberately forsake my particular calling to do the good which society demands of me, to save the universe from annihilation; and I believe that a like but infinitely greater steadfastness elsewhere is all that now preserves it. But I would not stand between any man and his genius; and to him who does this work, which I decline, with his whole heart and soul and life, I would say, Persevere, even if the world call it doing evil, as it is most likely they will.

I am far from supposing that my case is a peculiar one; no doubt many of my readers would make a similar defence. At doing something,—I will not engage that my neighbours shall pronounce it good,—I do not hesitate to say that I should be a capital fellow to hire; but what that is, it is for my employer to find out. What *good* I do, in the common sense of that word, must be aside from my main path, and for the most part wholly unintended. Men say, practically, Begin where you are and such as you are, without aiming mainly to become of more worth, and with kindness aforethought go about doing good. If I were to preach at all in this strain, I should say rather, Set about being good. As if the sun should stop when he had kindled his fires up to the splendour of a moon or a star of the sixth magnitude, and go about like a Robin Goodfellow, peeping in at every cottage window, inspiring lunatics, and tainting meats, and making darkness visible, instead of steadily increasing his genial heat and beneficence till he is of such brightness that no mortal can look him in the face, and then, in the meanwhile too, going about the world in his own orbit, doing it good, or rather, as a truer philosophy has discovered, the world going about him getting good. When Phaeton, wishing to prove his heavenly birth by his beneficence, had the sun's chariot but one day, and drove out of the beaten track, he burned several blocks of houses in the lower streets of heaven, and scorched the surface of the earth, and dried up every spring, and made the great desert of Sahara, till at length Jupiter hurled him headlong to the earth with a thunderbolt, and the sun, through grief at his death, did not shine for a year.

There is no odour so bad as that which arises from goodness tainted. It is human, it is divine, carrion. If I knew for a certainty that a man was coming to my house with the conscious design of doing me good, I should run for my life as from that dry and parching wind of the African deserts called the simoom, which fills the mouth and nose and ears and eyes with dust till you are suffocated, for fear I should get some of his good done to me,—some of its virus mingled with my blood. No,—in this case I would rather suffer evil the natural way. A man is not a good *man* to me because he will feed me if I should be starving, or warm me if I should be freezing, or pull me out of a ditch if I should ever fall into one. I can find you a Newfoundland dog that will do as much. Philanthropy is not love for one's fellow-man in the broadest sense. Howard was no doubt an exceedingly kind and worthy man in his way, and has his reward; but, comparatively speaking, what are a hundred Howards to *us*, if their philanthropy do not help *us* in our best estate, when we are most worthy to be helped? I never heard of a philanthropic meeting in which it was sincerely proposed to do any good to me, or the like of me.

The Jesuits were quite baulked by those Indians who, being burned at the stake, suggested new modes of torture to their tormentors. Being superior to physical suffering, it sometimes chanced that they were superior to any consolation which the missionaries could offer; and the law to do as you would be done by fell with less persuasiveness on the ears of those, who, for their part, did not care how they were done by, who loved their enemies after a new fashion, and came very near freely forgiving them all they did.

Be sure that you give the poor the aid they most need, though it be your example which leaves them far behind. If you give money, spend yourself with it, and do not merely abandon it to them. We make curious mistakes sometimes. Often the poor man is not so cold and hungry as he is dirty and ragged and gross. It is partly his taste, and not merely his misfortune. If you give him money, he will perhaps buy more rags with it. I was wont to pity the clumsy Irish labourers who cut ice on the pond, in such mean and ragged clothes, while I shivered in my more tidy and somewhat more fashionable garments, till, one bitter cold day, one who had slipped into the water came to my house to warm him, and I saw him strip off three pairs of pants and two pairs of stockings ere he got down to the skin, though they were dirty and ragged enough, it is true, and that he could afford to refuse the *extra* garments which I offered him, he had so many *intra* ones. This ducking was the very thing he needed. Then I began to pity myself, and I saw that it would be a greater charity to bestow on me a flannel shirt than a whole slop-shop on him. There are a thousand hacking at the branches of evil to one who is striking at the root, and it may be that he who bestows the largest amount of time and money on the needy is doing the most by his mode of life to produce that misery which he strives in vain to relieve. It is the pious slave-breeder devoting the proceeds of every tenth slave to buy a Sunday's liberty for the rest. Some show their kindness to the poor by employing them in their kitchens. Would they not be kinder if they employed themselves there? You boast of spending a tenth part of your income in charity: maybe you should spend the nine-tenths so, and done with it. Society recovers only a tenth part of the property then. Is this owing to the generosity of him in whose possession it is found, or to the remissness of the officers of justice?

Philanthropy is almost the only virtue which is sufficiently appreciated by mankind. Nay, it is greatly overrated; and it is our selfishness which overrates it. A robust poor man, one sunny day here in Concord, praised a fellow-townsman to me, because, as he said, he was kind to the poor, meaning himself. The kind uncles and aunts of the race are more esteemed than its true spiritual fathers and mothers. I once heard a reverend lecturer on England, a man of learning and intelligence, after enumerating her scientific, literary, and political worthies, Shakespeare, Bacon, Cromwell, Milton, Newton, and others, speak next of her Christian heroes, whom, as if his profession required it of him, he elevated to a place far above all the rest, as the greatest of the great. They were Penn, Howard, and Mrs. Fry. Every one must feel the falsehood and cant of this. The last were not England's best men and women; only, perhaps, her best philanthropists.

I would not subtract anything from the praise that is due to philanthropy, but merely demand justice for all who by their lives and works are a blessing to mankind. I do not value chiefly a man's uprightness and benevolence, which are, as it were, his stem and leaves. Those plants of whose greenness withered we make herb tea for the sick, serve but a humble use, and are most employed by quacks. I want the flower and fruit of a man; that some fragrance be wafted over from him to me, and some ripeness flavour our intercourse. His goodness must not be a partial and transitory act, but a constant superfluity, which cost him nothing and of which he is unconscious. This is a charity that hides a multitude of sins. The philanthropist too often surrounds mankind with the remembrance of his own cast-off griefs as an atmosphere, and calls it sympathy. We should impart our courage, and not our despair, our health and ease, and not our disease, and take care that this does not spread by contagion. From what southern plains comes up the voice of wailing? Under what latitudes reside the heathen to whom we would send light? Who is that intemperate and brutal man whom we would redeem? If anything ail a man, so that he does not perform his functions, if he have a pain in his bowels even,—for that is the seat of sympathy,—he forthwith sets about reforming—the world. Being a microcosm himself, he discovers, and it is a true discovery, and he is the man to make it,—that the world has been eating green apples; to his eyes, in fact, the globe itself is a great green apple, which there is danger awful to think of that the children of men will nibble before it is ripe; and straightway his drastic philanthropy seeks out the Esquimaux and the Patagonian, and embraces the populous Indian and Chinese villages; and, thus, by a few years of philanthropic activity, the powers in the meanwhile using him for their own ends, no doubt, he cures himself of his dyspepsia, the globe acquires a faint blush on one or both of its cheeks, as if it were beginning to be ripe, and life loses its crudity and is once more sweet and wholesome to live. I never dreamed of any enormity greater than I have committed. I never knew, and never shall know, a worse man than myself.

I believe that what so saddens the reformer is not his sympathy with his fellows in distress, but, though he be the holiest son of God, is his private ail. Let this be righted, let the spring come to him, the morning rise over his couch, and he will forsake his generous companions without apology. My excuse for not lecturing against the use of tobacco is, that I never chewed it; that is a penalty which reformed tobacco-chewers have to pay; though there are things enough I have chewed which I could lecture against. If you should ever be betrayed into any of these philanthropies, do not let your left hand know what your right hand does, for it is not worth knowing. Rescue the drowning and tie your shoe-strings. Take your time, and set about some free labour.

Our manners have been corrupted by communication with the saints. Our hymn-books resound with a melodious cursing of God and enduring him forever. One would say that even the prophets and redeemers had rather consoled the fears than confirmed the hopes of man. There is nowhere recorded a simple and irrepressible satisfaction with the gift of life, any memorable praise of God. All health and success does me good, however far off and withdrawn it may appear; all disease and failure helps to make me sad and does me evil, however much sympathy it may have with me or I with it. If, then, we would indeed restore mankind by truly Indian, botanic, magnetic, or natural means, let us first be as simple and well as Nature ourselves, dispel the clouds which hang over our own brows, and take up a little life into our pores. Do not stay to be an overseer of the poor, but endeavour to become one of the worthies of the world.

I read in the Gulistan, or Flower Garden, of Sheik Sadi of Shiraz, that "They asked a wise man, saying, Of the many celebrated trees which the Most High God has created lofty and umbrageous, they call none azad, or free, excepting the cypress, which bears no fruit; what mystery is there in this? He replied, Each has its appropriate produce, and appointed season, during the continuance of which it is fresh and blooming, and during their absence dry and withered; to neither of which states is the cypress exposed, being always flourishing; and of this nature are the azads, or religious independents.—Fix not thy heart on that which is transitory; for the Dijlah, or Tigris, will continue to flow through Bagdad after the race of caliphs is extinct: if thy hand has plenty, be liberal as the date tree; but if it affords nothing to give away, be an azad, or free man, like the cypress."

My Copy of Keats[1]

Richard Dowling[2]

The only copy of Keats I ever owned is a modest volume published by Edward Moxon & Co. in the year 1861. By writing on its yellow fly-leaf I find it was given to me four years later in September, 1865. At that time it was clean and bright, opened with strict impartiality when set upon its back, and had not learned to respond with alacrity to hasty researches for favourite passages.

The binding is now racked and feeble from use; and if, as in army regulations, service under warm suns is to be taken for longer service in cooler climes, it may be said that to the exhaustion following overwork have been added the prejudices of premature age.

It is not bound as books were bound once upon a time, when they outlasted the tables and chairs, even the walls; ay, the very races and names of their owners. The cover is simple plain blue cloth; on the back is a little patch of printing in gold, with the words Keats' *Poetical Works* in

[1] Reprinted from *Ignorant Essays*, by Richard Dowling, by permission of Messrs. D. Appleton & Co.

[2] Richard Dowling, born June 3, 1846, died July 28, 1898, commenced life as a journalist. In 1870 he joined the staff of *The Nation*, a Dublin publication conducted by Mr. A. M. Sullivan; for some years he edited *Zozimus*, and was the founder of a weekly, *Ireland's Eye*. In 1875 he went to London, where he joined *The Illustrated Sporting and Dramatic News*, and started a weekly paper, *Yorick*, which lived six months. In 1878 his first novel, *The Mystery of Killiard*, was brought out by Tinsley Brothers, which was followed up by *The Weird Sisters*, *The Sport of Fate*, etc. An obituary notice which appeared in one of the most important of London weeklies, said of him, "He was one of the kindest-hearted of men, and an admirable talker, whose wit and vivacity remained unimpaired almost to the end." His two most important volumes are *Indolent Essays* and *Ignorant Essays*, of which the latter is the best, from which our selection is taken.

the centre of a twined gilt ribbon and twisted gilt flowers. The welt at the back is bleached and frayed; the corners of the cover are battered and turned in. There is a chink between the cover and the arched back; and the once proud Norman line of that arc is flattened and degraded, retaining no more of its pristine look of sturdy strength than a wheaten straw after the threshing. . . .

If any owner of a cart of old books in Farringdon Street asked you a shilling for such a copy of Keats as mine, you would smile at him. You would think he had acquired the books merely to satisfy his own taste, and now displayed them to gratify a vanity that was intelligible; you would feel assured no motive toward commerce could underlie ever so deeply such a preposterous demand.

My copy will, I think, last my time. Already it has been in my hands more than half the years of a generation; and I feel that its severest trials are over. In days gone by it made journeys with me by sea and land, and paid long visits to some friends, both when I went myself, and when I did not go. Change of air and scene have had no beneficial effect upon it. Journey after journey, and visit after visit, the full cobalt of the cloth grew darker and dingier, the boards of the cover became limper and limper, and the stitching at the back more apparent between the sheets, like the bones and sinews growing outward through the flesh of a hand waxing old. . . .

My Keats has suffered from many pipes, many thumbs, many pencils, many quills, many pockets. Not one stain, one gape, one blot of these would I forego for a spick and span copy in all the gorgeous pomp of the bookbinder's millinery. These blemishes are aureolæ to me. They are nimbi around the brows of the gods and demi-gods, who walk in the triumph of their paternal despot on the clouds metropolitan that embattle the heights of Parnassus.

What a harvest of happy memories is garnered in its leaves! How well I remember the day it got that faint yellow stain on the page where begins the *Ode on a Grecian Urn*. It was a clear, bright, warm, sunshiny afternoon late in the month of May. Three of us took a boat and rowed down a broad blue river, ran the nose of the boat ashore on the gravel beach of a sequestered island and landed. Pulling was warm work, and we all climbed a slope, reached the summit, and cast ourselves down on the long lush cool grass, in the shade of whispering sycamores, and in a stream of air that came fresh with the cheering spices of the hawthorn blossom.

One of our company was the best chamber reader I have ever heard. His voice was neither very melodious nor very full. Perhaps he was all the better for this because he made no effort at display. As he read, the book vanished from his sight, and he leaned over the poet's shoulder, saw what the poet saw, and in a voice timid with the sense of responsibility, and yet elated with a kind of fearing joy, told of what he saw in words that never hurried, and that, when uttered, always seemed to hang substantially in the air like banners.

He discovered and related the poet's vision rather than simulated passion to suit the scene. I remember well his reading of the passage:

> " Fair youth, beneath the trees, thou canst not leave
> Thy song, nor ever can those trees be bare;
> Bold lover, never, never canst thou kiss,
> Though winning near the goal—yet, do not grieve;
> She cannot fade though thou hast not thy bliss,
> For ever wilt thou love and she be fair!"

He rehearsed the whole of the ode over and over again as we lay on the grass watching the vast chestnuts and oaks bending over the river, as though they had grown aweary of the sun, and longed to glide into the broad full stream.

As he read the lines just quoted, he gave us time to hear the murmur, and to breathe the fragrance of those immortal trees. "Nor ever can those trees be bare," in the text has only a semicolon after it. Yet here he paused, while three wavelets broke upon the beach, as if he could not tear himself away from contemplating the deathless verdure, and realising the prodigious edict pronounced upon it. "Bold lover, never, never canst thou kiss, though winning near the goal." At the terrible decree he raised his eyes and gazed with heavy-lidded, hopeless commiseration at this being, who, still more unhappy than Tithonus, had to immortality added perpetual youth, with passion forever strong, and denial forever final.

"Yet do not grieve." This he uttered as one who pleads forgiveness of a corpse—merely to try to soothe a conscience sensible of an obligation that can never now be discharged. "She cannot fade, though thou hast not thy bliss, for ever wilt thou love, and she be fair!" Here the reader, with eyes fixed and rayless, seemed by voice and pose to be sunk, beyond all power of hope, in an abyss of despair. The barren immutability of the spectacle appeared to weigh upon him more intolerably than the wreck of a people. He spoke the words in a long drawn-out whisper, and, after a pause, dropped his head, and did not resume.

I recollect that when the illusion he wrought up so fully in my mind had passed away in that long pause, and when I remembered that the fancy of the poet was expending itself, not on beings whom he conceived originally as humans, but on the figures of a mere vase, I was seized with a fierce desire to get up and seek that vase through all the world until I found it, and then smash it into ten thousand atoms.

When I had written the last sentence, I took up the volume to decide where I should recommence, and I "turned the page, and turned the page." I lived over again the days not forgotten, but laid aside in memory to be borne forth in periods of high festival. I could not bring myself back from the comrades of old, and the marvels of the great magician, to this poor street, this solitude, and this squalid company of my own thoughts—thoughts so trivial and so mean compared with the imperial visions into which I had been gazing, that I was glad for the weariness which came upon me, and grateful to gray dawn that glimmered against the blind and absolved me from further obligation for that sitting.

On turning over the leaves without reading, I find *Hyperion* opens most readily of all, and seems to have fared worst from deliberate and unintentional comment. Much of the wear and tear and pencil marks are to be set down against myself; for when I take the book with no definite purpose I turn to *Hyperion*, as a blind man to the warmth of the sun. Some qualities of the poem I can feel and appreciate; but always in its presence I am weighed down by the consciousness that my deficiency in some attribute of perception debars me from undreamed-of privileges.

I recall one evening in a pine glen with one man and *Hyperion*. It would be difficult to match this man or me as readers. I don't think there can be ten worse employing the English language to-day. I not only do not by any inflexion of voice expound what I utter, but I am often incapable of speaking the words before me. I take in a line at a glance, see its import with my own imagination apart from the verbiage, which leaves not a shadow of an impression on my mind. When I come to the next line I grow suddenly alive to the fact that I have to speak off the former one. I am in a hurry to see what line two has to show; so, instead of giving the poet's words for line one, I give my own description of the vision it has conjured up in my mind. This is bad enough in all conscience; but the friend of whom I speak now, behaves even worse. His plan of reading is to stop his voice in the middle of line one, and proceed to discuss the merits of line two, which he had read with his eye, but not with his lips, and of which the listener is ignorant, unless he happen to know the poem by rote.

On that evening in the glen I pulled out Keats, and turned at my friend's request, to *Hyperion*, and began to read aloud. He was more patient than mercy's self; but occasionally, when I did a most exceptionally bad murder on the text, he would writhe and cry out, and I would go back and correct myself, and start afresh.

He had a big burly frame, and a deep full voice that shouted easily, and some of the comments shouted as I read are indicated by pencil marks in the margin. The writing was not done then, but much later, when he and I had shaken hands, and he had gone sixteen thousand miles away. As he was about to set out on that long journey, he said, "In seven years more I'll drop in and have a pipe with you." It had been seven years since I saw him before. The notes on the margin are only keys to what was said; for I fear the comment made was more bulky than the text, and the text and comment together would far exceed the limits of such an essay as this. I therefore curtail greatly, and omit much.

I read down the first page without meeting any interruption; but when I came in page two on:

> "She would have ta'en
> Achilles by the hair and bent his neck,"

he cried out, "Stop! Don't read the lines following. It is bathos compared with that line and a half. It is paltry

and weak beside what you have read. 'Ta'en Achilles by
the hair and bent his neck.' By Jove! can you not see the
white muscles start out in his throat, and the look of rage,
defeat and agony on the face of the Greek bruiser? But
how flat falls the next line: 'Or with a finger stay'd Ixion's
wheel'? Besides, a crowbar would be much better than a
finger. It is a line for children, not for grown men. It
exhausts the subject. It is too literal. There is no question left to ask. But the vague 'Ta'en Achilles by the hair
and *bent* his neck' is perfect. You can see her knee in the
hollow of his back, and her fingers twisted in his hair.
But the image of the goddess dabbling in that river of hell
after Ixion's wheel is contemptible."

He next stopped me at

"Until at length old Saturn lifted up
His faded eyes, and saw his kingdom gone."

"What an immeasurable vision Keats must have had
of the old bankrupt Titan when he wrote the second line!
Taken in the context it is simply overwhelming. Keats
must have sprung up out of his chair as he saw the gigantic
head upraised and the prodigious grief of the gray-haired
god. But Keats was not happy in the matter of full stops.
Here again what comes after weakens. We get no additional strength out of

"And all the gloom and sorrow of the place
And that fair kneeling goddess.

The 'gloom and sorrow' and the 'goddess' are abomin-
ably anticlimacteric."

"Yes, there must be a golden victory;
There must be gods thrown down and trumpets blown
Of triumph calm, and hymns of festival
Upon the gold clouds metropolitan,

> Voices of soft proclaim, and silver stir
> Of strings in hollow shells; and there shall be
> Beautiful things made new, for the surprise
> Of the sky-children; I will give command:
> Thea! Thea! Thea! where is Saturn?"

"Read that again!" cried my friend, clinging to the grass and breathing hard. "Again!" he cried, when I had finished the second time. And then, before I could proceed, he sprang to his feet, carrying out the action in the text immediately following:

> "This passion lifted him upon his feet,
> And made his hands to struggle in the air."

"Come on, John Milton," cried my friend, excitedly sparring at the winds—"come on, and beat that, and we'll let you put all your adjectives behind your nouns, and your verb last, and your nominative nowhere! Why, man." this being addressed to the Puritan poet—"it carried Keats himself off his legs; that's more than anything you ever wrote when you were old did for you. There's the smell of midnight oil off your later spontaneous efforts, John Milton.

" When John Milton went loafing about and didn't mind much what he was writing he could give any of them points"—(I deplore the language) "any of them, ay, Shakespeare himself points in a poem. In a poem, sir" (this to me), "Milton could give Shakespeare a hundred and one out of a hundred and lick the Bard easily. How the man who was such a fool as to write Shakespeare's poems had the good sense to write Shakespeare's plays I can never understand. The most un - Shakespearian poems in the language are Shakespeare's. I never read Cowley, but it seems to me Cowley ought to have written Shakespeare's poems, and then his obscurity would have been complete. If Milton only didn't take the trouble to be great he would have been greater. As far as I know there are no English poets who improved when they ceased to be amateurs and became professional poets, except Wordsworth and Tennyson. Shelley and Keats were never regular race-horses. They were colts that bolted in their first race and ran until they dropped. It was a good job Shakespeare gave up writing rhymes and posing as a poet. It was not until he despaired of becoming one and took to the drama that he began to feel his feet and show his pace. If he had suspected he was a great poet he would have adopted the airs of the profession and been ruined. In his time no one thought of calling a play a poem—that was what saved the greatest of all our poets to us. The only two things Shakespeare didn't know is that a play may be a poem and that his plays are the finest poems finite man as he is now constructed can endure. It is all nonsense to say man shall never look on the like of Shakespeare again. It is not the poet superior to Shakespeare man now lacks, but the man to apprehend him."

I looked around uneasily, and found, to my great satisfaction, that there was no stranger in view. My friend occupied a position of responsibility and trust, and it would be most injurious if a rumour got abroad that not only did he read and admire verse, but that he held converse with the shades of departed poets as well. In old days men who spoke to the vacant air were convicted of necromancy and burned; in our times men offending in this manner are suspected of poetry and ostracised.

As soon as my friend was somewhat calmed, and had cast himself down again and lit a pipe, I resumed my reading. He allowed me to proceed without interruption until I came to

"His palace bright,
Bastion'd with pyramids of glowing gold,
And touch'd with shade of bronzed obelisks,
Glared a blood-red through all its thousand courts,
Arches, and domes, and fiery galleries;
And all its curtains of Aurorian clouds
Flushed angerly: while sometimes eagles' wings,
Unseen before by Gods or wondering men,
Darken'd the place; and neighing steeds were heard,
Not heard before by Gods or wondering men."

"Prodigious!" he shouted. "Go over that again. Keep the syllables wide apart. It is a good rule of water-colour sketching not to be too nice about joining the edges of the tints; this lets the light in. Keep the syllables as far apart as ever you can, and let the silentness in between to clear up the music. How the gods and the wondering men must have wondered! Do you know, I am sure Keats often frightened, terrified himself with his own visions. You remember he says somewhere he doesn't think any one could dare to read some one or another aloud at midnight. I believe that often in the midnight he sat and cowered before the gigantic sights and sounds that reigned despotically over his fancy."

"O dreams of day and night!
O monstrous forms! O effigies of pain!
O spectres busy in a cold, cold gloom!
O lank-eared Phantoms of black-weeded pools!
Why do I know ye? why have I seen ye? why
Is my eternal essence thus distraught
To see and to behold these horrors new?
Saturn is fallen, am I too to fall?
Am I to leave this haven of my rest,
This cradle of my glory, this soft clime,
This calm luxuriance of blissful light,
These crystalline pavilions, and pure fanes,
Of all my lucent empire? It is left

Deserted, void, nor any haunt of mine.
The blaze, the splendour, and the symmetry
I cannot see—but darkness, death, and darkness.
Even here, into my centre of repose,
The shady visions come to domineer,
Insult, and blind and stifle up my pomp—
Fall!—No, by Tellus and her briny robes!
Over the fiery frontier of my realms
I will advance a terrible right arm
Shall scare that infant thunderer, rebel Jove,
And bid old Saturn take his throne again."

"What more magnificent prelude ever was uttered to
oath than the portion of this speech preceding. 'No, by
Tellus!' What more overpowering, leading up to an overwhelming threat, than the whole passage going before
'Over the fiery frontier of my realms I will advance a
terrible right arm!' What menacing deliberativeness there
is in this whole speech, and what utter completeness of ruin
to come is indicated by those words, 'I will advance a
terrible right arm'! You feel no sooner shall that arm
move than 'rebel Jove's' reign will be at an end, and that
chaos will be left for Saturn to rule and fashion once more
into order. Shut up the poem now. That's plenty of
Hyperion, and the other books of it are inferior. There is
more labour and more likeness to *Paradise Lost*." And
so my friend, who is 16,000 miles away, and I turned from
the Titanic theme, and spoke of the local board of guardians,
or some young girl whose beauty was making rich misery
in the hearts of young men in those old days.

There is no other long poem in the volume bearing any
marks which indicate such close connection with any individual reader as in the case of *Hyperion*. *Endymion*
boasts only one mark, and that expressing admiration of
the relief afforded from monotony of the heroic couplets

by the introduction in the opening of the double rhyming
verses:

"Full of sweet dreams, and health, and quiet breathing
    Therefore, on every morrow, are we wreathing—"

The friend to whom this mark is due never handled the
volume, never even saw it; but once upon a time when he,
another man, and I had got together, and were talking of
the "gallipot poet," the first friend said he always regarded
this couplet as most happily placed where it appears.   So
when I reached home I marked my copy at the lines.   Now,
when I open the volume and find that mark, it is as good
to me as, better than, a photograph of my friend; for I
not only see his face and figure, but once more he places his
index-finger on the table, as we three sit smoking, and
whispers out the six opening lines, ending with the two I
have quoted.   Suppose I too should some day go 16,000
miles away from London, and carry this volume with me,
shall I not be able to open it when I please, and recall what
I then saw and heard, what I now see and hear, as distinctly as though no long interval of ocean or of months lay
between to-night and that hour? . . .

When I take down my copy of Keats, and look through
it and beyond it, I feel that while it is left to me I cannot be
wholly shorn of my friends.   It is the only album of photo-
graphs I possess.   The faces I see in it are not for any eye
but mine.   It is my private portrait gallery, in which hang
the portraits of my dearest friends.   The marks and blots
are intelligible to no eye but mine; they are the cherished
hieroglyphics of the heart.   I close the book; I lock up
the hieroglyphics; I feel certain the book will last my time.
Should it survive me and pass into new hands—into the
hands of some boy now unborn, who may pluck out of it
posies of love-phrases for his fresh-cheeked sweetheart—

he will know nothing of the import these marginal notes bore to one who has gone before him; unless, indeed, out of some cemetery of ephemeral literature he digs up this key—this Rosetta stone.

A Night Among the Pines[1]

Robert Louis Stevenson

From *Bleymard* after dinner, although it was already late, I set out to scale a portion of the *Lozère*. An ill-marked stony drove road guided me forward; and I met nearly half a dozen bullock-carts descending from the woods, each laden with a whole pine-tree for the winter's firing. At the top of the woods, which do not climb very high upon this cold ridge, I struck leftward by a path among the pines, until I hit on a dell of green turf, where a streamlet made a little spout over some stones to serve me for a water-tap. "In a more sacred or sequestered bower . . . nor nymph, nor faunus, haunted." The trees were not old, but they grew thickly round the glade: there was no outlook, except north-eastward upon distant hill-tops, or straight upward to the sky; and the encampment felt secure and private like a room. By the time I had made my arrangements and fed *Modestine*,[2] the day was already beginning to decline. I buckled myself to the knees into my sack and a made a hearty meal; and as soon as the sun went down I pulled my cap over my eyes and fell asleep.

Night is a dead monotonous period under a roof; but in the open world it passes lightly, with its stars and dews and perfumes, and the hours are marked by changes in the face of Nature. What seems a kind of temporal death to

[1] From *Travels with a Donkey in the Cevennes.*
[2] The donkey.

23

people choked between walls and curtains, is only a light and living slumber to the man who sleeps a-field. All night long he can hear Nature breathing deeply and freely; even as she takes her rest, she turns and smiles; and there is one stirring hour unknown to those who dwell in houses, when a wakeful influence goes abroad over the sleeping hemisphere and all the outdoor world are on their feet. It is then that the cock first crows, not this time to announce the dawn, but like a cheerful watchman speeding the course of night. Cattle awake on the meadows; sheep break their fast on dewy hillsides, and change to a new lair among the ferns; and houseless men, who have lain down with the fowls, open their dim eyes and behold the beauty of the night.

At what inaudible summons, at what gentle touch of Nature, are all these sleepers thus recalled on the same hour to life? Do the stars rain down an influence, or do we share some thrill of mother earth below our resting bodies? Even shepherds and old country-folk, who are the deepest read in these arcana, have not a guess as to the means or purpose of this nightly resurrection. Toward two in the morning they declare the thing takes place; and neither know nor inquire further. And at least it is a pleasant incident. We are disturbed in our slumber only, like the luxurious *Montaigne*, "that we may the better and more sensibly relish it." We have a moment to look upon the stars. And there is a special pleasure for some minds in the reflection that we share the impulse of all outdoor creatures in our neighbourhood, that we have escaped out of the *Bastille* of civilisation, and are become, for the time being, a mere kindly animal and a sheep of Nature's flock.

When that hour came to me among the pines, I wakened thirsty. My tin was standing by me half full of water. I emptied it at a draught; and feeling broad awake after this internal cold aspersion, sat upright to make a cigarette. The stars were clear, coloured, and jewel-like, but not frosty. A faint silvery vapour stood for the *Milky Way*. All around me the black fir-points stood upright and stock-still. By the whiteness of the pack-saddle, I could see *Modestine* walking round and round at the length of her tether; I could hear her steadily munching at the sward; but there was not another sound, save the indescribable quiet talk of the runnel over the stones. I lay lazily smoking and studying the colour of the sky, as we call the void of space, from where it showed a glossy blue-black between the stars. As if to be more like a pedlar, I wear a silver ring. This I could see faintly shining as I raised or lowered the cigarette; and at each whiff the inside of my hand was illuminated, and became for a second the highest light in the landscape.

A faint wind, more like a moving coolness than a stream of air, passed down the glade from time to time; so that even in my great chamber the air was being renewed all night long. I thought with horror of the inn at *Chaseradès* and the congregated nightcaps; with horror of the nocturnal prowesses of clerks and students, of hot theatres and pass-keys and close rooms. I have not often enjoyed a more serene possession of myself, nor felt more independent of material aids. The outer world, from which we cower into our houses, seemed after all a gentle habitable place; and night after night a man's bed, it seemed, was laid and waiting for him in the fields, where God keeps an open house. I thought I had rediscovered one of those truths which are revealed to savages and hid from political economists: at the least, I had discovered a new pleasure for myself. And yet even while I was exulting in my solitude I became aware of a strange lack. I wished a companion to lie near me in the starlight, silent and not moving, but ever within touch. For there is a fellowship more quiet even than solitude, and which, rightly understood, is solitude made perfect. And to live out of doors with the woman a man loves is of all lives the most complete and free.

As I thus lay, between content and longing, a faint noise stole toward me through the pines. I thought, at first, it was the crowing of cocks or the barking of dogs at some distant farm; but steadily and gradually it took articulate shape on my ears, until I became aware that a passenger was going by upon the high-road in the valley, and singing loudly as he went. There was more of good - will than grace in his performance; but he trolled with ample lungs; and the sound of his voice took hold upon the hillside and set the air shaking in the leafy glens. I have heard people passing by night in sleeping cities; some of them sang; one, I remember, played loudly on the bagpipes. I have heard the rattle of a cart or carriage spring up suddenly after hours of stillness, and pass, for some minutes, within the range of my hearing as I lay abed. There is a romance about all who are abroad in the black hours, and with something of a thrill we try to guess their business. But here the romance was double: first, this glad passenger, lit internally with wine, who sent up his voice in music through the night; and then I, on the other hand, buckled into my sack, and smoking alone in the pine-woods between four and five thousand feet toward the stars.

When I awoke again (*Sunday, 29th September*), many of the stars had disappeared; only the stronger companions of the night still burned visibly overhead; and away toward the east I saw a faint haze of light upon the horizon, such as had been the *Milky Way* when I was last awake. Day was at hand. I lit my lantern, and by its glow-worm light put on my boots and gaiters; then I broke up some bread for *Modestine*, filled my can at the water-tap, and lit my spirit-lamp to boil myself some chocolate. The blue darkness lay long in the glade where I had so sweetly slumbered; but soon there was a broad streak of orange melting into gold along the mountain-tops of *Vivarais*. A solemn glee possessed my mind at this gradual and lovely coming in of day. I heard the runnel with delight; I looked round me for something beautiful and unexpected; but the still black pine-trees, the hollow glade, the munching ass, remained unchanged in figure. Nothing had altered but the light, and that, indeed, shed over all a spirit of life and of breathing peace, and moved me to a strange exhilaration.

I drank my water chocolate, which was hot if it was not rich, and strolled here and there, and up and down about the glade. While I was thus delaying, a gush of steady wind, as long as a heavy sigh, poured direct out of the quarter of the morning. It was cold, and set me sneezing. The trees near at hand tossed their black plumes in its passage; and I could see the thin distant spires of pine along the edge of the hill rock slightly to and fro against the golden east. Ten minutes after, the sunlight spread at a gallop along the hillside, scattering shadows and sparkles, and the day had come completely.

I hastened to prepare my pack, and tackle the steep ascent that lay before me; but I had something on my mind. It was only a fancy, yet a fancy will sometimes be importunate. I had been most hospitably received and punctually served in my green caravanserai. The room was airy, the water excellent, and the dawn had called me to a moment. I say nothing of the tapestries or the inimitable ceiling, nor yet of the view which I commanded from the windows; but I felt I was in some one's debt for all this liberal entertainment.   And so it pleased me, in a half-laughing way, to leave pieces of money on the turf as I went along, until I had left enough for my night's lodging. I trust they did not fall to some rich and churlish drover.

Index

THE END